Reform and Reaction
in the Platine Provinces
1810–1852

To Alan Turner,

fellow student of

Platine history —

with all best wishes

David

Bushnell

University of Florida Monographs
Social Sciences Number 69

Reform and Reaction
in the Platine Provinces
1810–1852

David Bushnell

A University of Florida Book
University Presses of Florida
Gainesville

Library of Congress Cataloging in Publication Data

Bushnell, David, 1923–
    Reform and reaction in the Platine provinces,
1810–1852.

    (University of Florida monographs. Social sciences;
no. 69)
    "A University of Florida Book."
    Bibliography: p.
    Includes index.
    1. Law—Argentina—History and criticism. 2. Argentina
—Politics and government—1817–1860. 3. Liberalism—
Argentina—History. I. Title. II. Series.
KHA292.B87 1983   349.82'09   83–10490
ISBN 0–8130–0757–7   348.2009

UNIVERSITY PRESSES OF FLORIDA is the central agency for scholarly publishing of the State of Florida's university system. Its offices are located at 15 NW 15th Street, Gainesville, FL 32603.

Works published by University Presses of Florida are evaluated and selected for publication, after being reviewed by referees both within and outside of the state's university system, by a faculty editorial committee of any one of Florida's nine public universities: Florida A&M University (Tallahassee), Florida Atlantic University (Boca Raton), Florida International University (Miami), Florida State University (Tallahassee), University of Central Florida (Orlando), University of Florida (Gainesville), University of North Florida (Jacksonville), University of South Florida (Tampa), University of West Florida (Pensacola).

Contents

Glossary

Acta	Minute (of a meeting or resolution)
Alcabala	Sales tax
Capellanía	Chaplaincy, chantry
Censo	Ecclesiastical mortgage
Consulado	Merchant guild
De cuerpo presente	With the body present
Defensor de Pobres y Menores	Defender of the Poor and Minors
Estanciero	Owner of estancia; rancher
Fuero	Corporate privilege
Liberto	Freedman
Luces del siglo	Enlightenment of the age
Mayorazgo	Entail
Obedézcase pero no se cumpla	Obey but do not execute
Obras Pías	Pious foundations
Papeleta	Document of employment
Pardo	Person of part-African descent
Patente	License
Patronato	Patronage, civil, over church
Porteño	Native of Buenos Aires
Protector de Naturales	Natives' Protector
Quinto	Fifth (tax on metals)
Ramos estancados	Fiscal monopolies

Glossary

Recurso de nulidad e injusticia notoria	Appeal on grounds of glaring defect, against judicial decision in final instance
Suma del Poder Público	Sum of Public Power, i.e., supreme authority in all three branches of government
Vecinos, vecindario	Residents enjoying full political rights

Introduction

THERE WAS a time when the history of Latin America in its first century of independence was widely treated by historians—and others— as some combination of endless squabble among personalist leaders and epic clash of liberal and conservative principles. Today's historians—and others—are more interested in social and economic structures, "neo-colonial" dependency, and political culture as distinct from political ideas and government institutions. These new concerns are as valid as the old ones, if not more so. It is unfortunate, however, even if understandable, that the current generation of scholars has moved on to a new range of subject matter without first tying together some of the numerous loose ends their predecessors left—perhaps the most obvious of which have to do with the nature and aims of nineteenth-century conservatism. And it is not the primary objective of this study to remedy that gap, although it may throw some light on what conservatism was up against. For the immediate purpose is to say something more on Latin American liberalism, considered as a process of legal and institutional innovation. Liberalism is no longer a popular creed in much of Latin America, least of all Argentina, where it is a bad word. Nonetheless, it remains a significant portion of Latin America's heritage whatever one's views.

The Latin American liberalism of the last century can be and has been studied as an intellectual phenomenon, as a contending army in the civil warfare of the period, or as an expression of the interests and attitudes of particular social groups. All these and other possible approaches have advantages and pitfalls. But there is also some methodological wisdom in the words of Scripture "By their fruits ye shall know them," and one of

1

the most enduring of the varied fruits of nineteenth-century liberalism was a particular series of juridical and institutional changes, from freedom of worship to freedom of contract, introduced during or following the attainment of political independence. Many of these measures, all of which were in some sense intended to enlarge the sphere of individual liberty and initiative, also had the support of men identified by their own words, or retroactively by historians, as Latin American conservatives. Indeed *liberalism* in the sense used here—as a process of innovation—was never the exclusive possession of self-styled liberals. There are other problems, too, in this use of the term, but almost any use must be arbitrary in some respects, and I shall at least try to be consistent in order to minimize the damage.

Liberalism, however defined, did not appear in Latin America overnight with the coming of independence. Just as its intellectual roots are found in the thought of the Enlightenment, particularly the Iberian Enlightenment, its first manifestations in law and administration are to be found in the reforming tendencies of the late colonial period. Even so, the late colonial reforms derived from imperial strategy as well as from Enlightenment principles, and their scope was limited by the forces of tradition and inertia inherent in the structure of the colonial regime. Though the Jesuits might disagree, the essence of Bourbon (and Pombaline) reformism was more truly reflected in a new administrative style than in radical institutional changes. By contrast, the collapse of Spain's absolute monarchy in 1808 in the wake of the French invasion of the Iberian peninsula created the conditions for frontal attack on a whole series of laws and institutions that appeared outmoded, not only in Spanish America but obviously in Spain itself. Two examples perhaps suggest the difference. The famous intendant system, introduced first in Spain and later in the colonies by the Bourbon monarchs, represented an attempt to streamline and rationalize the administrative system, but in fact it reinforced the system's authoritarian nature; it did not offer the same degree of novelty as, say, the sudden introduction of representative assemblies and congresses in the second decade of the nineteenth century. Likewise it has often been noted that individual members of the free *pardo* population rose in status in the late colonial period with the aid of official policies such as the incorporation of pardo contingents into the militia with enjoyment of *fuero* and the sale of patents of legal whiteness. Yet all this merely riddled the colonial Jim Crow laws with a few more exceptions: it is not to be compared with the virtual scrapping of those laws by the new governments that came to power in 1810 and thereafter.

It could be properly observed at this point that the establishment of representative institutions or the granting of formal equality to pardos meant considerably less in practical than in legal terms. The same distinction between legal theory and everyday practice can naturally be made in other cases, too; yet there is no more reason a priori to assume that reform measures remained a dead letter, or were simply irrelevant in the Latin American context, than there is to believe the contrary propositions. Certainly they did not occur in a vacuum but bore a relationship to other developments of the same period. And, if someone cared enough to enact a law or decree, there may even be a slight presumption that something came of it. If in fact the enactment did not have practical effect, the fact of its adoption is still a significant datum for the study of legislative behavior and for studying the climate of opinion. And, before trying to assess whether an innovation was enforced—and if so, with what effect—one has to know that it was promulgated. For all these reasons, a concern with identifying the measures adopted does not seem out of place. Accordingly, except for incidental references, the "fruits" of liberalism to be considered here will be the written texts of laws and decrees. These texts do not constitute the whole story, but they are a significant part. Moreover, the fact that the historian can readily classify them both geographically (by place of issuance) and chronologically (by date) becomes a special advantage for purposes of comparative analysis.

In the process that forms the central theme of this investigation, the new Spanish American nations had for their point of departure not only a roughly homogeneous colonial system—homogeneous, at least, in the principles that underlay it—but also the influence of a liberal creed that exhibited a high degree of homogeneity by virtue of, among other things, a shared set of external models. It was a creed that contained more than a few logical contradictions—in particular, that between the liberal faith in individual freedom and constitutional government and the need to crush the resistance of entrenched traditional interests—as Charles Hale, for example, has shown so well in the case of Mexico.[1] Yet, to the extent that they welcomed and responded to this liberal influence, Latin Americans tried at least to eliminate or revamp those laws and institutions that appeared to curtail unduly the rights of the individual in political, religious, economic, and social areas. In this sense it was a somewhat negative creed, dedicated to rooting out abuses and preventing their recurrence, to creating conditions in which private citizens could forge a new and better society rather than creating such a society directly by governmental action. The effort may have been misguided, but on balance it did favor the forces of change; and it served, for better or worse, as an agent of Western-style modernization. Moreover, the fact that liberals were rooting out abuses contained in a common colonial heritage meant that the specific issues debated and measures taken (or rejected) were repeated in one country after another, at least in *Spanish* America. There were, of course, many differences in scope and timing. A reform adopted by gradual stages in one country might be introduced in toto, at the stroke of a pen, in another; identical measures might be introduced in different countries in different chronological order; and steps once taken could always be reversed. In short, each country had a profile of its own in the matter of liberal innovation or even a whole complex of profiles if, as in Argentina, the function of renovating or maintaining the juridical-institutional structure was entrusted primarily to provincial rather than national authorities.

Even without the special complication presented by the lack of a true national government in Argentina for most of the period from 1820 (when even the pretense of maintaining the region's traditional administrative unity was temporarily abandoned) to the overthrow of the dictatorship of Juan Manuel de Rosas in Buenos Aires in 1852, the Argentine profile offers several noteworthy characteristics. For Latin America as a whole, one can distinguish a first wave of liberal reform activity corresponding to the independence struggle and its immediate aftermath; then, a period of consolidation or even retrogression, which lasted roughly until mid-century; and a second wave, corresponding more or less to the third quarter of the century.[2] By the end of the century, the standard objectives of nineteenth-century liberalism either had been accomplished or were losing their relevance, or both, and a new set of issues was emerging. All these stages are readily identifiable in Argentina. In addition, the Rosas dictatorship has long been regarded as a classic example of Latin American reaction against the excesses of the first generation of reformers; in fact, it has been overrated as such. The Argentine manifestation of the first wave itself, lasting from the May Revolution of 1810 that began the independence movement through the ephemeral national presidency of Bernardino Rivadavia in the mid-1820s (though with a certain lull in 1815–20), can hardly be overrated, because liberal innovations were carried farther—at least on paper—than anywhere else in Latin America at that time. By contrast, the Argentine performance during the second broad wave of liberal reform shows relative moderation. The successors of Rosas were more aware of what their countrymen could and would assimilate than Rivadavia had been, or than were their contemporaries and counterparts in certain other countries.

In one important respect, the Argentine performance fell short even during the first wave: despite several false starts, no full-fledged written constitution was ever successfully established at the national level, as in other American nations. To be sure, provision for a rough separation of powers was included in the very *acta* of 25 May 1810 which launched the independence movement. That declaration temporarily ascribed executive power to the newly created Junta of Government and final judicial responsibility to the colonial Audiencia, which had not yet been abolished.[3] These initial arrangements later gave way to others, generally of makeshift variety, and in due course many individual provinces made for themselves some sort of written constitution; but except for strictly interim or stillborn inventions, Argentina did not achieve one until 1853. With or without a proper written charter of government, however, the relationship between liberal political precepts and actual political structures and practice ranged from not very close to unusually complex. Thus, because of the inherent ambiguities, and also because constitutional history has been so extensively examined by other historians, the form of government will receive only slight attention in the discussion here. One of the few exceptions will be the development of suffrage regulations, a detail which has not been studied as fully but which is important—not because elections were always meaningful but because the legal definition of voting rights reveals which segments of the population were deemed worthy of political participation and which were relegated to second-class citizenship. Any move to enlarge the suffrage will be an indicator of democratization (at least in principle), not necessarily of liberalism as understood at the time, but it may be interesting to note to what extent the two went together.

One other topic that will receive less attention than it intrinsically deserves is tariff policy. In the economic sphere, there was no more significant issue than this one, and the principal fluctuations between low-tariff and protectionist tendencies require mention as part of the context in which other policies were being made and unmade. But the tariff is another highly complex issue and one that is particularly resistant to a methodology built around the written text of laws and decrees; the rates themselves have little meaning until one takes account of the procedures used in valuation of merchandise, changing price levels, and many other factors. Then, too, the tariff, like constitutional history, has been extensively treated by other scholars,[4] and any attempt to say something new on the subject would require a separate study. The main emphasis here will be placed on certain other issues that have not been wholly overlooked but have seldom been treated systematically. The specific measures to be examined are not always of great practical importance; in some cases the importance is merely symbolic. But at least it will be symbolic of an intent either to modify or in some measure to revert to the colonial juridical-institutional heritage. Those measures studied will meet three criteria: that they be reasonably unambiguous in their significance, whether practical or symbolic or both; that they relate to larger issues and problems, even if dealing with transitory events; and that each should be one of a number of dispositions relating to the same issue or problem. The items that satisfy these requirements do not necessarily provide a balanced sampling, but they do cut across several areas of governmental activity.

Discussion on the period after 1820 will focus on a group of provinces. One of them, inevitably, is Buenos Aires. Five others—Entre Ríos, Corrientes, Mendoza, Salta/Jujuy, and Córdoba—have been selected partly on the basis of the adequacy of available sources, partly for purposes of regional and subregional coverage, as explained more fully in chapter 3. (As explained later, data for Salta are used up to the separation of Jujuy from Salta in 1834; thereafter, the analysis will be limited to Jujuy.) A last member of the group is Uruguay, an Argentine province that suffered Luso-Brazilian occupation until 1825 and became technically independent in 1828; but it more than satisfies the criterion of adequate sources and, at the same time, provides an instructive parallel to Buenos Aires— it could almost be called a control experiment. To facilitate both cross-referencing and wider comparisons, the relevant enactments of each province (and of the overall Platine authorities prior to 1820) are listed by political jurisdiction and date of issue in a series of appendixes. At least the first textual mention of any one enactment will be followed, in parentheses, by its respective number in the appendixes.

A final limitation of the analysis, which will become apparent but needs to be stated at the outset, is that it is more descriptive than explanatory. Naturally, there is an implicit assumption that the occurrence of particular changes at particular times and places reflects not only the appeal of certain guiding principles and efforts of individual standard-bearers but the presence of objective conditions creating an environment receptive to the measures in question. However, a full examination of those conditions and an attempt to relate them to the observed patterns of change would require more than this brief volume. The findings presented here should at least tend to confirm or to modify a number of familiar generalizations in Argentine history, and they are certainly meant to suggest new questions. Whether they also suggest any new answers will be for the reader to decide.

Research for this study began fourteen years ago with the help of a Fulbright-Hays faculty research grant and continued intermittently, with financial aid from the University of Florida and from the Organization of American States. As the research was carried out both in Buenos Aires and in archives and libraries of all the provinces mentioned except Entre Ríos, the individuals who gave assistance and advice are literally too numerous to mention, although I do want to place on record my special gratitude to two Argentine scholars who are no longer with us, Ricardo R. Caillet-Bois and Julio César González. I also wish to single out for thanks two colleagues at the University of Florida, Andrés Suárez and Neill Macaulay, who reviewed and commented on specific portions of the manuscript, as well as my constant companion in academic tourism and equally constant source of criticism and encouragement, Virginia Starkes Bushnell.

1. The First Decade: Initial Reforms and Brief Pause

In May 1810, Argentine revolutionaries established a governing junta at Buenos Aires that claimed to exercise supreme authority over the entire Viceroyalty of the Río de la Plata until such time as its component provinces could send deputies to agree upon a form of government for the area. In practice no full-fledged constitution was adopted until 1819, and none took effect until 1853. Nor did the May 1810 Junta in its original form even last out the year: junta followed junta; triumvirates and directorates rose and fell with distressing regularity. Nevertheless, a government of some sort, enjoying at least de facto independence, existed in what is now Argentina after 1810. And at the same time that its members worried about the threat of counterrevolution or possible invasion and squabbled among themselves, they also set to work to alter the institutional framework they had taken over from their colonial predecessors.

The First Round of Revolutionary Reforms

The call to the interior provinces to elect deputies to a constituent congress (issued 25 May 1810, the very day of establishment of the new regime) signified acceptance of the representative principle as a necessary point of departure for a new political organization. To be sure, the proposed basis of representation was scarcely innovative, for those invited to participate were the *"parte principal y más sana del vecindario."* The term *vecindario* or *vecinos* had traditionally designated property-owning heads of families, Spanish-born or Creole, and only the better elements of this already select minority were explicitly summoned.[1] Moreover, with a representative assembly slated to convene at some date in the not-too-

8

distant future, and with innumerable administrative and military details to contend with in the meantime, the Junta of May and its immediate successors did not see fit to undertake a comprehensive revision of inherited structures. The celebrated revolutionary activism of Mariano Moreno, secretary of the May Junta, found its principal expression instead in campaigns of political indoctrination, in protecting the new regime against its enemies, and in the creation of new subsidiary institutions, from the National Library to the Academy of Mathematics. The various interim authorities nevertheless did issue a number of decrees that deserve to be counted as reforms that altered the preexisting framework in some way. Some of these represented decisions concerning specific cases that had arisen in the course of day-to-day administration but that had wider implications; others frankly represented an attempt to deal with general issues that could not be left until the gathering of a constituent assembly.

Less than two weeks after establishment of a revolutionary junta, the new rulers of Buenos Aires had moved to integrate the Indian militia units into white battalions, all for the purpose, it was explained, of bringing military organization more into line with theoretical civil equality (I-1). The same integrationist policy was expressed in a measure of August 1812 that formally opened to "every class of persons" the town of Quilmes, which was the one ostensibly Indian community in the vicinity of Buenos Aires even though its population already consisted in large part of whites and mestizos (I-9). The decree provided, in effect, that the Indians of Quilmes should no longer be considered a distinct community with "privileges" (and obligations) different from those of other citizens; and it called for the eventual distribution of their communally owned lands as individual private property.[2] In between these two measures, that of September 1811 suppressed the Indian tribute; it was printed and distributed in Quechua as well as Spanish (I-4). (Perhaps as an afterthought, the army that went to liberate what is now Bolivia also freed all Indians of "Peru" from payment of parish fees.)[3] No similar commitment to civil equality was shown on behalf of black inhabitants, but the new regime at least prohibited the slave trade as of 9 April 1812 (I-6), and the following month it introduced the policy of giving freedom to token numbers of existing slaves as a way of marking the anniversary of the May Revolution (I-7).

By a number of separate acts, the revolutionary authorities likewise extended a cordial welcome to nonblack immigrants, offering them all the rights of citizens, the chance to acquire land, and the right to import mining equipment duty-free (I-2, 12). The First Triumvirate in September 1812 even ended the standing requirement that foreign merchants use native consignment agents rather than sell their goods directly in whole-sale commerce (I-13). This ruling did not greatly change anything, as the requirement had been widely disregarded, but it did place clearly on rec-ord the intention of opening the Río de la Plata to foreign trade and to foreigners' participation in the life of the region. Meanwhile, another se-ries of decrees and regulations abolished prior censorship of the press, ex-cept in matters of religion (I-3),[4] explicitly listed guarantees of civil rights and judicial due process (I-5), defined limits of the military fuero as en-joyed by members of militia units (I-8), and ended the practice of confer-ring certain types of municipal office in perpetuity, though "without prejudice" to current holders (I-10). A final order abolished the colonial tobacco monopoly, along with associated *ramos estancados* (e.g., playing-card monopoly) (I-11).[5]

As a group, these measures were in keeping with an emerging revolu-tionary ideology, but they were miscellaneous in content and in most cases not likely to generate serious opposition. Several were clearly ex-pected to win favor with groups whose good will was perceived as stra-tegically important. Extinction of the tribute would please the Indians of Upper Peru, where a first military expedition from Buenos Aires had been turned back in defeat. Abolition of the slave trade and the end to the consignment system (the only really controversial item) would please the all-powerful British. And the dismantling of the tobacco monopoly ful-filled a promise already made to the Paraguayans, who were the principal producers in the Platine area and had been coyly reluctant to recognize the claims of the authorities at Buenos Aires.[6]

A program that was at once more comprehensive and more controver-sial began to emerge when the Asamblea General Constituyente at last began to function in January 1813. This body came to be known in Ar-gentine history as the Assembly of the Year XIII, and the Jacobin nuances of such a designation are not undeserved for the assembly represented an early peak of radical reformist energy. One of its incidental accomplish-ments was to adopt the Argentine national anthem, including the memo-rable lines "O hear the sound of broken chains! / See noble equality en-throned!"[7] There was, of course, an element of hyperbole in such words; yet among the major and minor accomplishments of the assembly it is possible to detect a number that did in fact break different kinds of bonds for different classes of people. Above all, the formal adoption of a law of free birth, which went into effect 31 January 1813, started the ultimate eradication of black slavery (I-14). This law was supplemented by a *Re-glamento para la educación y ejercicio de los libertos*, enacted 6 March, specifying that male children of slave mothers would remain under the tutelage (*patronato*) of the mother's owner until age twenty and female children until sixteen or married, whereupon they would enter into full enjoyment of the freedom offered.[8] Still other slaves, born too soon to benefit from the free-birth principle, received a promise of freedom in return for military service in the cause of independence (I-21), and the assembly continued the practice of observing patriot festivals by freeing limited numbers of slaves.[9] Various restrictions on the Indian population were broken, too, at least in theory, by a law that reaffirmed both the suppression of the tribute and the Indians' juridical equality, while specifically ending the *mita* and any other involuntary service of the Indians on behalf of state, church, or private citizens (I-15).

The assembly combined further encouragement of immigration with the promotion of mining when it offered foreigners engaged in that industry the freedom of non–Roman Catholic worship in private homes (I-17). This provision was, at the same time, only one of those adopted by the assembly that affected the organization and practice of religion. Others formally abolished the Inquisition (I-16), fixed thirty years as a minimum age for professions in the regular orders (I-20), created a Comisaría General de Regulares to assume the powers previously exercised over different orders by their respective superior authorities in Spain (I-22), placed assets of hospital orders directly under secular control (I-23), and, last in practical though not necessarily symbolic importance, prohibited baptizing infants with cold water (I-24). On the same day that the deputies chose to regulate religious professions, they had also outlawed titles of nobility (I-18) and judicial use of torture, adding in the latter case that all instruments of torture were to be rendered unusable (I-19). The founding of entails was similarly outlawed, in another session, to complete the assembly's list of major prohibitions (I-25).

The blows against civil and ecclesiastical obscurantism mentioned are not the only measures of the Assembly of the Year XIII that served to win it an honored niche in Argentine liberal tradition; but even excluding any others, these easily overshadow any accomplishments along similar lines prior to the Rivadavian reforms of the next decade. It was, though, a rather brief spurt. The assembly itself continued its sessions intermittently for another year and a half, and the revolutionary movement remained for that period in much the same hands. But other concerns—such as the war in Uruguay and Upper Peru and the threat posed by post-Napoleonic European reaction—began to take precedence over the adoption of reform measures. Among the few and limited exceptions that need to be recorded are the decree of the Second Triumvirate of October 1813 against the whipping of schoolchildren (I-26) and that of Supreme Director Gervasio Posadas in September 1814 halving the rate of tithe payments in the provinces of Entre Ríos and Corrientes and in Uruguay (I-27). The former of these measures might be considered an educational analog to the assembly's abolition of torture. The other was justified as a measure to relieve those provinces of war-related economic hardships, and obviously it was intended to win support for the hard-pressed central authorities vis-à-vis federalist opponents. However, it was also a precedent for tampering with clerical income from the tithes on one pretext or another. And it tended to weaken the church as an institution, a side effect that was not wholly unwelcome in some circles.

Indeed, the most obvious difference between the scattered reforms issued by various executive bodies, from the start of the revolution to the meeting of the assembly, and those adopted in the course of its sessions had been precisely the inclusion among the latter of a number directly attacking the position of the Roman Catholic church. As mentioned, the assembly even took two rather cautious steps toward the introduction of religious toleration. It is true that merely eliminating the Inquisition did not make legal the open profession of heretical beliefs—it only removed a particular agency whose special duty had been to combat heresy—while the right to hold non–Roman Catholic services in private houses was limited to a small number of people, and foreigners at that. Yet these moves were symptomatic of a wider commitment to toleration, and the gradual appearance of de facto toleration on the shore of the Río de la Plata (not necessarily in the interior) outpaced the legislative progress made. (In the most common Argentine usage, the "interior" means those provinces lying outside the "Littoral," which comprises both Buenos Aires and the provinces bordering the Paraná River. Here, however, the word will cover all provinces other than Buenos Aires.) Other significant blows were struck at the religious orders, seen as a vast misapplication of human and material resources—a combination of social vagrancy and voluntary servitude under religious pretexts—and accordingly a particular target of Enlightenment thinkers in Europe and revolutionary liberals (and even some conservatives) in America. Some measures taken concerning the orders aimed simply to bring them more directly under national and secular control, but the move to limit professions, though ostensibly for the sake of improving discipline, suggested that such control might not always be exercised with benevolent intent. The outwardly trivial prohibition of cold-water baptism revealed perhaps a more general desire to bring ecclesiastical practices into line with the *luces del siglo* (secular enlightenment).

In social and economic matters the reforms of the assembly, like the decrees issued previously, moved toward a society where neither official monopolies nor individual and corporate privileges nor considerations of race and birth would hinder the free circulation of goods and services. With regard to slaves and Indians, the assembly merely advanced a few steps further: from abolition of the slave trade to the principle of free birth; from the liberation of a few individual slaves for ceremonial purposes to more widespread manumission in return for military service;[10] and from suppression of Indian tribute and the granting of equal status in militia service or property holding to the prohibition of all forms of Indian forced labor. The last provision, of course, was embedded in a legislative decree whose phrasing made a general and categorical declaration of Indian equality. The prohibition of entails and titles of nobility and the tendency at least to curb the military fuero all sought to lessen the weight of arbitrary privilege, just as the preceding measures struck at arbitrary disadvantage. And the moves to encourage immigration, starting in 1810, were somewhat comparable in principle, for they tended toward assimilation of those who differed in geographic rather than social or racial origin.

The free play of individual initiative was advanced by two admittedly minor pieces of tax relief: the abolition of state monopolies, and the partial, regional suppression of tithes, which was a fiscal as well as a religious measure. In terms of liberal economic theory, the tithes were not as arbitrary a form of taxation as the monopolies, but objectionable they certainly were, especially as they were levied on gross production rather than net income. Of even greater economic importance, obviously, was the handling of foreign trade during these same years. Although the tariff and related questions will not receive detailed examination, a definite congruence existed between trade policy and reform efforts generally in the period 1810–15. Throughout the half decade, while rates and procedures fluctuated repeatedly, the revolutionary authorities adhered to a policy that at least tended in the direction of freer trade.[11] This liberalizing process—and the weight of British influence—can likewise be seen in the decree of the First Triumvirate allowing foreign merchants to sell their goods without the use of native intermediaries.

A similar congruence is harder to demonstrate for political practices and institutions because of endemic confusion, on the one hand, and the inevitable use of arbitrary war measures, on the other. This area, too, is excluded from comprehensive consideration. But such scattered innovations as eliminating prior press censorship, attempting to define individual civil rights, prohibiting "perpetual" offices and judicial torture, and, for that matter, abolishing a legal nobility all point to a commitment to some form of liberal and republican polity alongside the intended regime of free-enterprise economics.

In a broader context, many of the reforms adopted by Argentine patriots were obviously being enacted concurrently by the first self-governing regimes established in other parts of Spanish America, to say nothing of the de facto government of Joseph Bonaparte and the opposing resistance governments of the mother country. Abolition of the Indian tribute and of the Inquisition are examples of measures so universally adopted that their appearance at Buenos Aires does not deserve special notice. In certain respects, the progress of innovation was actually more far-reaching in one or more of the other theaters of the Hispanic world than in the Río de la Plata. Spanish liberals made more sweeping changes at the expense of the religious orders, and in Mexico, Father Miguel Hidalgo offered slaves immediate freedom.[12] The Venezuelan First Republic of 1811 not only abolished the fueros—which Spanish liberals also sought to do but which the Argentines did not yet seriously attack—but proved considerably more forthright, at least on paper, in establishing the legal equality of all races. Indeed, Venezuela's constitution of 1811 was quite specific in eliminating the traditional disabilities that had been placed upon the free pardo population.[13]

In Argentina, though the principle of free birth was proclaimed earlier than in Venezuela (where it dated only from 1821), there was obvious ambivalence on the status of free subjects of African or part-African descent. The integration of Indian with white militiamen was accomplished by taking the former *out* of the units that contained the colored castes, on the ground that Indians were in every respect equal to whites; implicitly, it was recognized thereby that pardos were *not* equal and that forced association with them was demeaning to the Indians. True, a subsequent decree spoke of the need to extirpate "the degradation to which the accidental difference of color has until now condemned a part of our population which is as numerous as it is capable of any great undertaking."[14] But there was no strong impulse to implement the principle of equality for pardos. Thus racial segregation continued to exist in military organization,[15] and in the lack of specific measures to the contrary, it is safe to assume that discrimination also survived, de jure as well as de facto, in other aspects of social relations. The study of judicial records in the province of Córdoba clearly demonstrates that such was the case,[16] and that it was the case more generally is suggested by, among other things, the suffrage provisions of the *Estatuto Provisional* of 1815 (to be discussed).

It will also be noted that the liquidation of separate Indian communities

with their unique juridical status and collective landownership, a gener-
alized objective of nineteenth-century liberals in country after country of
Spanish America, was so far applied only in the atypical instance of
Quilmes rather than embodied in legislation applicable to all provinces
that had comprised the Viceroyalty of the Río de la Plata. Indeed, the
Quilmes decree was more a continuation of the piecemeal attacks on the
Indian communities, a familiar feature of the late colonial regime—
bringing that process to a successful culmination, as far as the province of
Buenos Aires was concerned—than a first installment of a wider reform.
It is not that the possibility of a more sweeping measure had not occurred
to anyone, for a draft constitution presented to the Assembly of the Year
XIII included a provision for the conversion of Indian communal lands
into individual private holdings throughout the former Viceroyalty and
now United Provinces of the Río de la Plata.[17] However, neither that nor
any other constitution was adopted. And before further action was taken
in the following decade, again on a piecemeal basis, the one region where
the issue was most significant on a practical level, Upper Peru, was irre-
trievably lost to Argentine jurisdiction.
    Even those measures concerning the Indians that were not expressly
limited in application to a single locality had only slight practical effect,
because during most of the independence period Upper Peru remained
under royalist control. With respect to the tribute, the Pampa Indians did
not pay but more likely received tribute as a bribe for good behavior.[18] Its
abolition is easy to minimize as a safe propaganda gesture because it
could have little or no impact on revenue entering the Buenos Aires treasury. Nevertheless, both the provisional government that first decreed it
in 1811 and the Assembly of 1813 that confirmed it—and confirmed the
exemption from payment of ecclesiastical fees for Indians of Upper Peru,
though not of other provinces[19]—were consciously acting for what is
now Bolivia as well as for Argentina proper. With no thought as yet of
accepting the establishment of an independent state in Upper Peru, the
men who made the decision believed they were doing something of practical importance—if not in the short run, at least for the happier day
when patriot arms would have successfully reached Lake Titicaca.
    Somewhat the same can be said on the prohibition of *mayorazgos* and
titles of nobility, which had never been much sought after in what is now
Argentina. Within that territory there appear to have been, at the time of
independence, at most six mayorazgos and two Creole title-holders.[20]
There were more of each in Upper Peru. In this case, unlike that of the
tribute or of Indian forced labor, it could not be assumed that the individuals directly affected by the reform would be grateful to the revolution-

ary legislators and thus more likely to embrace the patriot cause. Entails and titles were objectionable in and of themselves, the former incompatible with the free circulation of property rights, the latter incompatible not only with the concept of civil equality but with the basic republicanism that many members of the 1813 Assembly personally adhered to even if they were not yet ready to proclaim a republic. The fact that Upper Peru was unrepresented at the time both reforms were adopted may have contributed to an apparent lack of opposition (which offers an obvious contrast with the controversy the same two measures later stirred up in Chile); and this fact would lend some justification to the view that the legislators were seizing upon issues of no great moment to themselves in order to strike an enlightened pose. The fact remains that by the beginning of 1815, Argentine revolutionaries had already compiled a rather impressive record of innovations which, taken as a whole, overshadows that achieved anywhere else in Spanish America at a comparable stage in the struggle. Moreover, with minor exceptions it lasted, whereas the achievements of Hidalgo or of the Venezuelan First Republic were mostly wiped out by Spanish reconquest.

An Interlude of Moderation

The relative immunity of the Argentine heartland to royalist military action, and thus to a forcible rollback of revolutionary achievements, was not accompanied by immunity to internal dissensions, which continued to take their toll. Even so, the second five years of the revolution saw a somewhat greater continuity at the level of titular national authorities, not that these could always or everywhere make their will respected. The second national congress, which convened at Tucumán in March 1816 and moved to Buenos Aires the following year, did not finally dissolve itself until February 1820. It appointed a chief executive who set a new record for length of tenure: Juan Martín de Pueyrredón, who served as supreme director from July 1816 to June 1819. But this incipient and ultimately abortive stabilization was associated with a marked decline in the pace of institutional reform, first clearly evident during the transition year 1815. Few of the measures introduced earlier were revoked, but there was without doubt a lessening of fervor in implementing those that remained, and there was a virtual halt to further enactments.

The one evident advance, compared to previous years, was the adoption in May 1815 by an improvised Junta de Observación at Buenos Aires of an Estatuto Provisional that was to serve as temporary frame of government until the next national congress could write a permanent one (I-28). It was the first enactment that can fairly be called a written constitution, and the Congress of Tucumán was chosen in accordance with its terms.[21] The Estatuto was not a large step, in view of its frankly interim character. One of the few features that requires comment is the effort to codify the requirements for enjoyment of active citizenship and hence the suffrage—an effort that was not especially enlightened even for the period and is significant less for any consequences that occurred than for the attitudes revealed. Previously, revolutionary governments had been content to continue to use the traditional concept of vecino in some form in determining which inhabitants should be admitted to active political participation, and that concept by customary usage was restrictive though at the same time susceptible to varying applications in practice. The Estatuto's definition of citizenship was more detailed and thus more legally precise, despite its failure to say exactly what constituted a "lucrative and useful profession," in lack of which citizenship could be suspended. In context, the phrase doubtlessly was meant to refer to independent practitioners of a profession or trade and not mere hired hands. Yet the imposition of socioeconomic limits on the right to vote was not incompatible with early nineteenth-century liberalism, which neither in Latin America nor in Europe entailed a necessary commitment to political democracy. It was enough that in a free commonwealth anyone had the theoretical opportunity to improve his economic status and thereby meet the requirements; and the attempt to supply a written definition of what was required, something new for the Río de la Plata, was fully in accord with liberal principles.

The overt discrimination by the Estatuto against Afro-Argentines— required to meet the additional test of being freeborn sons of parents also born free—is a different matter, for not everyone had equal opportunity to change his skin color. This provision was stated in terms almost identical to those found in the Constitution of Cádiz of 1812, handiwork of the Spanish liberals,[22] but it appears to have no true parallels in the legislation of other Spanish American nations. It is thus one more sign of a curious ambivalence in applying revolutionary principles to the Afro-Argentines' situation. It cannot have made much practical difference, because to be excluded on the grounds of African ancestry the pardos first had to meet all other requirements for citizenship, which presumably not many did. The citizenship provisions of the Estatuto Provisional were incorporated, with only minor changes of wording, in the *Reglamento Provisorio* of 1817 (I-33), which was adopted, as another temporary expedient, by the national congress after its move from Tucumán to Buenos Aires. The provisions were implicitly reaffirmed by the Constitution of 1819—supposedly definitive but in fact stillborn—and they were to serve as points

of departure for treating the suffrage in most of the provinces after national unity dissolved in 1820.[23] They accurately reflect the fact that slaves
who directly or indirectly received their freedom because of the independence struggle (as in the case of blacks captured by Argentine corsairs
[I-32]) would join the free population in a condition of distinct inferiority.

The Estatuto Provisional contained a set of addenda that annulled both
the prohibition of using the lash on schoolchildren and the age limitations
placed on professions in the religious orders. No new attempt was made
to reform the orders for the rest of the decade, and two more acts of the
Assembly of 1813 affecting them were subsequently repealed. Elimination of the Comisaría de Regulares by the Congress of Tucumán (I-29) did
not mean a return of the orders to their previous subordination to superiors in Spain; but it did remove the intrusive hand of the politically created
Comisaría, leaving the way clear for the ecclesiastical ordinaries to exercise the necessary superior authority pending establishment of a new
chain of command that did not pass through Spain on the way to Rome.
This solution was more in line with standard church procedures, and it
safely removed the threat of "nullity," which was cited as a reason for
adopting it.[24] The decree of Pueyrredón returning their hospitals to the
control of the Bethlehemite friars (I-30) was even more straightforward
but would prove short lived, lasting only until the reforms of Rivadavia
in the following decade, as was true of the removal of the minimum age
for religious professions. Renewed authorization to whip schoolchildren
did not last even that long, canceled by the same Reglamento Provisorio of 1817 that in most other respects merely confirmed the Estatuto
Provisional.

A matching change of orientation occurred in tariff policy, where a
trend toward liberalization of foreign trade, evident in the first stage of
the revolution, gave way to a relative, and in its practical implementation
somewhat illusory, protectionism (I-31).[25] The retreat from liberal principles in the handling of foreign trade could be seen, too, in the decree of
Pueyrredón of 31 May 1817 that temporarily prohibited the operations of
the *saladeros* (meat-salting plants). Ostensibly designed to protect local
consumers by assuring adequate fresh meat supplies at reasonable prices,
it actually reflected a more complex rivalry between entrenched merchant groups and the emerging class of *estancieros*, whose position was
improving at the expense of the merchants in part because of new oppor-
tunities opened up by the development of salt meat exports.[26] Yet the re-
orientation of policy in foreign trade and other matters was not destined
to be permanent, much less absolute. As the decade closed, Pueyrredón's
interim replacement, José Rondeau, prohibited bullfights, a stroke of so-

cial and cultural innovation worthy of the Assembly of the Year XIII (I-34). Though strictly "liberal" only from the standpoint of the bulls, the measure was a harbinger of renewed reform of all kinds that was around the corner. A substantial groundwork had been laid, touching the principal areas of governmental activity yet consisting sometimes of half measures and leaving important gaps. Bernardino Rivadavia and his associates would work to bring loose ends together in Buenos Aires in the 1820s.

2. The Second Decade: Apogee of Buenos Aires Liberalism, 1821–1827

THE LULL in reforming activity ended abruptly in 1821. From that point until 1827, Argentina witnessed once again, as during the Year XIII, a series of institutional innovations bolder than any being attempted elsewhere in Spanish America. Now, however, reforms emanated principally from the Buenos Aires provincial executive and legislature. The last vestige of a national authority had expired in 1820; the effort to recreate a national government in 1825–27 proved unsuccessful and left few permanent traces. To the extent that the interior provinces underwent a comparable process of liberal reform in the decade of the 1820s, as discussed in chapter 3, it was largely by imitation of the province of Buenos Aires or by local initiative, not by command of a higher authority.

The program of reforms adopted in Buenos Aires is conventionally associated with the figure of Bernardino Rivadavia. Having already had a hand in the work of the First Triumvirate of 1811–12, he served as minister of government of the province from July 1821 to 1824, under the titular leadership of Governor Martín Rodríguez. Then with the title of president, he headed the abortive national administration during 1826–27. But it is not always clear how much credit or blame should be ascribed to Rivadavia for the adoption of a particular measure, especially during his service as minister of the provincial administration. There were a number of others, such as Minister of Finance Manuel José García (who stayed on even when Rivadavia temporarily stepped down from office in 1824) and key figures of the provincial legislature, who played a significant role in the formulation of policy. Rivadavia was simply the most forceful, or

20

most notorious, figure within a larger group of Creole business and professional men who aspired to see Buenos Aires and eventually the surrounding nation catch up willy-nilly with the progress of northwestern Europe. And there were still others, including the rising estanciero, saladerista, and rural militia officer Juan Manuel de Rosas, for whom the consolidation of domestic order was the highest political objective. However, order and progress were not inherently incompatible, especially as progress in the view of Rivadavia necessarily entailed both placing administration on a firm and efficient basis and protecting and advancing the province's dominant economic interests. Hence, Rivadavia and his collaborators were able to receive, if not a blank check, at least a large initial grant of confidence from Buenos Aires's social and economic establishment.[1]

Political Innovations

In political organization the province did not adopt a formal written constitution. It operated instead under an informal constitution of fairly conventional outline, with Governor, Junta de Representantes, and a Tribunal de Apelaciones which headed an ostensibly separate judicial power. The judiciary did, however, enjoy more real independence than in other Argentine provinces.[2] The one unusual feature of governmental structure, though it would soon be copied elsewhere, was the elimination (by a law adopted in 1821) of separate municipal governments, the *cabildos*, whose functions were assumed directly by the provincial legislative, executive, and judicial authorities (II-P4). This move was not unrelated to factional differences between the Buenos Aires cabildo and the provincial administration, but more fundamentally it was an effort to simplify and rationalize government by means of consolidation, doing so at the expense of the tradition-encrusted municipal institution rather than of the new or at least refashioned provincial organs.[3]

At the same time, the liberty and equality of individual citizens were receiving much verbal recognition, as they had since the start of the revolution, and in practice they were respected more fully than during most of the period from 1810 until after mid-century. They were also confirmed or extended by a few more measures—those dealing with the free circulation of ideas in print perhaps the least striking. A general law on press freedom, adopted in 1822, did little more than confirm the essential features of the pertinent reglamento of 1811 (I-3) while actually providing more summary judicial treatment of alleged abuses (II-P6).[4] Before this law was passed, an earlier decree of Rivadavia had expressly extended to importers of books (or paintings or engravings) the same freedom from prior censorship legally accorded to printers and publishers (II-P2). Another ended the requirement, logically inconsistent with the abolition of prior censorship, that printers obtain official permission for publishing the writings of any author not present in the province (II-P3).

Of somewhat greater significance was the series of measures culminating in the virtual elimination of jurisdictional fueros, so that henceforth the nature of the case, rather than the status of the individual, would determine which court had cognizance. First to go was the mercantile fuero, which had rested on the assumption that commercial actions were those performed by recognized merchants, with the merchant guild or *Consulado* in charge of adjudicating disputes. The Consulado itself ceased to exist as of 1 January 1822. In April of the same year Rivadavia assigned to a new Tribunal de Comercio full jurisdiction over *actos de comercio* regardless of the individuals involved, being careful to define what constituted an acto de comercio (II-P5).[5] The ecclesiastical fuero disappeared a few months later, under the terms of a general law of church reform (II-R12), and the military *fuero*, by the law of July 1823 that, with only minor exceptions, annulled all personal fueros in both civil and criminal cases. Ecclesiastical and military courts would continue to exist, but with jurisdiction respectively over those offenses "which can only be committed by members of the clergy" and over those of strictly military nature or committed in line of military duty (II-P7). Buenos Aires thereby affirmed the theoretical equality of its inhabitants with regard to judicial procedure, and at an earlier date than in any other Spanish American republic.[6] As Rivadavia himself emphasized, the reform further aimed at general simplification of the legal structure—a Benthamite goal of wide appeal to Latin American liberals of the period.[7]

The most intriguing of Rivadavia's political reforms is the 1821 law of universal male suffrage (II-P1). Its practical impact was limited by popular apathy and official manipulation; yet it was almost as unusual in Latin America at that time as was the extinction of both military and ecclesiastical fueros, and it was not adopted without misgivings. In one sense, it gave expression to the equalitarian strain that had been present, though far from dominant, in the revolutionary movement from the very start. But a democratic suffrage was embraced by the Rivadavians only as a lesser evil, in view of the practical difficulty of defining what special social and economic or educational qualities make a man fit for active citizenship.[8] Though in Buenos Aires the law remained in force with minor revisions until after the fall of Rosas, second thoughts among many of its original supporters led to the inclusion of rather different suffrage provisions in the national constitution that was drawn up in 1826 but never ratified. These provisions specifically deprived any hired servant or day laborer of full citizenship rights, including the suffrage, as well as any adults who were still illiterate as of fifteen years from the "acceptance of this constitution."[9] The constitution was simply not "accepted." Nevertheless, its suffrage provisions were undoubtedly in closer accord with the trend of thought of the dominant political and socioeconomic sectors of Buenos Aires (and of Latin America generally) than the election law of 1821 had been. Thus social and economic policy would be directed mainly toward creating the conditions in which individual enterprise could best prosper and so contribute to overall development, but without much attention to improving the situation of the common man directly in order that he might more effectively collaborate.

Socioeconomic Innovations

One constant feature of socioeconomic policy during the years 1821–27 was the attempt to assure individuals the right to make use of their property exactly as they saw fit. As Rivadavia noted in the preamble to one of his decrees, "Free use of property is as important for its increase as is security in its possession." On that occasion he was strengthening the principle in question by permitting anyone to slaughter his own cows (II-SE3).[10] On another occasion, a provincial law citing "the inviolability accorded to properties . . . of whatever ownership" served in effect to protect the property rights of enemy aliens, i.e., Spaniards (II-SE9). And, in two of the last decrees that he issued in 1827 before his fall from power, Rivadavia set out to end price controls on bread and meat, the main articles of popular consumption (II-SE17). This particular decree was repealed by his successors before the date it was to take effect (IV-SE2); but it did give classic expression to laissez-faire economic doctrine, as had Rivadavia's earlier removal of legal limitations on the rate of interest, which further connoted a freedom from conventional religious scruples in that it entailed conscious rejection of Roman Catholic teachings on usury (II-SE8). Not surprisingly, perhaps, freedom of interest rates was slyly introduced by administrative directive rather than openly through legislation.

Rivadavia's ending of the traditional practice of forcing urban artisans to do harvest labor (II-SE15) can be seen as a somewhat analogous application of the principle of economic liberty in the labor market. There, however, it was more than offset by his other decrees that restricted the mobility of apprentices and rural workers, seeking to curb the common man's innate indiscipline with elaborate contractual and pass requirements.[11] The latter, to be sure, do not require discussion under the heading of socioeconomic innovations because they were reinforcing colonial practice rather than breaking new ground.

One more limitation of personal freedom, contained in the decree of Rivadavia's cabinet colleague Manuel José García, permitted the ceremonial killing of bulls but only by special permission and on condition that they first be dehorned, all with a view to rooting out or at least curbing uncivilized traditions from the Hispanic past (II-SE7). And for a number of years bullfights ceased altogether.[12] But the most glaring instance of official restrictions on individual enterprise was the law of emphyteusis originally adopted by the province of Buenos Aires (II-SE10) and later extended, in principle, to the whole nation during the abortive restoration of national unity in 1826 (II-SE14). According to this legislation, public lands not yet alienated were to remain the property of the state, to be used on a kind of rental basis but not owned by private citizens. Concerning the objectives of the measure, there is agreement only that it was intended to provide a reliable source of revenue for the treasury. If the provincial (and subsequently national) authorities seriously hoped to affect the basic structure of landholding as well, they at least never followed through with effective implementation to prevent emphyteutic leaseholds from becoming in practice a mere extension of the system of large private estates. In any event, though emphyteusis stands out as an apparent exception to the thrust of Rivadavian economic policy, it made very little difference even as a fiscal device.[13]

Another group of measures continued the antislavery impulse of the preceding decade. These were, however, quite modest, and they were inspired not just by humanitarian sentiment and a desire to enlarge the scope of individual freedom in the labor market but also by military considerations. On the one hand, Rivadavia acted to tighten enforcement of the free-birth principle by prohibiting the removal of pregnant slave women to foreign lands (e.g., Brazil) where that principle might not apply; he also forbade removal of the free children of slave mothers who had not yet reached their age of effective emancipation (II-SE2). On the other hand, the war with Brazil over Uruguay that broke out in 1825 meant that slaves were taken for military service both within Argentina itself and by corsairs on the high seas, exactly as during the war of independence and with a promise of freedom as the ultimate reward (II-SE12, 13, 15). But freedom was naturally conditional on living through the conflict, and it would not take effect until a specified term of service was completed. Slaves taken locally were in worse condition in that they had both to reimburse the state for the indemnity it paid their former owners and to complete an additional fixed term of six years' service to the state itself. If taken by a corsair at sea, a slave did not have to worry about reimbursing his former owner, only his saviors. Certainly one highly questionable feature of Rivadavia's March 1827 decree on the subject is its unspoken assumption that *any* black found on board a Brazilian ship must be a slave. Then, too, overtly segregated schools and militia units continued to exist at Buenos Aires,[14] though at least the racial discrimination in voting rights that was formalized in the preceding decade (I-28) had been done away with by the election law of 1821.

Various changes in the structure of taxation round out the picture of socioeconomic reforms. Elimination of the colonial *alcabala* (II-SE5) and the ending of compulsory tithe payments as a by-product of ecclesiastical reform (II-R12) represented, from the standpoint of liberal economic thinking, the removal of two clearly obnoxious traditional burdens on production and distribution. The *sisa*, a consumption tax somewhat comparable to the alcabala,[15] may not have been literally a burden, but it was a nuisance, and likewise done away with, as was the *media anata* charged on salaries of new official appointees (II-SE11). Abolition of the alcabala was paired, however, with the introduction of a new direct tax on capital (II-SE4), exactly as was done, or at least attempted, in a number of other Latin American countries in the aftermath of independence.[16] With a statutory exemption for the first $1,000 or $2,000, the *contribución directa* was designed to extract a larger share of revenue from those who could best afford to pay, whereas the alcabala, indirectly paid by everyone, was socially regressive in its impact. The contribución directa is therefore uniformly ignored by those who dwell upon the indifference of early Latin American liberals such as Rivadavia to the interests of the common man. Admittedly, the new form of taxation was not put forward purely on the grounds of social justice, even though such motives were cited by its sponsors; it was supposed to have other advantages too, including that of permitting the state to reduce its overwhelming dependence on a single revenue source, the customs.[17]

Proponents of the contribución directa warned against an excessive reliance on customs duties, stressing the danger of a blockade that might cut off the flow of imports. At the same time, most of them favored lowering the tariffs as something desirable in itself, and in fact the trend in tariff policy was once again in the direction of liberalization, though not without minor fluctuations and inconsistencies. Literally "free" trade may have had some theoretical supporters in the Buenos Aires of the 1820s, but it never crossed the mind of anyone in authority to implant it: a compromise between quite moderate protectionism and a strictly revenue tariff was instead the norm. This was clearly reflected in the 1822 tariff (basic rate 15 percent ad valorem), which, with modifications, was to last out the decade (II-SE6). And just as fewer obstacles were being put in the way of foreign goods, immigrants from abroad were eagerly sought too, under a blanket authorization from the legislature (II-SE1). Not many came, but the encouragement of immigration—specifically from Protestant countries—was also one purpose of the formal establishment in 1825 of religious toleration (II-R19),[18] the culmination of the most controversial series of reforms of the Rivadavian period, those adopted in ecclesiastical affairs.

Religious Innovations

Measures altering the status of the established Roman Catholic church in the province of Buenos Aires began even before the appointment of Rivadavia to the ministry in mid-1821. In November 1820, for purposes of economic recovery, the Junta de Representantes decreed a temporary reduction in the rate of the tithes (II-R1),[19] and at some point the province also donated land for a non–Roman Catholic cemetery which officially opened in January 1821 (II-R2). The first of these two measures was then superseded by the article of the December 1822 "law of reform of the clergy" (II-R12)—the comprehensive enactment of Rivadavian anticlericalism—that put an end to the tithes altogether. The second measure was, of course, a further step in the direction of outright toleration for dissenters: it meant toleration at least for dead Protestants. In February 1825, the treaty between the United Provinces of the Río de la Plata and Great Britain explicitly granted freedom of religion to British subjects (II-R17), and in October of the same year a Buenos Aires provincial law extended toleration to everyone (II-R19). In so doing, Buenos Aires put final legal approval on a situation that had been developing de facto for some years. In the interior, by contrast, opinion was generally adamant against toleration in any form, and often, therefore, the provision of the 1825 treaty was specifically disowned by provincial authorities.[20]

Whereas religious toleration clearly served to enlarge the scope of individual liberty in society at large, a good many other enactments in religious matters served to place artificial constraints on the freedom of those drawn to a clerical vocation, and to that extent were thoroughly illiberal. These enactments exemplify a fundamental tension or inconsistency running through all Latin American liberalism of the past century, prepared as it was to curb the liberty of the institutional church for the sake, supposedly, of the greater liberty of the greatest number. A good example is the first significant decree of Rivadavia himself on an ecclesiastical question: in November 1821 he prohibited members of the clergy from enter-

ing Buenos Aires province without official permission (II-R3). This decree subsequently became the one item of Rivadavian anticlericalism to
be formally revoked in the interval between his departure from the ministry and his installation as president of Argentina (II-R18). By then,
however, it had already fulfilled its most important function, as sine qua
non for suppression of the smaller convents.

Rivadavia began his reform of the regular clergy in particular with a
series of measures, from December 1821 to July of the following year,
that removed them from any dependence upon the provincials of their
respective orders and placed them directly under control of the government or, in spiritual affairs, of the ecclesiastical ordinary (II-R4). Also in
July 1822, he suppressed the small Franciscan convent of Recoleta, whose
suburban site he proposed to use for a new cemetery (II-R7), and secularized the hospitals previously controlled by the Bethlehemite friars and
(for women) by the Hermandad de la Caridad (II-R9). The Bethlehemites themselves were given the option of continuing to perform hospital duties under state administration and on the state payroll or retiring
forthwith on a pension. But the capstone for this, as for other aspects of
ecclesiastical reform, was the general reform law of December 1822,
which formally suppressed the houses of the Bethlehemites and those belonging to other male orders that held less than sixteen members; set
maximum size limits as well for both the male and two female convents;
reiterated the dependence of the regulars upon the diocesan ordinary;
prohibited professions before the age of twenty-five; and encouraged the
ordinary to assist both friars and nuns who sought secularization.[21] The
property of suppressed houses passed automatically to the state, and the
real estate belonging even to those that satisfied the requirements for survival was to be exchanged for government obligations.

As things finally turned out, only the main Franciscan convent, among
those of the male orders, was able to escape closure. Thanks both to the
previous decree that made it impossible to call up reinforcements from
other provinces and to the overly cooperative attitude of the ordinary—
Provisor Mariano Zavaleta, who at one point told the remaining friars
either to opt for secularization or to leave Buenos Aires—the male orders
of Mercedarians and Dominicans were extinguished entirely, and one
other small Franciscan convent at the town of San Pedro was closed
down (II-R14, 15, 16). Nor were the assets of the religious orders the
only ecclesiastical property that passed into state hands; separate measures both before and after the "law of reform of the clergy" took possession of any property belonging to the sanctuary of Luján not directly
needed for purposes of the cult (II-R8), did the same with properties of

Buenos Aires Cathedral and its chapter (II-R13), and authorized debtors to redeem their mortgage obligations to the Dominican nunnery and to ecclesiastical *capellanías* by payment in treasury notes (II-R6, 11).

The preceding inventory still does not quite exhaust the Rivadavian program of ecclesiastical reform, which in all essentials was enacted into law and, in Buenos Aires at least, carried out. The basic law of reform had further included provisions for the abolition of the ecclesiastical fuero and for turning the diocesan seminary into a Colegio Nacional de Estudios Eclesiásticos under state auspices. A negative measure of some significance was the omission of any mention of religious orthodoxy from the statement of qualities required in teachers, part of a decree on primary education issued by Rivadavia in 1826 (II-R20). And, finally, there was the cemetery reform already mentioned.

Cemetery reform had attracted the attention of Rivadavia from the first months of his ministry; as early as December 1821 he ordered the construction of new public cemeteries outside the city limits of Buenos Aires, with a view to ending the unsanitary custom of interring cadavers within or directly adjoining church buildings (II-R5). The enforcement of the prohibition of burials inside churches was held in abeyance until such time as the new facilities could be inaugurated, but as already noted, the suppression of the Recoleta convent was expressly designed to provide space for cemetery construction. And when Rivadavia issued his detailed regulation for the new Recoleta cemetery, it provided that cadavers should not be taken into churches even for funeral services: they should go directly from mortuary to cemetery gates (II-R10).

Needless to say, many innovations relating to religion had more than religious significance. Toleration, as seen before, was part of the campaign to attract immigration, while suppression of the ecclesiastical fuero was one installment of the broader abolition of judicial privileges. The reduction, then elimination, of the tithes was also a tax reform. And the seizure of substantial amounts of ecclesiastical property—irreversible insofar as the government then sold off many of the assets it had taken[22]— was one means of expanding the sphere of individual as distinct from corporate enterprise, supposedly for the economic good of the province. Much the same can be said of efforts to encourage the redemption of ecclesiastical *censos*. For that matter, the campaign against the religious orders, which first subjected them to more rigorous control and then wiped them out except for one male convent and the city's two nunneries, derived in large part from the conviction that they represented a socially indefensible misapplication of human and material resources. The argument was difficult to apply in the case of the Bethlehemite friars, whose function of service to the community had to be acknowledged. Even so, it was widely assumed that their function would be more efficiently performed under secular control, just as the entire package of ecclesiastical reforms was designed to promote the secularization of society at the expense of a traditional church that appeared irrelevant at best and at worst a bulwark of obscurantism and reaction that needed to be curbed if the nation was to realize its potential. In fact, the ideal solution, from the Rivadavian standpoint, would have been to convert the church itself into nothing but a utilitarian agency for inculcating practical morality.[23] It is a revealing detail that, in his decree confiscating assets of the Luján sanctuary, Rivadavia observed in justification (and with unfeigned displeasure) that the sanctuary existed *only* to carry on the cult of an image.

The general secularizing tendency is equally well seen in Rivadavia's creation in 1823 of the Sociedad de Beneficencia, which took over not just the women's hospital but other church-connected activities, including various educational programs, and ran them with state support and lay personnel.[24] It is reflected, too, in his primary education decree of 1826 and in the conversion of the ecclesiastical seminary into a Colegio Nacional, which in turn was to form part of the University of Buenos Aires founded by Rivadavia in 1821.[25] Nor did it apply only to the living. Cemetery reform, which had been a prominent concern of the European Enlightenment and which was introduced to Buenos Aires by Rivadavia, did not strip burial of the dead of all religious trappings, but it did keep secular considerations uppermost in the placement of cadavers. As it happened, this was one of the measures of Rivadavia that in due course was most widely imitated in other provinces.

Looking at the entire reform program adopted at Buenos Aires from 1821 to 1827, though mainly during the first two years, one is hard put to find significant tenets of nineteenth-century Latin American liberalism not acted on in some way. Much, of course, had already been done by earlier revolutionary authorities, especially in the Assembly of 1813. The liquidation of religious orders and seizure of church property were not as complete as they would be in the later Mexican Reforma (or its Colombian equivalent of roughly the same period), but they were complete enough, particularly in light of the relative weakness of the church to begin with in Buenos Aires. A charge of timidity or lack of zeal in certain other areas would perhaps be easier to support, but there was some record of accomplishment almost everywhere.

Naturally the disparity in numbers of reforms respectively classified as political, socioeconomic, and religious does not in itself constitute an objective measurement of difference in emphasis, since not all individual enactments are of comparable importance, and not all matters of official concern lent themselves equally well to manipulation by means of formal legislation and decrees. However, it is no doubt significant that religious measures, even counting the "law of reform of the clergy" merely as one item, make up the largest single group. If it is just that in this area a great deal had been left undone by earlier revolutionary governments, then Rivadavia and his associates were prepared to make up for lost time. Indeed, they were prepared to tread far more boldly in religious matters than most other Latin American rulers of the period, including both rulers of other countries and those of the other Argentine provinces. Of course, the greater moderation of the hinterland with respect to liberal innovations extended to other issues besides religion—and there were differences of degree among those provinces themselves as well as between them and Buenos Aires.

3. The Progress of Innovation in the Other Provinces, 1820–1827

Like Buenos Aires, the provinces of the interior were left in full control of their own affairs as of 1820, and they were less affected by the temporary rebirth of a national government presuming to speak for all Argentina in 1825–27. This is not to say that each went its own way under unique local laws and institutions: unless specifically repealed or superseded by local ordinance, measures adopted for the nation as a whole during the first decade of the revolution remained everywhere technically in force. Also, similar problems call forth similar solutions. Nevertheless, there was room for differentiation, reflecting both problems that varied from one region to another and differences in local power structures and in degree of receptivity to the example of frenzied innovation being set by Buenos Aires.

The historian who seeks to analyze the differential process of innovation in the other provinces simply at the level of official enactments—let alone detailed implementation—is immediately faced with a problem of sources. Nowhere in the interior, though Corrientes and Mendoza came close, did a provincial government regularly publish as detailed and systematic a log of its activities as the *Registro Oficial de la Provincia de Buenos Aires*. Official gazettes in the interior tended to appear irregularly, and they were unevenly supplemented by an unofficial press. A number of provinces, such as La Rioja and San Luis, did not even have printing presses, and archival collections that might make up for the lack of printed documents are often incomplete as well. In certain cases retrospective compilations of provincial laws and decrees were issued later in the century (e.g., Entre Ríos, Córdoba, Jujuy), but these too have their limitations.

There are, nevertheless, at least some provinces for which a sufficient body of data on local legislation and executive decrees is available to follow the course of official policy and programs over substantially the whole period from 1820 to the definitive establishment of a national government in 1853. These are Entre Ríos, Corrientes, Santa Fe, Córdoba, Mendoza, San Juan, and Salta/Jujuy. The last two provinces are paired, since Jujuy was formed as an independent province only by secession from Salta in 1834. A better compilation of laws and decrees is available for the province of Jujuy than is available for Salta, but fortunately the data for Salta are somewhat better for the early years, and, since they were applicable to Jujuy prior to its separation, they can be combined with the later data for Jujuy alone to form a single series.

This group of provinces is obviously not a balanced sample, as it tends to exclude the least developed and gives disproportionate representation to the regions of the Littoral and Cuyo. The first of these drawbacks is at present beyond remedy, but the regional imbalance will be lessened in this chapter and in chapter 5, where the interior provinces are again considered, by carrying the process of selection one step further and eliminating San Juan and Santa Fe from consideration. San Juan, like Mendoza, is representative of the Cuyo region, and Santa Fe, like Entre Ríos, is part of the Littoral, but the quality of data is better for both Mendoza and Entre Ríos. Corrientes, of course, is also a Littoral province, but it had a sufficiently distinctive character and history to justify separate analysis. For the rest, the heart of the nation is represented by Córdoba and the northwest by Salta/Jujuy.

In an entirely separate category is the province of Uruguay, which in 1825 rose up to begin to throw off Brazilian rule and briefly rejoined Argentina, having been an integral part at the outbreak of the revolution against Spain. Uruguay's experience during its period of Luso-Brazilian captivity has little bearing on the comparative scheme of this study, but its experience as a restored segment of Argentina, and later as an independent offshoot, does merit attention. As noted in the Introduction, Uruguay offers full and readily accessible data. During the period of reunion, Uruguay's record in the matters under consideration may throw some light on the degree of integration with Argentina that was actually achieved. And it will likewise be of interest to observe whether the treatment of specific issues in independent Uruguay was significantly different from that in one or more of the provinces still forming part of Argentina. However, the latter question will not be directly examined in this chapter, since the period under consideration is 1820–27 only. Nor is chronological coverage for Uruguay, dating only from 1825, comparable to that of the other provinces. Precisely because it is a somewhat special case, Uruguay will be discussed before the others.

Transplatine Argentina: Uruguay

The history of Uruguay during the independence period diverged from that of other Argentine provinces in that it fell prey to Portuguese conquest. Also, Uruguay had in José Gervasio Artigas a leader who combined adherence to some rather conventional liberal objectives with an agrarian populism that had no close parallel elsewhere in the Río de la Plata. His "agrarian reform" would prove abortive, but it sets him and his movement apart.[1] (Naturally this side of Artigas's program aggravated the lack of understanding between him and the "despots of Buenos Aires," who watched the final Portuguese occupation with relative equanimity.) Another distinctive feature was the sheer extent to which the Uruguayan land and population were ravaged by the struggles of the period, again without parallel in the Río de la Plata region.

By the time Uruguay rebelled against the Brazilian empire and rejoined Argentina in 1825, the healing of the ravages of earlier fighting was well under way; Artigas was an exile in Paraguay; and the cadres of his movement were mostly co-opted or destroyed.[2] From that point until the coming of definitive independence in 1828, Uruguay was not always strictly subordinate to Buenos Aires, but then the same could be said of other Argentine provinces during the ostensible restoration of central rule. Not only that, but Uruguay had much in common both socially and economically with the province of Buenos Aires itself, which it broadly resembled in structure if not in scale. It, too, had an essentially pastoral economy oriented to export trade; a capital that was a principal port tending to look outward rather than inward upon its own hinterland; and a society in which such presumed bastions of traditional values as a hereditary nobility and the Roman Catholic church had been either nonexistent or relatively weak. The fact that the two provinces had so much in common—despite a disparity in total resources that protracted warfare had only aggravated—did not necessarily make it easier to bring them together under a single national government. On the contrary, Montevideo was a potential competitor whose incorporation the metropolis across the river would never tolerate on equitable terms. Yet neither should it be surprising that legal enactments on the two sides of the Río de la Plata were often similar.

Particularly since Uruguay was absorbed with the struggle against Brazil, its provincial assembly was in no position to adopt a comprehensive program of reforms in the manner of Buenos Aires during the

Rodríguez–Rivadavia administration; rather, its enactments were a mere advance installment of what Uruguayans would do once they attained full management of their own affairs. Even so, the parallels with what had already been done at Buenos Aires, both in the first years of the revolution and later, scarcely need underscoring. The establishment of universal male suffrage by Uruguay in 1825 (III-U1) was not quite so forthright as in the Buenos Aires law of 1821 (II-P1), because in the latter case elections were direct, and in Uruguay they were indirect, with only property owners allowed to serve as second-stage "electors." Moreover, by formally endorsing the abortive Argentine constitution of 1826, Uruguay officially abandoned the goal of democratic elections less than a year later (III-U7). But the suppression of tithes (III-U3) and cabildos (III-U6) and the treatment of press freedom—with abolition of prior censorship and creation of a jury to hear allegations of press abuses (III-U5, 8)— were almost identical.

Also nearly identical, at least in appearance, was an Uruguayan contribución directa (III-U9), although it seems never to have attained even the limited practical importance of the Buenos Aires original (II-SE4).[3] Uruguay further went on record as explicitly accepting both the gradual elimination of slavery (III-U2) and, as part of a special law of "guarantees," the principle of an economy without artificial restraints on individual initiative (III-U5). Less explicitly, it accepted the system of emphyteusis decreed by the national congress for the administration of public lands (II-SE14; V-U5). To the extent that Uruguayans engaged in foreign trade in the midst of war with Brazil, they were subject to the generally moderate tariff rates of the Argentine national government, in turn derived from those of Buenos Aires, and Argentine law superseded a February 1826 effort of Uruguayans toward protection of local agriculture (III-U4). (To be sure, neither were the national tariffs wholly lacking in protectionist features with respect to flour and grain.)[4] All the rest would come later. The fact remains that the thrust of local legislation would hardly support the thesis that Uruguay in the mid-1820s exhibited a distinctive nationality and that, as a result, reunion with Argentina was a purely artificial arrangement.

The Littoral: Entre Ríos

The province of Entre Ríos lived primarily from the livestock industry, as did the Littoral as a whole, and possibly nowhere else was the picture so uncomplicated by the presence of other economic endeavors. Having suffered (like Uruguay) more than its share of devastation in the strife of the revolutionary period, it entered the following decade with little more

than 20,000 inhabitants, mostly poverty-stricken.[5] Entre Ríos was also
the Littoral province closest to Buenos Aires, and except for the latter's
insistence that its port should preserve a monopoly of overseas trade—
something Entre Ríos was for the moment in no position to challenge—
the fundamental interests of the two provinces were not markedly different. Moreover, when Entre Ríos more or less settled down institu-
tionally, it was under the governorship of the *porteño* Lucio Mansilla
(1821–1824), who had previously served, not quite wholeheartedly, in
the forces of the *entrerriano caudillo* Francisco Ramírez. Little wonder then
that the policies pursued by Entre Ríos were generally compatible with
those of Buenos Aires, even in the era of Rivadavian reformism.

The one measure of Entre Ríos that most clearly betrays the influence
of Buenos Aires is the law on reform of religious orders that flatly prohibited "convents or monastic houses" (III-ER9). Since there weren't any
of these in Entre Ríos at the time the law was issued, their prohibition
could have no immediate application. It was a guideline for the future and
a statement of principle, and its outside inspiration was frankly acknowledged in the preamble: "There is nothing more just or fitting than to
imitate the conduct of peoples who precede us in the highroad of civilization. . . ."[6] The corollary provision of the law that called for secularization of individual friars serving within the province reflected not only the
Rivadavian example but also the appearance of specific requests for secularization and the encouragement of Provisor Mariano Zavaleta of Buenos Aires. However, permission to operate in Entre Ríos without opting
to secularize was in fact granted, e.g., to the notoriously ultramontane
Fray Francisco Castañeda, who had militantly opposed the Rivadavian
reforms in Buenos Aires and received the approval of Governor Mateo
García de Zúñiga in May 1827 to open a school at Paraná.[7] Neither did
Entre Ríos join Buenos Aires in granting religious toleration, but it did
follow Buenos Aires's lead in prohibiting church burials (III-ER7) and in
the abolition of the tithe system (III-ER6).[8]

The latter was about as far as the impoverished Littoral province dared
go in financial reform, unless one includes a tariff policy that featured essentially moderate levies on import trade (III-ER2).[9] Such a tariff merely
gave recognition to the pastoral nature of the economy and to the primacy of treasury interests, which were best served by encouraging imports. Where there was conflict between the requirements of economic
reconstruction and those of abstract liberalism, the former automatically
took precedence, so that more than once provincial legislation made the
enjoyment of landownership conditional on covering the land with cattle.[10] But there was no conflict when it came to increasing the number of

human inhabitants. In this case, the province took the theoretically more acceptable course of granting exemptions from taxation and military service to European immigrants, some of whom actually reached Entre Ríos—only to desert soon afterward to Buenos Aires (III-ER10).[11]

Entre Ríos also explicitly accepted the measures promulgated from Buenos Aires in 1812–13 against slavery (III-ER3, 5) and school lashings (III-ER8).[12] The antilashing decree was at first glance even strengthened. The 1811 press reglamento (I-3) was incorporated into provincial legislation too, though with additional and quite explicit warnings against seditious writings and those contrary to morality or Roman Catholicism (III-ER3, 4). Suffrage provisions, in the beginning, were as generous as in the Buenos Aires law of 1821, and they became only slightly less so when the formally democratic electoral regulation of *Jefe Supremo* Francisco Ramírez (III-ER1) was superseded by the provincial constitution of 1822, which required a useful occupation and, from a specified future date, literacy as well for the enjoyment of full citizenship (III-ER3). The abolition of cabildos did not figure among Entre Ríos's accomplishments because they had already ceased in the province almost without their demise being noted. Municipal institutions had never been deeply rooted, and they passed from the scene no later (and possibly earlier) than 1820, when Francisco Ramírez decreed the extinction of the municipality in Corrientes during his abortive annexation of the neighboring province. If Ramírez was also responsible for the end of the cabildos in his own province, as some have suggested, the motive would have to be found in his personal drive for aggrandizement rather than a conscious campaign of administrative centralization and rationalization as at Buenos Aires.[13]

Even counting the elimination of cabildos and suppression of nonexistent convents—and the adoption of a written constitution which Buenos Aires still lacked—the number of legal innovations recorded in Entre Ríos was far less than at Buenos Aires. In a province of such rudimentary economy and society, there was not really a great deal to reform or legislate. A similarly modest achievement would naturally be seen in other interior provinces, as compared with Buenos Aires, although in some provinces the greater weight of tradition was as much responsible as was mere simplicity of lifestyle.

The Littoral: Corrientes

The province of Corrientes, though also of the Littoral, presented a number of special features. It was comparable to Entre Ríos in size but had almost twice the population.[14] It too had suffered severely in the civil strife of earlier years, as well as from the indiscriminate slaughter of livestock for hides with the definitive opening of the region to non-Spanish trade. But Corrientes was farther removed from Buenos Aires and economically more diversified. Livestock was the principal industry, yet agriculture was noticeably more important than in Entre Ríos. And the "city" of Corrientes, with something over 5,000 inhabitants, was older and had more of an urban identity than any of the settlements in the neighboring province. Corrientes even had significant household and artisan industries, shipbuilding among them.[15] Finally, there was social and cultural diversity. At one extreme stood a small upper class that, in the words of the brothers Robertson, considered themselves the descendants of noble *conquistadores* and on that ground naturally superior to newly rich porteños.[16] At the other extreme could be found not only slaves but some remnants of the Spanish colonial mission network, which lingered on at the beginning of the 1820s in the form of separate Indian communities with their own lands and institutions. In a larger national context, Corrientes stands out for its vigorous support of the principle of tariff protection both in its own legislation and, later on, in interprovincial negotiations.[17] Corrientes is notable also for its military-political struggle against the dictatorship of Juan Manuel de Rosas, whereas Entre Ríos continued to function as a satellite of Buenos Aires through the greater part of Rosas's reign. But even during the years that immediately followed the collapse of national unity in 1820, Corrientes's profile of innovations was observably different in several respects from that of Entre Ríos.

It was no doubt praiseworthy, in the context of the period, that Corrientes extended full citizenship to all free adult males, as in Buenos Aires, and did so through a formal written constitution broadly similar to that of Entre Ríos (III-CS1). Cabildos were suppressed, or resuppressed (III-CS2), and otherwise there is little of note from a purely political standpoint. No concessions were made to religious toleration either in the constitution or in other legislation. Corrientes did join the movement to prohibit burials in churches (III-CS5), and the provincial government, at least on paper, took over the assets of the Dominican convent (III-CS7). Unlike Entre Ríos, however, Corrientes did not cite any outside example for its "reform" of this one convent, nor was any action taken concerning the Franciscan and Mercedarian houses also existing in the provincial capital; immediate practical considerations, notably the virtual abandonment of the convent in question, rather than abstract anticlericalism, appear to have been the motivating force. At most there may have been a trace of anticlericalism in the law that called for a provincial system of education under strictly secular direction—particularly in light of Governor Pedro Ferré's original proposal emphasizing the logical distinction between public instruction and religious worship (III-CS8).

In social and economic matters Corrientes's chief originality lay in the fact that it had some Indian communities to liquidate, whereas Entre Ríos had none and Buenos Aires had disposed of its only one some years earlier (I-9). The various laws and decrees relating to the two communities of Itatí and Santa Lucía not only converted the Indians into small private property owners (though with temporary suspension of alienability of their farm plots) but further abetted their amalgamation with the Creole population by making provision for non-Indians who so desired to obtain a share of the former community lands (III-CS4, 6, 9). (Indians nevertheless continued to enjoy a separate and favored legal status in the payment of parish fees.)[18]

For the rest, Corrientes also expressed interest in the encouragement of immigration by the terms of the revised 1824 constitution, offering newcomers a temporary subsidy (III-CS2) with little, if any, practical effect. But economic policy in general was not necessarily liberal. Quite apart from its strict adherence to tariff protection of local crafts (III-CS3), the provincial government did things such as requiring rural inhabitants to plant crops,[19] the equivalent of Entre Ríos's legal requirement that landowners introduce cattle. While the emphasis on agriculture would have pleased Rivadavia and his circle, the attempt to use overt compulsion in the matter would clearly have gone against their professed creed.

Cuyo: Mendoza

The Cuyo region, consisting of the two provinces of Mendoza and San Juan at the foot of the Andes as well as the outlying province of San Luis, had been transferred from the jurisdiction of Santiago de Chile to that of Buenos Aires only in the late colonial period, and in the immediate post-independence era it retained close economic as well as social and cultural ties with the trans-Andean republic. The economy centered around livestock and irrigated agriculture, yet commerce was also important, especially for Mendoza. The region had contributed a disproportionate share of men and supplies to San Martín's epic crossing of the Andes, but on the whole Cuyo suffered less from the war with Spain and attendant civil conflict than had the Littoral. Indirectly, it is true, the coming of independence administered a blow to the Cuyo economy through the opening of the port of Buenos Aires on a regular basis; the resultant sharp increase in sales of European wine largely displaced the wines of Mendoza and San Juan from the porteño market. It took some time to accomplish the needed shift of emphasis to other lines of production such as cereals and livestock—an adjustment that Mendoza made somewhat better than San Juan. In both Mendoza and San Juan there were entrenched landowning and mercantile elites who enjoyed clear predominance over the other social sectors. They did have to accommodate a certain number of military upstarts, some of whom would at times get out of hand, but they no longer had to worry much about the interference of outside bureaucrats in their affairs.

These local patriciates—above all the younger members—were not unreceptive to the liberal ideas that now flowed in freely from Santiago as well as from Buenos Aires.[20] Indeed, in 1825 San Juan briefly threw discretion to the winds and flatly suppressed both the fueros (military and ecclesiastical) and the religious orders under the leadership of its own Rivadavia, Dr. Salvador María del Carril, and formally embraced freedom of religion. No other interior province imitated the work of Buenos Aires reformers quite so closely as this, but it soon turned out that however receptive to new ideas the rulers of San Juan might be, they did not enjoy the same freedom of operation as their porteño counterparts. Rival political and military leaders, with the aid of Facundo Quiroga from neighboring La Rioja, quickly answered the outraged cries of a less enlightened general populace.[21]

In Mendoza, too, there was an *inquietud de reformas*, as reflected in such things as the establishment of a quasi-official society to promote the cause of education through the teaching method of Joseph Lancaster and a revised curriculum that was perceived by some as dangerously unorthodox.[22] Nevertheless, the rulers of Mendoza were a bit more timid than those of San Juan, or perhaps they had more common sense. Their policy preferences were sometimes comparable, but their liberalism was hardly absolute and specific enactments were generally moderate; thus nothing was done in Mendoza to trigger a massive outburst of public indignation.

Mendozan legislators and provincial executives were given to piecemeal approaches and a certain amount of backtracking. In the effort to implant a contribución directa of its own, for example, in replacement of the alcabala and various other taxes (III-M9), Mendoza came closer to the purely fiscal model of Buenos Aires liberalism than did any other province.[23] But the reform was short lived,[24] and it must be set against the attempt—even more quickly abandoned—to reintroduce the colonial playing-card monopoly (III-M4, 5). Moreover, the taxing of imported merchandise was unabashedly protectionist, with the alcabala, once restored, charged at a much higher rate on competing goods from outside the province (III-M4, 13).

Politically, Mendoza created the usual sort of provincial government, with three powers directly or indirectly of popular origin and technically separate even if scarcely equal. The province stopped short of giving itself a formal written constitution, and it dismantled the cabildo only by stages, though rapidly once started (III-M8, 11). The fueros were only slightly restricted (III-M1). A racially discriminatory suffrage remained in effect, at least in the letter of the law, until 1827, when Mendoza stopped observing the formula first consecrated by the Estatuto Provisional of 1815 (I-28) and drew up its own regulation that made the right to vote conditional upon occupational and professional qualifications or, in their lack, some outstanding service to the common good, eliminating any sort of explicitly racial considerations (III-M14).[25] As for the treatment of press freedom, Mendoza's record was even more contradictory than the examples given in the Appendix might suggest: warnings and the official prohibition of ill-defined abuses (III-M2) alternated with reaffirmation of the 1811 reglamento (III-M3) and the suppression (for reasons of "enlightenment" and "decency") of specific newspapers (III-M15).

As in Buenos Aires, the most controversial reforms were those that concerned the church, with the religious orders bearing the brunt of them. Mendoza had more different orders active in its territory than did the province of Buenos Aires, and of these only one was eliminated entirely. However, the others were not in very healthy condition, and one reason was precisely the attempt of the civil authorities, with apparent sincerity, to improve discipline among them by insisting on the rule of common life (III-M6). Many friars preferred to secularize instead, and the Augustinians were then left with an almost empty convent that the government chose to suppress (III-M10).[26] Mendoza further joined Buenos Aires in setting a minimum age for professions, in requiring governmental permission for religious to enter the province, and in asserting diocesan authority over the orders (III-M12). However, the minimum age (twenty-two years) was somewhat lower than in Buenos Aires, and apparently subordination to the ordinary was never really effective in Mendoza.[27]

There was frequent tampering with the tithes as well, and on at least one occasion, when the tithe receipts were diverted to finance the amortization of counterfeit currency (III-M7), Mendoza drew down upon itself formal protests from both civil and ecclesiastical authorities of Córdoba, to whose diocese the province belonged.[28] What Mendoza did with the tithes was not really unique—it was just a bit more blatant than usual. Diversion of tithe receipts was always on a short-term, ad hoc basis, and the province did not tamper with the rate of the tithes, much less make them purely voluntary. Neither did Mendoza have qualms about joining the other two Cuyo provinces in the Pact of Guanache of April 1827, which, among other things, specifically pledged the continued exclusion of non–Roman Catholic cults.[29] All in all, as an ecclesiastical historian expressed it, the example of Buenos Aires was certainly felt, but what happened in Mendoza was "a weak and distant echo of the Rivadavian reform."[30]

The Northwest: Salta

The Northwest—whose geographic definition is flexible, depending on whether Tucumán is included—had in common with Cuyo a mixed economy based on both agriculture and grazing. To a greater extent than in Cuyo, artisan crafts were also important. The region had been much more ravaged by war, and its trading connection with Upper Peru (now Bolivia) diminished in relative importance while that of Mendoza with Chile was increasing. Yet here, too, the prerevolutionary elites largely maintained their position. How receptive they were to liberal innovations varied from one province to another and from time to time, but certainly in the case of Salta the climate was more favorable than otherwise. Moreover, the fact that until 1834 Salta included the present province of Jujuy naturally added to its relative importance. It also added a substantial Indian population that had retained much of its traditional culture and sociopolitical organization.

During the Rivadavian era, Salta enjoyed in Buenos Aires the reputation of being a bastion of progressive thought and action in the far interior. While this reputation was based in large part on Salta's stand on national issues, as a supporter of Buenos Aires leadership, it was not wholly unjustified from the standpoint of institutional reform within the province. But it must be noted that in Salta, as in Mendoza, the process was rather uneven. When the province adopted a written constitution in 1821, it was a decidedly rudimentary one, and the national charters of 1817 and 1819 remained in force on a wide range of matters not dealt with explicitly, as did the 1811 reglamento with regard to treatment of the press (III-S3). The suppression of cabildos in Salta by a subsequent law of 1825 was incomplete as well as tardy: it applied only to the municipal government of the capital city and not to the subordinate towns of Jujuy and Orán, ostensibly lest their citizens be deprived of an immediate mouthpiece for complaints against official abuses (III-S8).[31]

The first installments of ecclesiastical reform were of mostly minor importance. To some extent they were only preparation for more definitive measures whose time had not yet come: the vote of the provincial legislature to plan, but not yet build, a public cemetery outside the Salta urban area (III-S10), and the law requiring the regular orders to obtain approval of the diocesan ordinary before alienating convent properties, the intent being to keep such properties intact until the government was ready to dispose of them properly (III-S5). This law was part of a more general effort, as in a number of provinces, to bring the orders under control of the diocesan or secular clergy, an especially attractive goal for Salta, itself the seat of a diocese. Another expression of this policy was the province's refusal to recognize the legitimate superiors of the two Franciscan convents, named by the respective provincial chapter, so that the authority of the ordinary might be unobstructed (III-S14). It is not certain, of course, just how rigorously this official veto of the Franciscans' own leadership was enforced, nor whether a similar step was taken with convents of other orders. Then again, while Salta moved to facilitate the redemption of *censos de capellanías*, the measure was only permissive, allowing the executive to enter into agreement for that purpose with those who owed the censos, if both parties desired (III-S6). The real push to lay hands on the capital of censos for the benefit of the provincial treasury would come later (V-S2).

The law of December 1825 that extended a general welcome to foreign enterprise, guaranteeing protection of foreigners' property and freedom and offering special tax exemptions to mining entrepreneurs (III-S13), is another measure that was more important as evidence of a policy decision than for its immediate practical effect. Despite publication in three languages, the law ushered in neither a wave of European immigrants nor a Salta mining boom, but this was not for lack of interest in liberal approaches to economic and social development on the part of local leaders. The province's stagnant economy was enough to discourage immigration, and readily exploitable mineral resources were unspectacular. The handling of Indian common lands was something that Salta had more direct control over than the decisions of European investors and prospective immigrants, but the law authorizing division of those lands as private property—both as a reward to the Indians for their services to the cause of liberty and as another stimulus to economic development (III-S12)—did not really settle matters, and the status of Indian lands would continue to concern the province of Jujuy after it broke away from Salta. Nevertheless, again at the level of public policy and taken in conjunction with comparable measures adopted in Buenos Aires and Corrientes, the law further demonstrates the repudiation of the traditional collective landholding system in what is now Argentina. Its immediate pretext was a request by the lieutenant governor of Jujuy, who suggested that dividing up the common lands would put an end to bothersome disputes among the Indians themselves,[32] yet the measure was also in line with the ringing attack on "that absurd system" made by the provincial executive in an earlier message to the legislature.[33]

Though Salta was not prepared to follow the example of Buenos Aires in legally freeing the rate of interest (II-SE8), by prohibiting moratoria to debtors save by consent of their creditors (III-S11) it acted in another way to protect the liberty and property of moneylenders. Salta thereby anticipated one of the subsequent measures of Rosas in which he most closely conformed to classical liberal economic thinking (IV-SE16). To be sure, Salta also stands out as the first among the provinces under consideration to backtrack from the abolition of fiscal monopolies, as it restored the playing-card monopoly in 1820 and again in 1821 (III-S1), but this was only a brief relapse, and Salta is the province which, after Buenos Aires, made the most forthright attack on the fueros. Salta suspended the military fuero in civil cases (and that of fiscal employees, save as concerned actions in line of duty) (III-S7) and ruled that no fueros should apply in police questions (III-S9). Governor Alvarez de Arenales later spoke as if all fueros had been ended, which technically does not appear to have been the case,[34] but the tendency was clear enough. Salta followed the lead of Buenos Aires still more closely in treatment of the suffrage, granting the vote to all free men by a regulation of 1823 (III-S4). (This was after the province's constitution had first implicitly adopted the socially and racially restrictive provisions approved by the late national congress.) And another of Salta's governors issued an edict—whose practical effect remains uncertain—against the degrading tradition of bullfighting (III-S2).

The Center: Córdoba

The one province with resources even remotely matching those of Buenos Aires was Córdoba, which could boast one portion of the vast pampas, its own agricultural zones, some important artisan industries, a little mining, and a population of approximately 76,000 that included what was far and away the most important urban nucleus of the interior.[35] With the oldest (prior to independence, the only) university in Argentina, the city of Córdoba was also an intellectual center, but it was attuned to traditional Spanish and Catholic thinking, not to the latest fads of Western Europe, unlike Buenos Aires in the 1820s. The classic comparison sketched by Sarmiento between liberal Buenos Aires and conservative, traditionalist Córdoba[36] is overdrawn but contains a considerable measure of truth. Córdoba was significantly less receptive to institutional change than Salta and Mendoza, even though its socioeconomic structure had much in common with theirs.

Cordobés conservatism was conspicuously expressed in the resolution of the provincial legislature in 1820 that reaffirmed the right of citizens to be buried inside churches, in effect heading off a cemetery reform such as Buenos Aires and various other provinces would soon be adopting (III-CA1). Not quite six years later a revision of the provincial constitution eliminated the formal religious oath to defend the Roman Catholic church (and otherwise carry out the duties of his office) which the governor had previously been required to take (III-CA10). This change was intended, as the debate in the legislature made perfectly clear, as a bold, modernizing gesture, but it would be too much to assume that Córdoba had somehow lost its traditional moorings. In fact, the first provincial constitution adopted in 1821 (III-CA2) set a tone of Roman Catholic exclusivism that was never challenged in any substantive way. The new gubernatorial oath showed a regard for enlightened opinion and not much more. Córdoba's reaction to the 1825 treaty between the United Provinces and Great Britain, a flat refusal to accept the article that provided religious toleration for the subjects of each state in the territory of the other (III-CA8), was a better indication of the climate of opinion.

The practice of honoring the May Revolution by setting free a token number of female slaves purchased by the government (III-CA9) combined a regard for appearances with at least some concrete effect, but it is less noteworthy in a comparative perspective than the decision of Córdoba to maintain overt racial discrimination in regulating the suffrage. The province's constitution not only contained a socially and economically restrictive formulation of voting rights but subjected all those of African descent to the additional test contained in national regulations of the previous decade. Cordobés historians have extolled the liberality of their forebears in allowing any pardos to vote at all,[37] yet no other province (either of the sample here or of all those that worked out their own suffrage legislation after 1820) adopted the same discriminatory approach.[38]

In fiscal matters, Rivadavia himself would have approved of the nominal elimination of the alcabala and certain lesser taxes by the tariff law of 1822 (III-CA3) as a first step toward rationalization and simplification of the tax system. However, it was only a small first step, and later steps (some of which will be mentioned in chapter 5) tended to be in reverse direction. Moreover, the tariff law itself was distinctly protectionist. At the same time, rationalization of local administration by eliminating the cabildos (III-CA7) was accomplished, and the Córdoba constitution reflected a tendency to restrict the military, if not the ecclesiastical, fuero by granting the former only to members of the disciplined militia, not the milicia cívica or home guard, and only during active service.

The constitution further combined a declaration of responsibility to the disadvantaged with a guarantee of protection for individual enterprise. Though one of the more carefully drafted provincial charters, it did not deal explicitly with freedom of the press; but after a printing press was reestablished in Córdoba in 1823, Governor Juan Bautista Bustos issued his own regulatory decree that purported to safeguard free expression even as it prohibited attacks on either the political authorities or the established church (III-CA4). Some months later, Bustos withdrew his press decree (III-CA5) and disputed with the legislature on whether to put it back in effect or to issue a new law, and in the absence of any legal guarantees whatever, the province's newspapers temporarily stopped publication.[39] Finally, in November 1824, a press law was adopted along quite conventional lines, declaring the 1811 national regulation in force (III-CA6). So after some strange gyrations the legal treatment of press freedom in Córdoba ended on an acceptable note. Indeed, all things considered, Córdoba was not impervious to the winds of change, but neither was it an infatuated imitator of Buenos Aires.

A Comparative Overview

The preceding examination of individual provinces (including that of Buenos Aires as given in chapter 2) reveals numerous points of difference and similarity, not all of which readily lend themselves to comparative analysis. In some cases there is no problem: any one province did or did not restrict religious professions or church burials, and the different responses to these issues can be directly compared. On the other hand, the fact that Corrientes moved to liquidate Indian communal landholdings and Entre Ríos did not has little relevance because Entre Ríos had none to liquidate. One can equally well question the comparability of outlawing convents where none existed (as in Entre Ríos again) and suppressing them where they were active and important (as in Buenos Aires). Yet anticonvent measures did reflect in each instance a similar and unfavorable view of the monastic life, and they were analogous in policy intent if not immediate impact. Indeed, it is not too much to say that there is an analogy in terms of policy between the liquidation of Indian communal holdings in Corrientes and, say, the abortive move to lift government controls from the price of bread and meat in Buenos Aires. Both measures sought, in different ways, to enlarge the sphere of individual initiative. And the advantage of increasing the number of possible comparisons between provinces may sometimes justify the methodological liberty of grouping rather different enactments as expressions of a single policy orientation.

TABLE 3.1. Political-Judicial Innovations

	Buenos Aires	Cór- doba	Corrien- tes	E. Ríos	Men- doza	Salta	Uru- guay
Written constitution	0	+	+	+	0	+	−ᵃ
Suffrage extension	+	0	+	−	−	+	+
Guarantee of press freedom	+	−ᵇ	0	+	−ᵇ	+	+
Abolition of fueros	+	−	0	0	−	−	0
Abolition of cabildos	+	+	+	+	+	−	+
Combined scores	8	6	6	7	5	8	7

+ = adoption (2 points).
− = partial or temporary adoption (1 point).
0 = no adoption (0 points).
a. Referring to Uruguay's acceptance of the *national* constitution. Since Buenos Aires's provincial government had been abolished, Buenos Aires was unable to do as much; hence it may appear unfair to give Uruguay a higher rating on this item. However, Buenos Aires, unlike Uruguay, had had more than ample time to give itself a provincial constitution and had failed to do so.
b. Based on averaging of contradictory measures.

Whether comparison is made in terms of specific measures or more general policies, there are cases in which strict dichotomization is not applicable. A province might enact for itself only a limited version of something done elsewhere, or it might reverse the action almost as soon as taken, and in such cases an intermediate classification will be most appropriate. It is also quite conceivable that in some cases the apparent failure to take action one way or the other on a given issue may reflect nothing more than the inadequacy of available sources. Least of all can it be assumed that merely counting reforms adopted, not adopted, or adopted in part will give a scientific measurement of the extent to which any one province underwent a process of change. Despite these and other limitations, however, tables 3.1–3.3 are perhaps useful as rough representations of the performance of the various provinces in broad spheres of governmental activity. For each province in each table, and at the risk of giving a specious appearance of mathematical precision, the results are converted into a single numerical score.

In the first, or political, table (table 3.1), the existence of any sort of written constitution, quite apart from its specific provisions, is one of the items compared on the ground that the adoption of such a device for limiting arbitrary power, however ineffective in practice, was a standard requirement of nineteenth-century political liberalism; it also serves the purpose of providing at least one line on which Buenos Aires can be awarded a zero. Broadening of the suffrage is included as a separate item, with the already noted reservations as to how far it can be considered an indicator of liberalism.[40] And press freedom refers here to some reaffirmation of the principles contained in the reglamento of October 1811, including exemption from prior censorship: this area is noted for frequent and wide gaps between theory and practice, but also as one that produced a large number of official enactments. The remaining two items are self-explanatory, even though the abolition of fueros is admittedly more than a strictly political reform.

It is in the representation of social and economic reforms, in table 3.2, that grouping of somewhat different actions under a combined policy heading becomes expedient. Freedom of enterprise is thus a catchall designation encompassing several distinct measures taken at Buenos Aires, the liquidation of common lands ordered in Corrientes and Salta, and (for partial credit) the declarations of economic principle in Córdoba and Uruguay. Similarly, the liberation of interest rates in Buenos Aires and Salta's antimoratorium law, which in effect served to facilitate foreclosures, are lumped together as one item signifying greater freedom for moneylenders. Tax reform refers here to such things as abolition of the alcabala, creation of a contribución directa, or both (as in Buenos Aires and, briefly, Mendoza) but not mere elimination or reshuffling of nuisance taxes. Neither does it cover tariff policy, which is featured separately. The other items are, once again, largely self-explanatory, even though it should be emphasized again that the encouragement of immigration in Salta or Corrientes does not mean that immigrants came. The ecclesiastical reform table 3.3, which concludes the set, requires no special comment.

The tables do show clearly enough that the contrast between Buenos Aires and the other provinces as a group is substantially greater than differences among the other provinces themselves. This result is hardly surprising, and neither is the fact that the sharpest contrast is to be found in religious matters. The latter detail suggests that Catholic traditionalists have been basically correct in harping upon Rivadavian anticlericalism as a critical aspect of the cleavage between Buenos Aires and the rest of Argentina.

TABLE 3.2. Social-Economic Innovations

	Buenos Aires	Cór- doba	Corrien- tes	E. Ríos	Men- doza	Salta	Uru- guay
Greater freedom of enterprise	+	−	+	0	0	+	−
Freedom of interest/ foreclosures	+	0	0	0	0	+	0
Further moves against slavery	+	−	0	−[a]	0	0	−[a]
Reform of tax system	+	+	0	0	−	0	+
Tariff moderation	+	0	0	+	0	−[b]	−
Promotion of immigration	+	0	+	+	0	+	0
Emphyteusis	+	0	0	0	0	0	+[c]
Combined scores	14	4	4	5	1	7	7

+ = adoption (2 points).
− = partial or temporary adoption (1 point).
0 = no adoption (0 points).
a. Representing the mere reaffirmation of previous national legislation.
b. The data consulted on Salta's tariff policy are so scanty that this is an inference based in considerable part on lack of contrary evidence and on the extrapolation backward of subsequent data for Jujuy (see chapter 5).
c. Representing the enforcement in Uruguay of national legislation (see V-U5).

Even though the differences among the other provinces are not clear-cut, certain gradations do appear. Entre Ríos and Salta were obviously more "liberal" in the context of the period than was Córdoba, thanks chiefly to the latter's conspicuous lack of receptivity to religious reform. Salta would rank even higher if the prohibition or restriction of bullfighting were included in one of the tables. On its part, Mendoza—which shares with Córdoba the illiberal end of the spectrum—would also rank higher if the period covered by the data ended in 1825 instead of mid-1827, thus giving the Cuyo province less time to undo some of its more progressive attainments. It may also be that the particular set of cross-provincial indicators featured for comparison understates Mendoza's brand of moderate reformism; even so, the results of the comparison do point to the need for caution in describing the impact of liberal ideologi-

TABLE 3.3. Ecclesiastical Innovations

	Buenos Aires	Cór-doba	Corrien-tes	E. Ríos	Men-doza	Salta	Uru-guay
Abolition of tithes	+	0	0	+	−ª	0	+
Lesser convents suppressed	+	0	−	+	+	0	0
Other church assets taken	+	0	0	0	0	0	0
Religious professions limited	+	0	0	+	+	0	0
Redemption of censos facilitated	+	0	0	0	0	+	0
Prohibition of church burials	+	0	+	+	0	−	0
Religious toleration	+	0	0	0	0	0	0
Combined scores	14	0	3	8	5	3	2

+ = adoption (2 points).
− = partial or temporary adoption (1 point).
0 = no adoption (0 points).
a. Representing partial appropriation of tithe receipts to other purposes, by formal legislative action.

cal currents on Mendoza. Uruguay, which had little time in which to compile any record of innovation, and Corrientes, fall somewhere in the middle. Except for Mendoza, none of these relative standings is truly surprising. But if they generally agree with the traditional wisdom, they at least do so on the basis of a specific and verifiable (though admittedly limited) set of data. And they further provide a point of departure for assessing the differential impact, province by province, of the new climate of reaction and retrenchment that set in by stages following the collapse of the Rivadavian presidency in mid-1827.

4. The Reaction in Buenos Aires

THE BRIEF heyday of porteño reformism of the Rivadavian variety came to an end in mid-1827, when Rivadavia resigned from the presidency of Argentina. His resignation and subsequent departure into voluntary exile also signaled an abandonment, for the present, of the attempt to create a true national government. Once again each province assumed full control of its affairs, and in the province of Buenos Aires the immediate beneficiary was the local faction of Federalists, led initially by Manuel Dorrego and then by Juan Manuel de Rosas. Though federalism and liberalism are associated in conventional interpretations of nineteenth-century Latin America, Argentina is commonly cited as an exception—a country where the self-styled Federalist Rosas bitterly denounced and sought to undo the work of the liberal centralist Rivadavia. Yet in practice the rejection of liberalism by Rosas was never as complete as portrayed in the works of either Argentine liberals who hate him still or Argentine revisionists of the right and left who choose to praise him. Nor, of course, did the definitive version of the Rosas dictatorship take shape until 1835.

Earlier Phases, 1827–35

The departure from government of Bernardino Rivadavia led first to the transitional regime of Vicente López y Planes, who did little more than acknowledge the evident collapse of central authority. He proceeded to turn over his office—downgraded from presidency to governorship—on 13 August 1827 to the highly popular but somewhat erratic Federalist chieftain Dorrego, who had little time or opportunity to accomplish

50

much before he was overthrown and executed in December 1828. During the Dorrego interlude a few of the measures of the preceding period were rescinded, but the new governor was no reactionary; Dorrego was essentially a liberal, but less doctrinaire than Rivadavia and more in touch with popular sentiment. The regime of Dorrego's successor and executioner, General Juan Lavalle, did not accomplish much either, again for lack of time and opportunity. Though Lavalle and his collaborators considered themselves the heirs of Rivadavia, they were mostly preoccupied with trying to fight off Dorrego's heir, Rosas. Rather quickly, Rosas prevailed.

The first governorship of Rosas, from December 1829 to December 1832, saw a further retreat from the accomplishments of the Rivadavian era, but there was no wholesale rejection of Rivadavian reform. When he took the title "Restorer of the Laws" (*Restaurador de las Leyes*), Rosas intended no blanket exclusion of laws issued during a past administration. Indeed, he had been generally a supporter of the regime of Governor Martín Rodríguez, in which Rivadavia had served as minister.[1] Rosas abhorred the later excesses of Rivadavia, once the latter turned his attention from government of the province to overly ambitious schemes of national organization and development. Moreover, while Rosas frankly clothed himself with dictatorial powers—five days after his installation as governor he was voted "extraordinary faculties" for the purpose of "restoring" provincial institutions—he used them with what must be called, in comparison with his later performance, a spirit of moderation. He was least moderate in his adamant insistence on those powers as a condition for governing, so that when faced with their loss he took leave of the governorship. He did not return to office until early 1835, and in the intervening years of turmoil, with the province headed successively by three lesser members of the party of Dorrego and Rosas, a part of what antiliberal reaction had occurred since 1827 was quietly undone.

The period from the resignation of Rivadavia to the second governorship of Rosas thus brought little net change in legal and institutional frameworks. There was considerable rescinding and reissuing of laws and decrees, and no lack of minor tinkering, but the record of the period as a whole, compiled in an atmosphere of almost constant civil strife and hardening of factional antagonisms, was curiously inconclusive. Even so, that record forms part of the larger story of innovation and concomitant reaction that began with the revolution of 1810, and it provides a necessary frame of reference for assessing the policies and actions of the mature Rosas regime of 1835–52. To facilitate comparison with reforms of the Rivadavian period being reacted against, or in certain cases built upon, measures will again be considered in broad political, socioeconomic, and religious categories, as in chapter 2.

Political Innovations, 1827–35

Politically, one characteristic of the period 1827–35 is the disproportionate number of measures that concern the status of the press, an obviously sensitive matter during the years in which Juan Manuel de Rosas was rising to supreme power. Though it would have been possible to have a sharp decline in press freedom or other freedoms without a formal change in liberal legislation, legal changes appear closely synchronized with changes in the practical state of affairs. Generally, the press freedom established earlier suffered obvious erosion, starting during the governorship of Dorrego with a law containing no important procedural changes but spelling out more fully what was forbidden, among other things, attacks on the state religion, writings that encouraged disobedience to the provincial authorities, and whatever might "appear obscene" (IV-P2).

At the conclusion of the civil war unleashed by the overthrow of Dorrego, Acting Governor Juan José Viamonte went a step farther in October 1829 by forbidding all press criticism of the agreement between Rosas and Lavalle that had put an end to the hostilities with Viamonte himself installed as temporary head of government (IV-P4). This was followed, after Rosas became governor, by the public burning—ordered by the Junta de Representantes—of publications that had defamed both Dorrego and Rosas (IV-P5). In due course, Rosas unveiled his full solution to the problem of press abuses: by a decree of February 1832 he forbade anyone to set up a printing press or produce a periodical without express authorization, specified that no foreigner could obtain such permission without first renouncing all claim to diplomatic protection, and made editors fully and personally responsible for anything they printed (IV-P7).[2] When Rosas temporarily stepped down from the governorship, the legislature annulled this extreme decree and put the law sponsored by Dorrego back into effect (IV-P8). However, the unsettled state of the province led authorities a few months later to suspend all publication of what were vaguely referred to as "political writings" (IV-P9). Though the suspension was soon lifted (IV-P11), the representatives ultimately voted in September 1834 to reinstate the highly restrictive 1832 press decree (IV-P12) as pressure increased for the return of Rosas to office on his own terms. The decree was to remain in force until after Rosas fell from power.

The grant of universal male suffrage also suffered erosion during the brief Dorrego interlude, under a law excluding the military rank and file, though not officers, from the right to vote (IV-P1). The ostensible objective in this case was to make the suffrage of remaining voters more effective by ending bloc voting by the military in favor of official candidates.[3] A more serious instance of political retrogression was, of course, the granting of "extraordinary faculties" to Rosas as governor. Unlike the subsequent grant of dictatorial powers in 1835, the powers granted Rosas during his first governorship did not involve a sweeping transfer of supreme legislative and judicial authority to the governor, but instead only removed some of the normal limitations on executive authority.[4] Indeed, such powers had been granted repeatedly and almost routinely to previous governments, and the grant was a temporary arrangement, the non-renewal of which provoked Rosas's resignation. Nevertheless, while in possession of these faculties, Rosas imposed restrictions on the press, sought to tighten official control of personal movements by strict enforcement of a passport requirement for travel within as well as outside the province (IV-P6), and established the notorious requirement (3 February 1832) that professional people, including priests and medical doctors and not just government employees, wear the *divisa punzó*, the Federalist red ribbon.[5] And these measures were in addition to his often heavy-handed conduct of the province's business in still other matters.

Whether Rosas really deserves credit for relative moderation during his first governorship, it is noteworthy how far his immediate (interim) successors abandoned the course he had charted. They did not rescind the decree for wearing of the red, however much enforcement of it may have been relaxed, but they preferred Dorrego's press law. Likewise, General Viamonte, once more installed as acting governor in 1833, largely overthrew Rosas's restrictions on freedom of movement by lifting the passport requirement for travel within the province for persons other than rural hired laborers, who would still need a pass from their employers (IV-P10). A comparable move noted below (IV-SE10) enlarged the freedom of personal correspondence. In both instances Viamonte was, if anything, more liberal than Rivadavia, whom the same Viamonte, for self-evident reasons of expediency, refused to allow back from exile. The abortive return of Rivadavia prompted the legislature to notify other exiles that they would need express permission to reenter the province (IV-P13), and throughout the 1827–35 period there were additional abridgements of political liberty never dignified by being made the subject of a general law or decree. Such abridgements occurred under different provincial administrations and were directly related to the civil warfare that remained at least latent at all times. But they were not yet a daily occurrence.

Viamonte had demonstrated some concern for liberal principles during his initial brief stint as governor in 1829, prior to Rosas's first inauguration. On being invested with "extraordinary faculties" himself, Viamonte was careful to promise that he would refer all measures taken by virtue of these powers to the next legislature.[6] He was prepared to tamper with press freedom, yet his judicial decree of October 1829, directing that "extraordinary" appeals be handled solely by the *Cámara de Apelaciones* (IV-P3), was a small but suggestive step in the direction of more effective separation of powers. The measure referred specifically to the *recursos de nulidad e injusticia notoria*, which were appeals from ostensibly final court decisions. Such appeals had formed an integral part of Spanish legal tradition but were objectionable to liberal constitutionalists because they represented an exceptional procedure and provided a ready opportunity for the executive, who often took part in hearing the appeals, to interfere with judicial decisions. Rivadavia had thought of ending them, but he never got around to it.[7] Viamonte did not end them either, but he did refer them exclusively to the judiciary itself so as to avoid both executive interference and undue procedural delays. His decree was not consistently observed in practice; nevertheless, this is one instance, as will be seen, in which Rosas eventually returned to Viamonte's more "liberal" solution.

Socioeconomic Innovations, 1827–35

Although the new Federalist rulers took a less theoretical and less ambitious approach to socioeconomic issues than had their immediate predecessors, the class interests and prejudices represented were not markedly different. As already mentioned, the passport decree of Viamonte exempted everyone but rural laborers, and, generally, measures of a more purely social or economic nature reveal little interest in ameliorating conditions for the common man. The one clear-cut example of a more "populist" approach was Dorrego's nullification, before the measure had a chance to take effect, of Rivadavia's last-minute effort to lift price controls from bread and meat (IV-SE2).[8] Curiously, the provincial legislature later tried to reenact the same reform, throwing in the price of water for good measure (IV-SE13), almost on the eve of Rosas's return to the governorship, only to have the measure signed by Provisional Governor Manuel V. de Maza but never implemented.[9] *Obedézcase pero no se cumpla*: thus a belated return to a more doctrinaire variety of economic liberalism was nipped in the bud.

Just as measures relating to the press predominate in the political category for the years 1827–35, measures relating to the status of slaves and freedmen (*libertos*) are foremost in the socioeconomic category. Several of the measures concern the conditional liberation of slaves captured during the war with Brazil or else the forms of military service required of freedmen—a class of people who, according to Rosas, were under special moral obligation to perform such service for the land that had helped them out of bondage (IV-SE1, 8, 12). These measures differ only in detail from measures adopted earlier, but they are notable as evidence of continued overt segregation by race in the Buenos Aires militia (IV-SE5, 8), part of a larger pattern of formally acknowledged separation of the races in official and quasi-official services. Another example is the rejection, during the administration of Acting Governor Juan Ramón Balcarce, of a petition to admit "colored" children to the "common" schools, on the ground that they already had a school of their own in which they would receive an education more appropriate for their needs.[10] Also suggestive was the tariff of ecclesiastical fees approved in September 1832, which in certain instances provided for different amounts to be paid by whites, Indians, and slaves for the same priestly functions.[11] In the latter case, discrimination was of material benefit to the nonwhites, and slavery as such continued to decline under the impact of ad hoc bursts of generosity (as in a law empowering the government to set free a number of hospital slaves who were, in effect, state employees [IV-SE6]) and impressment of slaves into military service, with freedom as an eventual reward.[12] Long-established Creole slaves as well as recent war captives were subject to impressment, and the fact that military service of any kind could be a heavy price to pay for freedom is suggested by a Balcarce decree condemning to regular army duty any *free* man who tried to pass himself off as a slave simply to evade enlistment in the Buenos Aires militia. The same decree established a lesser penalty for falsely claiming ownership of a black who was in reality free: whoever did so must purchase two slaves for army duty and eventual freedom (IV-SE7).

And yet the most striking of all the measures on slavery is the ministerial decree of 15 October 1831, which permitted foreigners to sell slaves legally brought into the province as personal servants in the local market (IV-SE9). Though not signed by Rosas personally, the measure was justified to the Junta de Representantes by Rosas with the implausible, if not downright cynical, argument that the purpose was "to facilitate to the slaves of other countries who arrive to our shores the means of alleviating their condition."[13] In subsequently revoking the measure, Viamonte explained that it had in fact been used to open a gaping loophole in the abolition of the slave trade (IV-SE11). Rosas's fame as a special friend of the blacks obviously does not rest on the preceding or any other decree. And was it coincidence that in the same year, 1831, the police registries of freedmen whose quasi-liberty derived from capture by Argentine corsairs were somehow lost? The fact that captives not impressed into the armed forces had been assigned to fixed terms of service with private individuals made the wartime practice of seizing Brazil-bound slave ships a partial substitute for the abolished slave trade itself, and George Andrews has logically posed the question of whether the loss of records did not facilitate an indefinite prolongation of servitude.[14]

The few remaining items fall into no clear pattern. The move of Rosas to revive the colonial office of *Protector de Naturales*, which had at some point fallen into disuse, and attach it to that of *Defensor de Pobres y Menores* (IV-SE4) could perhaps be cited as an instance of concern for disadvantaged elements of society, symbolizing a degree of paternalistic interest in the Indians, as distinct from the orthodox liberal position of presuming to treat them as equal citizens. But it is not certain that the Indians benefited, and more likely that political manipulation was the main objective. The cancellation of outstanding immigration contracts ordered by Lavalle shortly after he seized power formally recognized the disappointing results of officially sponsored immigration campaigns in Buenos Aires. The time had not yet come for immigration on a large scale, and this acknowledgment was rounded out by Rosas's subsequent abolition of the official Comisión de Inmigración (IV-SE3). Lavalle might have tried again eventually, but certainly the encouragement of immigration was not one of the priorities of the Rosas regime. Then again, Viamonte's decree of 1833 that partially abolished the official monopoly of the mails by allowing letters for overseas to be delivered directly to ships without passing through the post office first (IV-SE10) was practical recognition of the fact that in international correspondence the state provided no true service but only taxed the service that private shipmasters were providing. The decree served to eliminate some petty government interference, for the stated purpose of facilitating commercial transactions, and as such it represents an admittedly minor stroke of economic liberalism under Federal auspices.

Religious Innovations, 1827–35

Religious innovations of the previous period were impressive in both number and scope, but from 1827 through 1834 the status of the church failed to receive the same concerted attention. One would hardly expect a similar record of ecclesiastical reforms, but in view of the extent to which Federalist spokesmen in Buenos Aires and the interior used the religious issue as a club to attack the godless Unitarios (as the Rivadavians were coming to be known), one might have expected a greater effort to correct the numerous wrongs supposedly inflicted on the church. In practice, nothing very substantial was attempted.

The 1822 law of reform of the clergy, cornerstone of Rivadavian anticlericalism, was formally modified in two minor respects: by requiring that the redemption of censos pertaining to *obras pías* be made in metallic currency or its equivalent (IV–R2) and by raising the maximum number of nuns permitted in the Dominican convent from thirty to forty (IV–R1). Both measures were adopted during the brief Dorrego regime.[15] The first obviously served to protect the church against giving up real assets in exchange for depreciated paper currency, although there is no indication that this had been a major problem.[16] In one other respect the implementation of the basic reform law was relaxed, but without overtly amending its provisions: a decision of Rosas's minister of government, Tomás Manuel de Anchorena, allowed an individual Bethlehemite friar to function as such despite the suppression of the order in Buenos Aires (IV–R8). Yet these moves amount to little in the last analysis, compared to the government's conspicuous failure to restore any of the suppressed convents or to return sequestered church assets, which continued to be sold or reallocated as the government saw fit (IV–R10, 13).

More dramatic evidence of reaction on the religious front can be seen in efforts to establish strict standards of orthodoxy in educational institutions and in the printing and sale of publications. A decree of Acting Governor Balcarce in February 1831 required primary schools to hire only teachers of known moral conduct and Catholic orthodoxy and to teach catechism every Saturday (IV–R7), thus countermanding the Rivadavia decree of 1826 that omitted any references to religious belief in setting qualifications for teachers (II–R20). Dorrego's press law, already mentioned, made clear that the 1825 law of religious toleration (II–R19) did not necessarily extend to the use of the press. And during the governorship of Rosas, a decree of Minister Anchorena sought to correct wrong interpretations of Rivadavia's 1821 decree on the free introduction of books, paintings, and engravings (II–P2) by expressly prohibiting the sale or circulation of anything that would "tend to attack the wholesome morality of the Gospel, the truth and holiness of the religion of the State, and the divinity of JESUS CHRIST." For good measure, the decree added that it was forbidden even to let someone look at a work of obscene art (IV–R9). A Catholic of strongly traditional leaning, Anchorena went so far as to sponsor the public burning of irreligious literature.[17]

However, not all officials were as zealous in combating bad books as was the minister of government, and freedom of worship per se was not challenged. After all, Governor Rosas himself was responsible for giving the British community the land for an Anglican church, whose cornerstone was laid in April 1830 (IV–R4), and not long afterward the Presbyterians began construction too, with an impressive number of government dignitaries turning out for the cornerstone ceremony (25 February 1833).[18] These favors were obviously more a matter of deference to British subjects than of deference to Protestantism, and much the same can be said of the increasing acceptance of religiously mixed marriages, which normally involved a foreigner as one of the partners. The law that authorized waiving of restrictions on such marriages—passed by the narrow margin of one vote while Rosas was not personally occupying the governorship—directly referred only to the impediments of civil law, but it put implied pressure on church authorities to be more generous in granting dispensations from canon law as well (IV-R12).[19] Foreigners may have been the main beneficiaries of these moves, but the fact remains that nowhere else in Argentina was anything similar taking place, and in only a few parts of Latin America.

Less remarkable, but significant complements to the reforms of Rivadavia, were the decree of Rosas extending the cemetery reform of Buenos Aires to the outlying town of San Nicolás (IV-R5) and the reduction of full religious holidays to twelve, decreed by Bishop Mariano Medrano at Rosas's instigation (IV-R11).[20] These measures more than offset the partial rollback of Rivadavian funeral regulations by Balcarce's decree repealing the prohibition against taking cadavers into church for funeral services (IV-R6). Although not highly controversial, the reforms in question were conventionally regarded as corollaries of the luces del siglo, toward which Rosas was often suspicious—without, however, being unalterably opposed. To be sure, the abundance of holidays was not only a monument to ancient superstitions but an artificial impediment to efficient use of manpower in a community short of labor. Hence the reduction in holidays was as much an economic as a religious reform, and it was the economic benefit that mainly appealed to Governor Rosas.

The Developed Dictatorship

Clearly, the reaction of Rosas during his first term as governor of Buenos Aires had been limited in both scope and degree, and other Federalist leaders who occupied the governorship during the period 1827–35 were even less inclined to restore the laws and institutions that had prevailed in the Río de la Plata in 1810, or, for that matter, in 1820. However, the seeming laxness of those other governors in such matters as control of press abuses had, in Rosas's opinion, seriously undermined public tranquility, and when he returned to the governor's office in 1835, he was convinced that a different and harder line was necessary. Rosas feared his enemies would take advantage of any signs of weakness, and he came to feel, as Tulio Halperín Donghi observes, that political order was dependent on maintaining the unity and partisan exaltation of his followers at a constant high pitch; this need caused him to require strict standards of Federal orthodoxy, rejecting any thought of compromise in policy or tactics.[21]

In March 1835, Rosas was granted the *Suma del Poder Público* by the Junta de Representantes and invested with final authority in matters pertaining to all three branches of government, being limited only by the stipulation that he defend the Roman Catholic apostolic religion and the cause of federation (IV-P14). The formal political structure of the province was greatly simplified—now anything Rosas wished to do was legalized in advance, as was the way he wished to do it. Though both the legislature and the courts continued in existence, they were not as relevant as they once were, and it is not surprising that from 1835 to the end of the Rosas regime few significant measures were formally adopted as law by the Junta de Representantes; more took the form of executive decrees. Yet even these became less frequent as years passed, to the point that the *Registro Oficial* of Buenos Aires province would for some months consist of nothing but the tables of treasury balance and shipping movements. If there was a section of other official documents, it might well consist only of an exchange of messages with "Our Great and Good Friend" Queen Victoria on some event in the life of the British royal family.[22]

Particularly in light of the Suma del Poder Público, one obviously cannot assume from the lack of a law or decree on some subject that things were being left exactly as before. There are examples of legal provisions that simply fell into disuse, as also happens under nondictatorial regimes. Nevertheless, the decline in rate of issuance of legal enactments (including both statutes of the legislature and executive decrees) is in keeping with the fact that Rosas never attempted to make his mark as a lawgiver. To repeat, he was known as "*Restorer* of the Laws," albeit a somewhat selective restorer. In this capacity, he did sign a relatively large number of measures on a wide range of subjects during the first years of his new administration, finishing business left pending at the end of his first governorship and correcting errors of the governors who had succeeded him. Thereafter he settled into a kind of immobilism as far as either legal innovation or explicit reaction was concerned. He did not become idle, for he continued to devote himself to the details of administration with fanatical energy.[23] But his handling of details seldom altered those fundamental principles that had been established at the outset of his renewed dictatorship.

Political Innovations, 1835–52

Although the use of "extraordinary faculties" or other kinds of emergency powers had been a common device since the start of the revolution against Spain both at Buenos Aires and in the other provinces—obviously limiting the practical scope of any political reforms of liberalizing tendency—the grant to Rosas of the Suma del Poder represented a formal abandonment of liberal political faith. Arrangements which had been regarded as exceptional, at least in theory, now became the norm. Thus equipped, Rosas seldom found it necessary to introduce further changes in the political system of Buenos Aires. His own restrictive press decree of 1832 had been reinstated even before his return to the governorship, but he hardly needed it to keep a tight rein on political and other expression. On his own authority now, he restored his earlier control of internal travel, which had been superseded when Governor Viamonte boldly suppressed the passport requirement (IV-P15). Rosas also further extended both the required use of Federal slogans and insignia (an area in which examples could be multiplied ad infinitum)[24] and the official requirements for political-religious orthodoxy in such fields as teaching (IV-P18).

Still, Rosas did not basically alter the outward form of provincial government. The Junta de Representantes continued to exist even after signing away all real power,[25] and it continued to be elected under the 1821 law of universal male suffrage, even though the suffrage continued to be manipulated by the provincial executive—as Rosas had the refreshing honesty to acknowledge, unlike his predecessors. He not only frankly drew up and circulated lists of approved candidates but attacked earlier governments for hypocritically professing liberal ideals while in fact interfering with free electoral expression (IV-P16). The previously existing court system continued too, however much its independence may have been further undermined.[26] That same court system was supplemented in 1838 by creation of the Tribunal de Recursos Extraordinarios (IV-P17), which is perhaps the most interesting of all the judicial measures of the Rosas regime. An obvious antecedent for it was the decree of Viamonte directing that extraordinary appeals (those lodged after the handing down of a decision in "final" instance) be handled by the highest regular appeal court, the Cámara de Apelaciones. Yet under Rosas these appeals were still being made, in practice, directly to the governor, and he complained of the excessive workload involved in his having to create special commissions to study the cases. So with additional urging from Rosas's cousin Nicolás Anchorena, who had a personal stake in one such appeal, the Junta de Representantes established still another and higher level of judicial authority, all of whose members were appointed by the governor to indefinite terms, to deal with the cases in question.[27] The establishment of the Tribunal amounted to a more regular method for handling a fundamentally irregular procedure and thus exemplifies a hallmark of the Rosas regime: the orderly administration of arbitrary power.

Socioeconomic Innovations, 1835–52

Another hallmark of the Rosas dictatorship was its relative lack of doctrinaire preconceptions in dealing with economic matters. Here Rosas's greatest attention was always devoted to fiscal and monetary problems, which he handled with some skill, as is generally agreed, whether or not he served the greatest good of the greatest number. Since his tax measures concerned the administration of revenues already in existence—no significant forms of taxation being added or subtracted—and since the management of money supply does not come within the scope of this survey, the items to be considered here do not constitute a representative cross section of economic and social policy during the period 1835–52. But they do suggest certain policy characteristics.

The most renowned economic measure of Rosas's second administration was the avowedly protectionist December 1835 tariff, best remembered for its folkloric prohibition of the importation of ponchos that might compete with those of Córdoba and other interior provinces. But the tariff was more important for its increased duties on the agricultural and industrial products of Buenos Aires (IV-SE15), and it formed part of a cyclical movement toward greater tariff protection, which had been making headway erratically since Rosas's first term as governor. The new tariff was the first instance of truly systematic protection, but whether it reflected a sincere commitment to protectionist doctrine or only political expediency remains subject to debate. Most likely the protectionism of Rosas was sincere, but in the long run it could not withstand the financial (and other) complications resulting from civil and foreign war or the overriding interest of Rosas's own estanciero class in a liberal trade policy.[28]

While the details of Rosas's gradual emasculation of his own tariff protectionism cannot be presented here, the retreat is quite compatible with the general tendency of his economic policy, which was always pragmatic yet, on balance, essentially liberal in the nineteenth-century sense. Thus his decree of 1836 that prohibited the granting of judicial moratoria to delinquent debtors (IV-SE16) calls to mind the similar legislation in Venezuela that the misleadingly titled Conservative Oligarchy adopted as a supplement to its notorious "Law of the 10th of April" on freedom of interest rates.[29] At Buenos Aires, Rivadavia had already taken care of interest (II-SE8); thus Rosas had only to complete the antidebtor and procreditor laissez-faire package, and he did so without stirring up the controversy that eventually arose in Venezuela. The political system under Rosas simply was not conducive to public controversy, but it is reasonable to suspect that the relative weight of mercantile interests and the dynamic condition of the economy of Buenos Aires would have lessened the impact of the debtor-creditor issue in any case.

Perhaps more striking is Rosas's accomplishment, though with obvious limitations, of Rivadavia's scheme to free the price of meat. He did so technically by implementation of the January 1835 law, which had been suspended almost as soon as adopted; noting both the dangers of monopoly and the fact that cattle prices had risen, so that it was unfair to continue imposing a fixed price for meat, Rosas permitted the price to fluctuate with market conditions so long as it did not rise above a figure to be set by a special citizens' committee (IV-SE18). Nothing similar was done with regard to the price of bread and water (as contemplated in the 1835 law), which again suggests the primacy of ranching interests. The step was in full accord with a proposal for remedying deficiencies in meat supply through greater freedom of competition that the estanciero Rosas had authored as far back as 1818.[30]

Meanwhile, the administration of public lands under a system of emphyteusis (II-SE10) was allowed to decline steadily through conversion of emphyteutic leaseholds into private property, although the system was not formally ended until after Rosas fell from power.[31] This reform of the Rivadavian era was one that had the effect of restricting individual property rights, so that its virtual demise did not make Rosas any less liberal in economic policy. Another instance of the Rosas regime's practicing a more consistent economic liberalism than that of Rivadavia can be seen in its abrogation of the legal requirement that limited liability corporations be established only with specific governmental permission. It is not clear just when this requirement (affirmed as recently as 1826) fell into disuse, but it was a spokesman for the Rosas dictatorship who, in September 1837, officially proclaimed its nullity on the ground that formation of such companies was a purely private act (IV-SE19). As a specialist in legal history said of the elimination of the same requirement in Colombia in 1853, such freedom "would not have been remarkable in the United States," where some states allowed incorporation without prior approval even earlier. But it was noteworthy in the Colombian context, and it must be accounted noteworthy that Buenos Aires in 1837 thus anticipated one of the policies that Colombia's ultraliberal mid-century administration would introduce from Bogotá.[32]

Conclusive evidence that a particular law or decree was no longer being observed is not always available, and one should not assume that only the more restrictive measures were allowed to lapse. Nevertheless, even the state of war emergency usual in the province could as well redound to the benefit of untrammeled private enterprise as the other way around: thus the fiscal belt-tightening of 1838, inspired by the first French blockade, entailed a reduction in governmental services, including virtual abandonment of free state-supported education in favor of a system financed by private tuition.[33] Adopted ostensibly for a temporary emergency, these economy moves did not prove temporary in fact. By contrast, Rosas was not content just to withdraw official support from the tradition of carnival; in 1844 he decreed its abolition (IV-SE22). That came as the culmination of a series of decrees—going back to the colonial period and taken up by Rosas during his first administration[34]—which placed limits on what carnival celebrants could lawfully do. These decrees were, in one sense, only police measures. Nevertheless, the yearly waste of time, energy, and resources was also an economic loss to the province which greatly concerned don Juan Manuel, and to that extent the prohibition was adopted for economic reasons. Although an interference with individual liberty, the abolition of carnival had "developmentalist" objectives and did not lack precedents. Disheartened traditionalists could take consolation from another revival of bullfighting, which figured in Buenos Aires's joyous celebration of the conferral of the Suma del Poder Público (IV-SE14).

Finally, Rosas failed to break any important new ground in the treatment of slavery and race relations. This time he refrained from making loopholes in the abolition of the slave trade and instead signed a treaty with Great Britain against the trade (IV-SE21). In 1836 he ended, at least temporarily, the compulsory militia enlistment of libertos (IV-SE17). Yet he also made it more difficult to purchase the libertos' release from services still owed during their period of conditional freedom: henceforth only their legitimate parents could do so (IV-SE20). And Rosas continued to the end to take official note of ethnic differences in such matters as license fees.[35] But at least the maintenance of public school segregation became moot, once he had essentially phased out public schools.

Religious Innovations, 1835–52

During his second governorship, Rosas can be said to have carried out—basically in the years 1835–38—a counterreform of the clergy. True, the coming of the Jesuits, which would have been the keystone of this undertaking just as it earlier crowned the achievements of the Counter-Reformation in Europe, rather quickly proved a disappointment to Rosas, who found them too independent. He welcomed them back initially in 1836, gave them a monthly subsidy and authorization to teach (IV-R18), and returned to them the church of San Ignacio (IV-R21) and the building that had housed the Jesuit college of Buenos Aires prior to the expulsion decree of Charles III (IV-R16). But in 1843, like any mid-century anticlerical liberal, Rosas expelled them all over again (IV-R22). Well before the actual expulsion, the work of the Jesuits at Buenos Aires had been badly disrupted by growing official hostility.[36] On the other hand, Rosas's restoration in 1835 of the suppressed Dominican convent, in order to "repair the evils caused to religion, to morality, to the Republic in general and most particularly to this province by the unnecessary, unjust, and violent measure" that had forced it to close some twelve years earlier, was destined to endure. He permitted the Dominicans to observe the same rules as before the law of reform of the clergy and equipped them with needed resources of capital and real estate (IV-R14). Likewise the Franciscans, whom not even Rivadavia had managed to suppress, received numerous benefits. These included not just restoration of their Recoleta convent (IV-R25), which became the headquarters of a city parish staffed by Franciscans from 1844 to 1853,[37] but such favors as the assignment of a building for their novitiate, which had been closed since early in the revolutionary period, and the prompt expulsion to Europe of one batch of troublemaking friars at the father guardian's request.[38]

The other orders eliminated by Rivadavia, the Mercedarians and the Bethlehemites, were beyond restoring, but encouragement of the religious orders was only part of the ecclesiastical policy of Rosas, who frankly sought to promote old-time religion as a cure for social and political disorders.[39] Thus numerous decrees appeared on the subject of religious orthodoxy and good moral standards in the theater, in citizens' speech, and above all in education (to which Rosas was not wholly indifferent after all). These measures included a police order that established military service (in the case of slaves, a mere hundred lashes at first offense) as the punishment for use of obscene language (IV-R15); creation of a special committee, with the diocesan provisor as an ex officio member, to review all theatrical productions in advance of presentation (IV-R20); the decree already referred to that imposed a test of political and religious orthodoxy for anyone engaged in the business of instruction (IV-P18), and another decree creating a textbook review commission for much the same purpose (IV-R26). In a comparable matter, it may be pertinent to note that Rosas gave full support to Bishop Medrano in the latter's effort to revive more traditional patterns of behavior among the clergy themselves. When, in October 1835, the bishop put out an order for strict observance of standard ecclesiastical dress, he pointed to an unfortunate decline in clerical discipline which he professed to have hesitated to correct with vigor lest he stir up passions unduly; but now, since "happily our situation has changed," he found it possible to take corrective measures.[40] Rosas even tempered his solicitude for foreign Protestants by a somewhat less generous administration of the 1833 law on civil dispensations for religiously mixed marriages: he was prepared to grant civil dispensation but only after the individuals concerned had first obtained the requisite ecclesiastical dispensations. What is more, Protestant schools for a time had to close in view of the test of religious orthodoxy imposed on teachers; they were allowed to reopen, but on condition that they not admit Roman Catholic children—not even children of English Catholic parents.[41]

All this is not to say that religious toleration in a strict sense was ever questioned. In 1837 a Methodist chapel took its place alongside the Anglican and Presbyterian churches, headed by a missionary from the United States whom the government had licensed to operate.[42] In exercising the control of foreign relations delegated to him by the other provinces of the Argentine Confederation, which in his interpretation included final authority in all matters related to the ecclesiastical patronato, Rosas objected to the papal decree erecting the new bishopric of Cuyo on the ground that it made specific reference to the prohibition of other cults.[43] Furthermore, he felt free to keep pressing the ecclesiastical authorities for abolition of superfluous holidays, to the point that Medrano eventually slashed the list of full religious holidays other than Sundays to an irreducible minimum of four (IV-R27).[44] Rosas continued the work of rationalizing funeral practices and related customs—not to mention carnival, as seen—by civil fiat. Rosas's prohibition of funeral masses *de cuerpo presente* (IV-R17) is particularly noteworthy, since it involved reinstating Rivadavia's regulation which had been revoked in December 1830 (IV-R6). Rosas flatly forbade the holding of wakes, for reasons of health and "good customs," and the observance of overly elaborate and expensive mourning procedures (IV-R23). He also continued to do as he pleased with sequestered church property, returning only certain assets that he placed at the disposition of the orders.

Rosas thus demonstrated that he was committed to the traditional system of civil patronage in ecclesiastical affairs, and as patron-in-chief, he clearly claimed last word in anything that did not touch essential religious doctrine. After all, as far back as 1832 he had required priests to wear the Federalist insignia like any civil employees. During his mature dictatorship he continued to expect the clergy to serve as active partners in the "Holy Cause of Federation," which he of course headed, and this expectation was one cause of his trouble with the Jesuits. Yet the bulk of the clergy, from Bishop Medrano down, saw in the Rosas regime a welcome relief from the anticlericalism of Rivadavia and the Unitarios. Rosas may have been overbearing, but he did not interfere to the detriment of essential interests, in the view of the average clergyman.

Whether Rosas wholly deserved the plaudits of Medrano, or of later conservative revisionists who would credit him with saving religion from its worst enemies, is another matter. His religious policy was coherent and comprehensive, but it was not one of unrelieved reaction: from his hands the Roman Catholic church got back neither its fuero nor its legal monopoly of religious practice, and only a fraction of its lost property. Buenos Aires continued to conform more closely to conventional liberal goals in religious policy than did the great majority of Latin American states. Indeed, the same could be said concerning the economic policy of Rosas, in spite or because of its essential pragmatism. As suggested before—and with the notable exception of his political management—Rosas was a better liberal than either his admirers or his detractors generally admit.[45]

5. The Reaction Outside Buenos Aires, 1827–1852

During the rise to power of Rosas and at the height of his dictatorship, there continued to be significant differences between Buenos Aires and the other provinces, as well as among the other provinces themselves, from the standpoint of "liberalizing" innovations. If the differences between Buenos Aires and the interior tended to become less sharp, it was largely because the interior was more conservative to begin with, and Buenos Aires under Rosas's auspices was, on the whole, moving in a conservative direction. One cannot speak so appropriately of a reaction occurring in the interior because there was less to react against, but some of the more modest innovations adopted in the Rivadavian era were annulled, often by spontaneous local initiative well before the consolidation of the Rosas regime. Instances of direct imposition or imitation of measures first promulgated by Rosas for Buenos Aires occur, but less frequently than one might expect considering Rosas's success in fastening his political control on the whole nation. Rosas's whims were not equally binding throughout the Argentine Confederation, even at the height of his power, and regarding some matters—even in Buenos Aires, but more so elsewhere—he was quite indifferent.

The pruning away of liberal innovations adopted earlier in the interior also diminished contrasts from one province to another, because certain provinces had been more receptive to such innovations in the first place. A shared desperation in financial matters, aggravated by the frequent civil warfare and continued monopolization of national assets by Buenos Aires, had the same effect, as is evident in the proliferation of such makeshift and retrograde expedients as government playing-card monopolies.

To be sure, there was room for differences of degree, and these broadly repeated those of the preceding period. A striking change can be seen only when the analysis is extended to Uruguay, which was no longer an Argentine province but an independent state after 1828. Paradoxically, in everything but political affairs, Uruguay became the area that conformed most closely to the pattern of Buenos Aires.

Uruguay

Assured of independence by the Argentine-Brazilian peace settlement of 1828, Uruguay adopted a national constitution in 1830. Both before and after its adoption and by the provisions of the constitution, the new nation quickly moved to alter its political, economic, and social institutions. Most of these changes moved the nation in a liberal direction, as though Uruguayans were consciously imitating the work of Rivadavia just when Buenos Aires was falling into the hands of Rosas. In this respect it hardly mattered which of the Uruguayan parties, *Blancos* or *Colorados*, happened to be in control, and the fact that Rivadavia spent part of his exile at Montevideo is mainly of anecdotal interest. More important, the region's economic and social structure had much in common (as noted before) with that of Buenos Aires, where much of Rivadavia's handiwork had in fact survived the advent of Rosas. This structure, based on a pastoral industry geared to export trade, was effectively dominated by a small number of large landowners in alliance with domestic and foreign mercantile interests, as in Buenos Aires. The populist experiment of Artigas was by now almost forgotten, and Uruguayan liberalism felt no need to make concessions to democracy—not even to the extent of a manipulated democratic suffrage, as across the river.

By ratifying the abortive Argentine constitution of 1826, in the midst of the struggle against Brazilian rule, Uruguay had begun a retreat from the formal democracy implicit in the electoral regulations of 1825 (III-U7). The retreat culminated, once the war was over, in the terms of the first Uruguayan constitution (V-U9), which denied the right to vote to all hired servants, day laborers, common soldiers, and (after 1840) illiterates. Treatment of the suffrage essentially replicated that of the 1826 Argentine text,[1] and resembled that of a number of provinces of the Argentine interior which chose to be less progressive—or possibly less hypocritical—than Buenos Aires continued to be even under the regime of Rosas. Presumably the new nation's leaders no longer saw any advantage in a populist pose, and certainly restriction of the electorate was not inconsistent with the political liberalism of the time. Having a formal, written constitution, which Buenos Aires still had not attained, was more clearly in accord with liberal precepts. Nor was constitutionalism in Uruguay an empty gesture. It is quite true that, as political conflict intensified over the next two decades, there were numerous instances in which constitutional procedures and guarantees were brazenly violated or interrupted. Press freedom, for example, governed by legal provisions approximately the same as in Buenos Aires before the rise of Rosas (V-U3), gained further protection in the national constitution, yet it was subject to notorious exceptions such as President Manuel Oribe's decree prohibiting attacks on a friendly foreign power, in effect, the government of Buenos Aires (V-U17).[2] Nevertheless, Uruguay was spared the ignominy of being ruled with the Suma del Poder. And in Montevideo a measure of free discussion and of legislative independence persisted under the control of the Colorados and their Unitario allies even through the period of the "Great War" with Rosas.[3]

Appropriately enough, Uruguay went just as far in the liquidation of fueros as Buenos Aires, though the abolition process dragged on from 1831, when the measure first passed the Chamber of Representatives,[4] to 1838, when it was signed into law by Oribe (V-U8, 20). Indeed, Uruguay went further and abolished the Montevideo Consulado—as a "legacy of the colonial system" and contrary to needed administrative unity and simplicity—and created a court of trained jurists to handle the cases formerly brought before the Consulado (V-U23).[5] Buenos Aires had eliminated the commercial fuero but had retained a commercial court staffed by members of the mercantile profession, an unacceptable compromise of the principle of citizen equality in the view of proponents of the Uruguayan reform.[6] Uruguay similarly improved upon Buenos Aires's example in a measure that regularized the handling of cases of nulidad e injusticia notoria. To limit the arbitrary use of an exceptional procedure, Governor Viamonte of Buenos Aires had referred these cases to the highest appeal court, while Rosas later created a separate and still higher court (whose members he appointed) for the cases in question (IV-P3, 17). Uruguay followed Viamonte's approach, but the empaneling of "eight good men" alongside three professional judges, as called for by the Uruguayan regulation of 1829 (V-U4), served as further insulation against executive interference in the judicial process and foreshadowed the constitutional requirement for general introduction of the jury system—which, however, does not appear to have been acted upon.

Uruguay deserves credit too for progress toward total emancipation of slaves, more so than any part of Argentina prior to the fall of Rosas. The date conventionally given for the abolition of slavery in Uruguay is 1842, when the Colorado regime entrenched in Montevideo declared slavery legally ended but then immediately impressed all male slaves capable of bearing arms into military service (V-U27). Or one could cite the abolition law issued in 1846 by the Blanco besiegers of Montevideo (V-U30), and the comparison would still favor Uruguay. Both measures were somewhat deceptive, leaving a substantial part of the black population— all but soldier-slaves, according to the law of 1842—in the hands of the previous owners under a form of legal tutelage that was ended only by a reunited country in 1853.[7] And both measures were frankly inspired in considerable part by the need to recruit slaves for the military.[8] It is also true that despite reaffirmation as a sovereign nation of the principle of free birth and the abolition of the slave trade (V-U6), Uruguay compiled a record of appalling laxity in its enforcement of the latter, particularly in the years before 1842, when a treaty signed with Great Britain against the trade (V-U25) was finally ratified.[9] Still other measures relating to slavery showed concern for the interests of slaveowners, including Brazilians seeking the return of runaways: though slaves who fled from Brazil or were captured during the struggle for Uruguayan independence were declared free (V-U7), subsequent fugitives were to be extradited (V-U18). And all free blacks or pardos were required to have valid work contracts and to carry a document certifying their status (V-U22), as were rural peons in Uruguay[10] and in the Argentine provinces. Although no Argentine province managed to do as much as Uruguay in the matter of slave emancipation, Corrientes came closest (V-CS22) and was directly influenced by the Uruguayan example.

In other aspects of social and economic policy, Uruguay did not exceed measures taken in Buenos Aires but did accomplish more than most provinces of the Argentine interior. As already noted, Uruguay during the era of Rosas moved to catch up with what Buenos Aires had accomplished during Rivadavia's regime or even before then. An obvious case in point is the liberation of interest rates, which in Uruguay was by formal legislation and thus rather more straightforward than at Buenos Aires (V-U21). Liberation of interest rates does not appear to have been highly controversial in Uruguay, as the only serious argument in congress concerned such tangential details as the rate to be paid when interest was required by law but was not set by a specific contractual provision.[11] The official encouragement of immigration by advancing passage money and the like (V-U14), elimination (even if short-lived) of bullfighting (V-U15), and abolition (in principle, for it was not implemented) of the alcabala (V-U2) could be cited as further examples of liberal progress. Likewise, the liberation of bread prices (V-U19) in Uruguay was a partial fulfillment of a goal Rivadavia had sought for both bread and meat, and that goal in Buenos Aires, too, received partial fulfillment under Rosas. The reform was suspended in Uruguay when bread was established as an outright state monopoly (V-U29), a temporary fiscal maneuver adopted during the long siege of Montevideo.

The Uruguayan provisions concerning emphyteusis bore direct relation to the program of Rivadavia. The preconstitutional provisional government explicitly affirmed that the public lands were subject to the system imposed by the Argentine law of 1826 (V-U5). Indeed, emphyteusis became one of the techniques used to regularize claims to ownership of small and medium-sized parcels on the basis of revolutionary grants from Artigas. Such claims were not expressly upheld or denied; they were converted into emphyteutic leases (V-U12).[12] The law did not, however, intend to make the system permanent, for it held out the prospect of eventual sale of the lands in question, much as happened in Buenos Aires. The law authorizing sale of the *ejido* or town commons of Montevideo (V-U11) is additional evidence of an ultimate commitment to individual ownership of landed property, even though the immediate motive was to obtain funds for the treasury.[13] The measure has no precise counterpart in the legislation of Buenos Aires but is analogous to the liquidation of Indian communal lands where they existed. In Uruguay there were no Indian communal lands, at least not in the usual legal sense. Neither, apparently, were there any entailed estates, but this did not stop the framers of the Uruguayan constitution from including a prohibition against founding entails, a measure that, in the Río de la Plata region, went back to the Assembly of the Year XIII (I-25).

Once in control of its own affairs, Uruguay enacted a tariff policy of low to moderate duties with a maximum of 25 percent (V-U1). This system resembled that of the late Argentine national administration, itself a carryover from Buenos Aires provincial policy. Uruguay showed less interest in imitating the later protectionist tariff that Rosas imposed in Buenos Aires. Far from facing any strong demand for tariff protection, Uruguayan authorities, seeking to make Montevideo a rival entrepôt for the trade of the Platine region, had everything to gain from a consistently liberal trade policy.

A similar commitment to liberal precepts was evident in religious policy. Independent Uruguay, while making Roman Catholicism a state religion, carefully refrained from prohibiting other cults in its constitution (V-U9). If this omission is seen as an implicit grant of toleration, then the only one of Spain's ex-colonies that attended to the matter even earlier was Buenos Aires. Attacks on Roman Catholicism in the press, on the other hand, were forbidden (V-U3); and the definitive establishment of toleration can be said to date only from the cornerstone laying of the first Protestant church of Montevideo, in 1844 (V–U28). Uruguay also imitated Buenos Aires in prohibiting church burials, at least in Montevideo (V–U16); in abolishing the clerical fuero; and in liberating interest rates, which had a religious dimension too (as noted before) in that it signified an explicit rejection of traditional Catholic doctrine on usury. The one regular convent in Uruguay was ordered closed on the familiar ground of understaffing, and its inmates, Franciscan and otherwise, told to leave the country (V–U24). This action did not vanquish all the religious orders though, as the Piarist fathers opened and maintained a school in Montevideo,[14] and the Jesuits were allowed to do the same when they began to enter the Banda Oriental in 1841 (V–U26). From the standpoint of the Colorado faction ruling in Montevideo at the time of the Jesuits' arrival, they had one recommendation that presumably overcame the standard anti-Jesuit prejudices of nineteenth-century liberals: they had just been chased out of Buenos Aires by Rosas.[15]

Another and somewhat curious case in which the object of Rosas's wrath automatically gained favor with his enemies concerns the institution of carnival, which the Buenos Aires dictator finally prohibited outright in 1844 (IV–SE22) after growing tired of piecemeal restrictions. To *El Nacional* of Montevideo, which was fanatically anti-*rosista*, this prohibition was another instance of arbitrary misuse of political power and socially and economically harmful, because carnival—by providing an interlude of rest and relaxation—was a needed antidote for social ills.[16] The editorialist forgot that Uruguay had actually anticipated Rosas's prohibition as early as 1831 (V–U10), but the Uruguayan prohibition had not taken hold, giving way to a renewal of efforts to control specific carnival abuses.[17] However, the reduction in number of other holidays was rather more important, and here the influence of Buenos Aires's example was evident in the context of the measure and was explicitly acknowledged. In 1833, Apostolic Vicar Dámaso Larrañaga exempted the inhabitants of the countryside from attending mass on minor holidays and limited the number of major festivals, setting a lower number for "the Indians, blacks, pardos and other castes that compose the major part of our laborers and artisans" than for the Creole faithful; presumably the nonwhites could less easily be spared from their work. The following year he extended dispensations to all inhabitants on equal terms, observing that he was thereby bringing Uruguayan practice into line with that of Buenos Aires and further implying that it was only right to do so, since until recently Buenos Aires and Uruguay had formed one nation

(V-U13).[18] In this detail—and many others—the association remained strong.

The Littoral: Entre Ríos

The province of Entre Ríos lay even more directly within the orbit of Buenos Aires than did Uruguay. As a sparsely settled area whose one significant industry, livestock, suffered devastating losses in the first decade of revolution, Entre Ríos had become the faithful client of Buenos Aires at a time when the latter was a focus of liberal innovation in the Rivadavian manner, and it continued to follow closely the leadership of Buenos Aires during the rise and consolidation of the Rosas regime. The savage Unitarios might make incursions from Uruguay or Corrientes and on occasion seize control of the provincial government, but they had no solid or lasting strength in Entre Ríos, and sheer proximity to Buenos Aires continued to influence events. Proximity to Santa Fe, directly across the Paraná River to the west and stronghold of the Federal patriarch Estanislao López until his death in 1838, was an added factor keeping Entre Ríos in line. Indeed, Pascual Echagüe took control of the province in 1832 as a client of López, who in turn was a quasi-client of Rosas. But as the years passed a perceptible change occurred in Entre Ríos's position. The recovery of cattle stocks, the troubles into which Santa Fe was plunged after López's death, and the stimulus derived from technically illicit trade on the Paraná and Uruguay rivers during the French and English blockades that caused hardship in Buenos Aires and elsewhere—all these factors and others helped the province evolve from the status of satellite-to-a-satellite to that of Rosas's primary ally in the Littoral region. Finally, after Justo José de Urquiza succeeded Echagüe as governor, Entre Ríos assumed the role of organizing Rosas's overthrow. These changes were not, in general, accompanied by major changes in legal and institutional structure, yet some modifications did occur.

If one begins by looking for examples of a post-1827 "reaction" in Entre Ríos against specific reforms adopted earlier, there are just three reasonably clear-cut cases. The mandatory payment of tithes, suspended in 1823, was restored in 1833 on the grounds that the "grave causes" leading to the original suspension had ceased and that support for the cult was inadequate (V-ER2); it was to suffer interruption again as a result of civil war and other special circumstances (V-ER8), but apparently on an irregular and informal basis, as the requirement remained at least nominally in effect. The law of 1825 that prohibited the establishment of convents was never formally rescinded—perhaps because it never occurred to anyone to establish one—but the intent that lay behind it was surely overriden by the invitation extended to the Jesuit order in 1837 to begin educational work in the province (V-ER7). Despite the fact that no Jesuits came and that the earlier law had never prevented individual members of religious orders from serving in Entre Ríos, the invitation itself was a reactionary move in light of that antecedent. But as far as religious affairs are concerned there was not much else to override. Toleration had not been proclaimed before and was not now; instead there were inspections for heretical books on entering the province (V-ER1) as well as continual attention to orthodoxy in education.[19] The purpose of the former, according to the vicar-delegate of Paraná, was to prevent Entre Ríos from being reduced "to the unfortunate state of France in Europe and of the major part of Buenos Aires."[20] Entre Ríos did tardily attempt to emulate the Buenos Aires of Rosas in reducing religious holidays, extracting an episcopal decree from Bishop Medrano (V-ER9), and in attempting to rationalize and simplify the practice of mourning, although on an optional basis (V-ER14). But these were quite modest steps, as was Urquiza's roughly comparable prohibition of carnival (V-ER10), which had its own rosista precedent.

The third example of an Entre Ríos "reaction" concerns the tariff. Though Entre Ríos for a time continued the generally moderate duties it had imposed in the previous period,[21] its February 1836 customs law set something of a record for speed in bringing the province's policy into line with the policy—in this case frankly protectionist—of Buenos Aires. It prohibited foreign ponchos, exactly as the Buenos Aires tariff of December 1835, as part of a long list of prohibitions and restrictions on overseas imports (V-ER4). In his zeal for the promotion of local agriculture, Urquiza later turned the same protectionism against the sister provinces of the Confederation, in the form of 50 percent duties on competing farm products, completely prohibited if coming from abroad (V-ER11).

The granting to Governor Echagüe of what closely approximated the Suma del Poder Público, even if not called by that name (V-ER6), took longer than the imitation of Rosas's 1835 tariff and represented less of a reaction against earlier policy, being the culmination (as in Buenos Aires itself) of a long-established custom of "extraordinary faculties," only more sweeping. The grant of the Suma del Poder was followed by extensions and new delegations that filled the rest of the period under consideration.[22] It was also followed by the granting, to Echagüe, of the title "Illustrious Restorer of Public Serenity" (*Ilustre Restaurador del Sosiego Público*),[23] which recalled the comparable title of Rosas but symbolized the fact that in Entre Ríos political stability was more important than laws.

The province of Entre Ríos anticipated the work of Rosas in Buenos Aires by ordering, though not immediately implementing, the establishment of a Tribunal de Recursos Extraordinarios as early as 1836 (V-ER5, 12). The most striking judicial innovation, however, was the abolition in 1849 of both military and ecclesiastical fueros (V-ER12). In Buenos Aires this reform was one of Rivadavia's that Rosas was content to let stand. Yet he showed no interest in exporting the reform to other provinces, and its adoption in Entre Ríos came when Governor Urquiza had begun to show signs of independence vis-à-vis the Buenos Aires dictator. Hence it is probably safe to attribute the measure to an internal innovative impulse, whose appearance foreshadowed more trouble to come between the Entre Ríos of Urquiza and the Rosas regime. The liberality of the law is further indicated by its simultaneous elimination of imprisonment for debt, at least for those independently employed.

In the same year, 1849, *El Progreso de Entre-Ríos* extolled the material progress of the province and attributed it to the fact that under the leadership of Urquiza, Entre Ríos was now practicing "that beautiful economic principle—laissez-faire."[24] One example of that principle, and another instance of applying a Rivadavian reform in Entre Ríos, is the 1850 authorization given to meat suppliers to sell at any price they wished (V-ER13); whereas conditions of shortage traditionally had been cited in justification of more stringent price-fixing, in this case free-market forces were called upon to *overcome* a temporary shortage.[25] Nevertheless, clearcut examples of economic liberalism were greatly outnumbered in practice by instances of illiberal regulation of economic activities, whether under Urquiza or his predecessors. Scattered throughout the *Recopilación de leyes, decretos y acuerdos de la provincia de Entre-Ríos* are countless laws and decrees limiting or prohibiting, for shorter or longer periods, the slaughtering of different kinds of livestock, processing of various animal products, or exporting these products or the animals themselves.[26] Such measures were adopted to conserve the province's principal natural resource, and they have counterparts in Buenos Aires and elsewhere. But in Buenos Aires they are less numerous—and tend to diminish with time. In Entre Ríos regulatory measures were the target of a January 1835 law designed to give *hacendados* free use of their property, but the law was suspended almost immediately and became only a declaration of principle and long-term objective (V-ER3). The 1835 law did not prevent the continuance of ad hoc restrictive measures, although restrictions tended to diminish with time, just as in Buenos Aires, but to a lesser degree. Neither did Entre Ríos's tariff measures reflect a true commitment to the goal of free trade. Urquiza showed a tendency toward freer trade in transactions with foreign merchants that violated the restrictions on river navigation laid down by Rosas in Buenos Aires's interest,[27] but the tendency was not reflected in the decrees Urquiza issued.

Urquiza must also receive credit or blame for one of the most extreme decrees of the period on regimentation of rural labor. Extreme not so much in its provisions—the usual prohibition of vagrancy, requirement that peons carry a *papeleta*, etc.—as in its "whereases," the decree cites "the little subordination and loyalty with which the individuals of the laboring class serve in their contracts [*conchavos*], to the extreme of abandoning their work just when they are most necessary, sometimes suddenly and capriciously demanding higher wages, sometimes proclaiming other trifling motives. . . ."[28] The insinuation that demands for higher wages, at a time when Rosas's paper money emissions were having an inflationary effect beyond the frontiers of Buenos Aires, might be only a pretext of troublemakers betrays a strong sense of social hierarchy and vested interest. The decree on rural labor contrasts with Urquiza's stand on slavery, manifested not through further legal innovations but by his refusal to extradite runaways from Rio Grande do Sul and even lending money from the treasury for slaves to buy their freedom.[29] However, the decree on laborers is compatible with the exclusion of day laborers from the abolition of imprisonment for debt, and it helps define and delimit whatever liberal impulse may have been stirring in Urquiza on the eve of his break with Rosas.

The Littoral: Corrientes

The distinctiveness of Corrientes among the Littoral provinces became more evident during the rise and apogee of the Rosas regime. Under its most notable leader of the first half of the nineteenth century, Pedro Ferré, the province initially took a strong stand for federalism, but for a federalism based on genuine provincial autonomy and respect for the interests of the interior, not the rosista brand that ill concealed a narrow dedication to the welfare of Buenos Aires. Finding more covert sympathy than effective cooperation among other provincial leaders, Ferré and his immediate followers eventually ended up in the camp of the Unitarios, who used their province as a base of operations and thus brought down on Corrientes the redoubled fury of (as Ferré put it) "the carnivorous tyrant of Buenos Aires."[30] Through the arm of his Entre Ríos ally, Justo José de Urquiza, Rosas managed to prevail over Corrientes. But Urquiza was able to detach Corrientes from Rosas, which was more easily accomplished than the earlier unwilling obedience. Corriéntes was the first province to join Entre Ríos in the final crusade against Rosas, and the most enthusiastic.

The frequent civil warfare of the period exacted a heavy toll in Corrientes but did not alter the essential characteristics of its traditional society or its economy, based primarily on livestock but with an appreciable admixture of agriculture, forestry, and small craft industries. Although the measures of successive provincial governments brought no fundamental transformation either, they do show that *correntinos* were prepared to take time out from local and national power struggles to tinker with provincial institutions. The results of the tinkering, to be sure, were often short-lived: the abortive 1839 constitution that explicitly recognized freedom of religious conscience (if not of worship) and extinguished the military fuero lasted three months (V-CS11), and the law of 1840 boldly proclaiming that Corrientes would never again be governed with "extraordinary faculties" lasted two months (V-CS17). However, the law on "extraordinary faculties" did express a genuine reluctance to grant total authority to the governor for an indefinite period as in Buenos Aires under Rosas. Ferré had earlier been given the Suma del Poder but with a time limit of one year (V-CS14), which the Buenos Aires dictator would have considered a contradiction in terms. And abolition of the fuero was reenacted in 1847, to apply to both the clergy and the military (V-CS25), under the auspices of anti-rosista Governor Joaquín Madariaga. The law's validity was then called into question after Urquiza's conquest of Corrientes, on the ground that the legislation bore the "stamp of the savage Unitarios,"[31] but the reform was reiterated under the correctly Federal auspices of Urquiza's ally, Governor Benjamín Virasoro. In any event, Corrientes must be counted as the first province of the Argentine interior to eliminate the fueros.

Earlier, Corrientes had become the first province of the interior to emulate the Rivadavian system of emphyteusis by its own legislation. A law of 1830 established that public lands would be given out only in emphyteutic leases (V-CS2). But the measure was less significant than at Buenos Aires and gradually abandoned.[32] Corrientes was also the first— and only—province to legislate the liberation of interest rates (V-CS13). The text of the law, issued in October 1839, intimated that Corrientes was doing only what other provinces had done, yet certainly other provinces had not done so by formal legal enactment—not even Buenos Aires, only Uruguay. The Corrientes law was soon revoked, but by a measure which appears to leave the substance of the reform intact: any "interest" on loans was forbidden, but charges could be made both for the "rent" of capital and for insurance against risk (V-CS15).

The formal abolition of slavery was debated by the provincial legislature in 1843 at the urging of Governor Joaquín Madariaga, who cited the Uruguayan law of the previous year as a precedent (V-U27) and stressed the military advantage of automatically conscripting freedmen into the provincial armed forces.[33] But the law that finally resulted was more limited than its Uruguayan model: though freeing able-bodied males in return for military service, it made no change in the status of other slaves, and once Madariaga was overthrown, the soldier-freedmen were ordered back to slavery (V-CS22). The province sought to guarantee observance of the free-birth legislation of 1813 by ordering priests to report all libertos who had been baptized (V-CS4), and to reduce the cost of manumission through purchase by eliminating the alcabala on such transactions (V-CS23). These commendable moves were countered by a law providing that libertos be assigned to appropriate jobs by the government at age 14 (V-CS3), not necessarily a benefit, and a consciousness of Corrientes's exposed position and concomitant need to preserve the goodwill of neighboring slave societies in Brazil and Paraguay made the treatment of fugitive slaves less than generous (V-CS10, 20). One measure did waive extradition for runaways serving in the armed forces but offered compensation to owners in such cases. Finally, attempts were made to remove explicitly racial categories in the designation of military units (V-CS12) and in setting ecclesiastical fees (V-CS7). This approach represented a conceptual advance but did not automatically redound to the nonwhites' short-term advantage; neither was it consistently followed (V-CS27).

In other aspects of socioeconomic policy, Corrientes continued to practice a rather sweeping tariff protectionism (V-CS6) and to offer inducements to new settlers (V-CS5). The province adopted prohibitive duties and outright prohibitions against foreign goods on behalf of other provinces' products as well as its own,[34] and newcomers were promised public lands in emphyteusis—presumably to encourage migration from other provinces more than in the hope of attracting immigrants from overseas. Neither immigrants nor native citizens were offered religious toleration beyond the freedom (whether explicit or implicit) of personal religious views. Nevertheless, the institutional position of the Roman Catholic church continued to deteriorate, more under the impact of harsh necessities than of doctrinaire anticlericalism. The appropriation of the assets of capellanías in 1828 by the provincial treasury, which agreed to pay 3 percent a year in return on the principal amount (V-CS1), was repealed in 1847, but that was probably too late to do much good for the church, and the repeal was presented simply as a move to enhance private property rights (V-CS24). There was also a steady erosion of the tithe system, with first special exemptions for hardship cases (V-CS9), then a more general suspension for one year (V-CS16), and finally de facto abolition of the tithes until the return of civil peace (V-CS21). In practice the tithes were not reestablished until January 1853, only to be abolished definitively by the Argentine constituent congress later that same year.[35] The decline of religious orders continued too, with both the Dominican convent and that of the Order of Mercy abandoned and assigned other uses (V-CS18, 19). But this process was not hastened by further governmental action. On the contrary, various efforts were made, unsuccessfully, to recruit new religious from other provinces. And while no formal invitation was issued to the Jesuits to establish a permanent base of operations in Corrientes, they did conduct a traveling mission.[36]

The reduction of religious holidays (V-CS26) and abolition of carnival (V-CS8) in Corrientes are part of a larger pattern and not unusual. The bishop of Buenos Aires issued the decree for reduction of holidays, exactly as for Entre Ríos, and the prohibition of carnival was decreed by Governor Atienza during an interlude of rapprochement between Corrientes and Rosas, who had not yet gone so far in his campaign against the custom. Nothing else accomplished or attempted in Corrientes was particularly unique, but the province is distinctive, compared to one like Entre Ríos, in the number of things attempted.

Cuyo: Mendoza

The province of Mendoza, like Cuyo generally, enjoyed a greater degree of tranquility in the Rosas era than did the Littoral. It was farther removed from both Buenos Aires and anti-Rosas operations in Uruguay. Mendoza did share in the upheavals that accompanied and followed the collapse of Rivadavia's national administration, ultimately joining the bloc of Unitario provinces headed by Córdoba's José María Paz, but from the middle of 1831 to the fall of Rosas the predominance of Federalism was never seriously threatened. Federalism was exercised by local allies of Rosas who were vociferously orthodox in their public allegiance but less ferocious—as often happened in the interior—in practical implementation of Federalist hegemony. An exception was the ex-friar José Félix Aldao, whose career as a Federalist caudillo in and around Mendoza provided Sarmiento with a memorable example (however luridly exaggerated) of provincial "barbarism." But the political style of Aldao did not represent the norm among rulers of the province.

In Mendoza the traditional landed and commercial oligarchy (to which Aldao belonged despite Sarmiento's insinuations to the contrary) had never lost its grip and further consolidated its position during the late 1830s and 1840s, helped by a relatively prosperous economic situation (which in turn reflected that of Mendoza's immediate neighbor to the west, Chile) and by Mendozan producers' successful shift of emphasis from wine and spirits for the market of Buenos Aires to livestock for the Chilean market. The tariff policy of Buenos Aires, which failed to give Mendoza adequate protection against European competitors in the age of Rivadavia, continued to fall short of expectations under Rosas. Nevertheless, in both periods Mendoza—with a few exceptions—managed to maintain pragmatically good relations with the dominant faction at Buenos Aires. Thus Mendoza, having accepted a less ambitious version of porteño liberal activism when the latter was in its heyday, now came to exemplify a milder version of rosista reaction, always strongly influenced by local circumstances.

Despite the number and variety of enactments on a broad range of topics, the laws and institutions of Mendoza did not change appreciably from the fall of Rivadavia to that of Rosas. As in Buenos Aires under Rosas, there were months when only tabular data filled the official gazette, the *Registro Ministerial*. And as in Buenos Aires, the system of government was not formalized in a written constitution, although the conventional three branches continued to function, supposedly independent of each other but in practice dominated by the executive. That domination was perhaps greater now than earlier, but the difference was only of degree, particularly as the Suma del Poder Público, though used (V-M20), was not a permanent fixture as in Buenos Aires. In 1845 the Sala de Representantes even turned down a request for such power from the governor on the ground that the legislators had done their job so well that nothing of the sort was needed.[37] The political system continued to rest, in theory, on a moderately restrictive suffrage as provided in 1827 (III-M14), but the extent of participation varied widely in practice. In November 1827 a rule was adopted that whenever less than 200 voters took part in Mendozan elections, the results were void and the Sala de Representantes would be responsible for the election. Yet some 7,800 persons voted in a plebiscite of November 1849 on Rosas's continuation at the head of the Argentine Confederation, with only three voting no.[38]

The gradual demise of the fueros, begun in Mendoza in the early 1820s, continued into the 1840s with the abolition of minor fueros and related privileges (V-M10) and with the exclusion of the military and ecclesiastical fueros from police cases (V-M2), robbery, and murder (V-M24). However, the province did not attain complete abolition of the fueros. The erosion of press freedom, on which Mendoza's earlier record had been erratic, continued too. The publication of anonymous writings was prohibited, then permitted again (V-M4), and there were numerous instances of the prohibition of specific subversive publications. On one occasion Governor Aldao decreed the public burning of papers from Chile

(V–M21). Needless to say, the ones he meant were the "filthy libels of the Savage Unitarios."[39]

In socioeconomic policy the record was mixed but marked by little net change in the end. For example, the measure of 1835 that recognized the freedom of Mendozan slaves who had touched the free soil of Chile on legitimate business (V–M11) was new and wholly admirable, but it cannot have affected many individuals, and another decree of the same year weakened the law of free birth by extending to age twenty-five the service owed by libertos to their mothers' masters. The extension of service was supposedly to protect young girls from vice but seems to have been applied to boys as well (V–M13). Mendoza's tampering with the free-birth legislation might be regarded as analogous to the Buenos Aires decree issued during Rosas's first administration that opened a loophole in the prohibition of the slave trade (IV–SE9). Mendoza also reneged on the decree of 1812 abolishing fiscal monopolies when in 1832, and again in 1838, it created a monopoly of yerba, tobacco, and playing cards (V–M7). But there was a local precedent from the previous decade for this vacillation regarding monopolies (III–M4), and the sheer inadequacy of ordinary taxes, rather than any commitment to state capitalism, is sufficient explanation. The monopolies did not last, and neither did the formal restoration in 1846 of that noble fiscal experiment of the 1820s, the contribución directa (III–M9; V–M26).

A further instance of experimentation in fiscal matters was the six-year elimination of taxes on mining, proclaimed in 1835 (V–M14) and part of a series of exemptions granted the industry.[40] The tax exemption reflected a commitment of the provincial authorities to the promotion of economic development and a special interest in mining. A similar interest in the local production of wine and *aguardientes* can be seen in the sweeping import prohibitions imposed on alcoholic beverages in the early 1830s (V–M6), within the general framework of a continuing tariff protectionism. Unfortunately, the wine of Cuyo needed more protection in Buenos Aires than at home, and the purpose of such protectionism in Mendoza, as in most interior provinces, was basically to defend beleaguered existing industries rather than to promote the development of new industries. These measures had in common the manipulation of tax policy for broader economic objectives, and whether it was done in a theoretically liberal or illiberal direction did not much matter. Neither was theory important to perhaps the most interesting economic enactment of all, the law of 1836 (which lasted less than four years) reducing the rate of interest from 5 to 3 percent (V–M16, 19). The wording of this measure was general enough to cover any kind of credit transaction, but it can hardly have been expected to have much effect on commercial usury. Concerned very definitely with ecclesiastical censos, including those of the provincial colegio which was ecclesiastical in origin, the purpose of the measure was simply to provide relief from short-term economic difficulties.[41]

No attempt was made to tamper with the principle of the censos, another indication that occasional interference with church income was neither the result of doctrinaire anticlericalism nor part of a concerted attack on the economic position of the church. The law cited was, to repeat, a means of giving relief to the propertied class and the provincial government, which had assumed responsibility for interest payments on some of the censos. In another connection the government was quite as prepared to appropriate the yield of the tithes for itself (V-M5, 12) as to reduce or suspend the obligations of private citizens. In general, interference with the tithe system was also for the purpose of short-term relief, and it had numerous precedents; nevertheless, interference was a source of controversy, especially when the Sala de Representantes decided to discontinue compulsory payments altogether as of the beginning of 1830 (V-M5).[42] This suppression was short lived, as products other than livestock were soon made subject to the tithes again (V-M8), and in 1836 the exemption of livestock was ended, though the basic rate was cut from $\frac{1}{10}$ to $\frac{1}{15}$ in that same year (V-M12, 15). It was the former friar Aldao who put the tithes back on their original footing for at least part of the following decade (V-M23). The reduction of religious holidays (V-M9) and prohibition of burials inside churches—or bringing the body to church prior to burial (V-M3, 22)—were not inspired by conscious anticlericalism either, although ranking as modernizing innovations. Prohibition of church burials had somehow been omitted during the brief interlude when Mendoza was directly exposed to Rivadavian reformism but was finally introduced in mid-1828; even then there was a wait of almost two decades for a cemetery to be built.

Only a few instances of legislation pertaining to religious matters were unequivocally a reaction against previous errors of omission or commission. One example, of symbolic significance, was the rewriting of the representatives' oath of office, which was adopted in March of 1822 with no reference to religious duties but was reformed in 1835 to include a solemn pledge "to defend the Catholic Apostolic Roman Religion."[43] Another example is the decree of September 1827 that reasserted traditional discipline of the religious orders and placed them again under the rule of their "legitimate provincials." Restoring the orthodox chain of command may have made little difference in the daily life of Mendoza's friars; but it had symbolic value as a statement of faith in the traditional ways of the church, and potentially it gave the friars a greater degree of protection against governmental interference.[44] But the current rulers of Mendoza were not tempted to resume the task of reforming the orders: on the contrary, conditions were now clearly favorable to the orders, and an attempt was also made to restore the Jesuits within the province (V-M17). The first initiative launched by Governor Pedro Molina not long after the Jesuits' return to Buenos Aires came to nothing when his successor failed to share his enthusiasm for Jesuits.[45] However, the upshot was a general invitation from the Sala to members of *all* religious orders to come to Mendoza (V-M18). Jesuits were not excluded, but the intent of the new law was evidently to lure other religious who could perform the same functions. This initiative did not prosper either, as things turned out. Hence in the 1840s a further attempt was made to attract the Jesuits, after they had already been expelled again from Buenos Aires, though not yet from Córdoba. The invitation this time was solely the work of the provincial legislature, where the Jesuits enjoyed strong support, and was passed over the objections of Governor Pablo Segura.[46] The governor did try to make the invitation less controversial by specifying that Jesuits would have to come to Mendoza on an individual basis rather than as a "community" (V-M25). But Rosas was not mollified: his government denounced the Mendoza law as a flagrant violation of his expulsion order, supposedly binding on the entire Argentine Confederation since it dealt with external relations; no Jesuits came.[47]

The Northwest: Salta/Jujuy

The Northwest generally, including the province of Salta, coped less successfully than Mendoza with the conditions that followed independence. Mendoza had reestablished a mutually beneficial trade with Chile, but Salta bordered Bolivia, where economic prospects were less favorable and political developments had troublesome side effects and reverberations in neighboring countries. Problems with Bolivia came to a climax in 1837, when Argentina, like Chile, declared war on the Peru-Bolivian Confederation of Andrés Santa Cruz; inevitably, the Northwest bore the brunt of the struggle on the Argentine side. Nor had Salta yet found a formula for prosperity within the Argentine economy itself. To complicate matters further, in the factional struggles of the period—at least until the 1840s—Salta was always an actual or potential troublespot. The Unitario leanings of the province during the days of Rivadavia did not disappear easily, and even ostensibly Federalist regimes sometimes had a crypto-Unitario flavor. Hence Salta was heavily involved in each of the civil wars that racked the Argentine interior, and it was the scene of much unsettling intrigue between wars.

What has been said of Salta is applicable as well to the province of Jujuy, which separated from Salta in November 1834. Jujuy had long been restive as a dependency of Salta; other towns of less significance had become provincial capitals in the general process of political fragmentation under way since early in the independence struggle, and it was only natural for Jujuy to do the same. The new province contained an impressive range of geographic and cultural diversity: from subtropical lowlands to the frozen uplands of the Puna de Atacama, and from gauchos and Creole land barons to Indian communities having far more in common with Indians on the Bolivian side of the border than with the rest of the province's population. The Indians of Jujuy remained resistant to full assimilation even if not immune to exploitation, and the regulation of their status is a prominent thread running through the institutional history of the province. As stated, the sources for provincial legislation and decrees of the period are better for Jujuy than for Salta, and from 1835 on, analysis will focus on the newly independent political unit.

Among the pertinent measures adopted by the province of Salta while Jujuy still formed part of it, the most important and most numerous concerned ecclesiastical property. These measures sought to curb efforts by the prelates of local convents to dispose of their assets independently (V-S1) and attempted (in 1831) to liquidate both real estate and mortgage holdings (censos) of chantries and pious foundations (V-S2). The result fell short of an across-the-board seizure of church property, but it was a good start. Under the circumstances of the period, furthermore, the recognition of assets taken as a debt upon the provincial treasury (which would pay 5 percent yearly interest) was dubious compensation, even though the Salta cathedral chapter professed to be satisfied with the arrangement when the disamortization law was passed.[48] Particularly hard hit were the religious orders. The orders were not harassed, as in Buenos Aires and Mendoza, with membership quotas and restrictions on the age of profession, but they were mostly dying out anyway due to the disruption conventual life had suffered since the start of the independence period and due to the virtual disappearance of recruits. Expressly because of their decline, the orders were the target of still another disamortization law in 1834 (V-S6), and in Jujuy neither the Franciscans nor the Order of Mercy managed to survive.

By the time Jujuy became independent, the Franciscan community had only a single friar, who later moved to Salta. The government continued to sell or simply appropriate whatever was left of the convent's properties

(V-J15), and when the Franciscans made a request to return, the authorities turned them down. If the friars came back, it was asked, how could they expect to support themselves? Seemingly no one thought to provide the answer by granting reparations for assets the state had been taking. Though talk of restoring Jujuy's Franciscan community recurred, this was not achieved until 1861.[49]

Once separated from Salta, Jujuy also showed little respect for church interests in its treatment of the tithes. The various exemptions granted on behalf of particular groups of individuals or local industries—militiamen of specified towns (V-J17), the wool and cheese production of the Puna (V-J24)—probably did not greatly reduce the total yield, but in practice, that yield was largely appropriated by the government. The greatest loser was the clergy of the diocesan see city of Salta, to which Jujuy remained subordinate ecclesiastically even if not politically: the see's share now went entirely to the provincial treasury (V-J10). The creation in 1844 of Jujuy's own Sociedad de Beneficencia, though suggestive of that founded by Rivadavia in Buenos Aires, was an effort to fill part of the gap left by the decline in the church's capabilities rather than a conscious attempt to displace the church from its traditional role in welfare and education.[50] The reform of burial procedures dealt a further blow to Catholic traditions, though not a grievous one. In this matter Salta first pointed the way with a decision to build a proper "pantheon" for the capital city (V-S3); Jujuy tardily followed suit in the mid-1840s with a general prohibition of church burials in either urban or rural parishes (V-J22).

The most distinctive feature in the institutional history of Jujuy is the treatment of the Indian communities, which were concentrated in the western and northern portions of the province and which still preserved a system of communal landholding and much of their traditional culture. The government of Salta, prior to the separation of Jujuy, had moved to liquidate the common lands of the Indian communities as was done during the 1820s in Corrientes (III-CS4, 6; V-S5), but the lands involved were more extensive in Salta/Jujuy and the Indians more numerous and less integrated into the broader society. Thus the measure appears to have remained largely a threat, never effectively implemented. Politically, the provincial legislature of Salta did not even try to bring the administration of the Indian communities into line with that of the province as a whole. Rather it enacted a complex special procedure for the selection of *caciques gobernadores*: heads of families in each Indian community were directed to name electors, who in turn would propose eight names; the cabildo of Jujuy would reduce the eight to a *terna* of three; and the governor of Salta would make the final choice.[51] The constitution and laws of Jujuy do not indicate how the administration of these Indian communities was handled after the new province was created, but the government did suspend the threat of sale or alienation hanging over the Indian lands (V-J8), in what appears to have been a conscious bid for the Indians' allegiance.[52] The regulation of 1836 that freed militiamen from the obligation to pay rent for the use of Indian community lands in the Quebrada de Humahuaca may have weakened the integrity of the Indians' traditional land system but not critically, and the regulation included a guarantee of the Indians' continued possession of the lands they had been exploiting (V-J12). In any case, a new and ingenious approach was inaugurated three years later, with the conversion of communal lands of the Quebrada into emphyteutic leaseholds (V-J19). Information is lacking on details of the operation, or whether it was extended to any part of the Puna, but the provincial treasury did not derive much rent from this source.[53] At least the system was more in keeping with Indian traditions than fee-simple ownership. Further, the province could pledge the lands in question as security for loans, as in Buenos Aires. The system technically remained in effect until 1855, when the problem of Indian lands was reopened.[54]

It was not only in regard to land that the Indian population received special treatment. In fiscal policy, Jujuy joined the ranks of those Latin American governments (e.g., Peru and Bolivia) which abolished and then restored the Indian tribute with little more than a change of name. The original abolition dated from the earliest phase of the independence movement (I-4); restoration came in 1840. The tax was restored with the name of contribución directa (V-J20), but it had nothing in common with the tax on capital by the same name in Buenos Aires. Nor was it adopted only for financial reasons. One motive, clearly reminiscent of the Spanish colonial tribute, was to affirm to the Indians through the symbolism of the tribute that they were now subjects of the province of Jujuy rather than wards of Salta, as in the past. Still another motive was to recognize the Indians' preference for a cash payment in lieu of military service. The fact that the Indians of the Quebrada de Humahuaca and Valles de Tupa *did* perform such service explains why the tribute was enacted only for inhabitants of the Puna. The restoration of the tribute in Jujuy thus displayed certain peculiarities, but it is nevertheless one of the most striking examples of reaction against, or retreat from, an earlier reform that can be found in Argentina during the Rosas era.[55]

At the same time, Jujuy solemnly reaffirmed, in the face of evident nonobservance, another reform that dated from the early independence period, the abolition of Indian forced labor (I-15). The decree of 1836 that forbade landowners to require labor service in addition to payment of rent (V-J13) did not make direct reference to the Indians, but it is reasonable to assume that they were the main victims of the practice being forbidden, and the later prohibition of forced labor for priests and magistrates did refer expressly to demands made upon the Indian population of the Puna (V-J23). Whether these measures solved the problem of forced labor (and one may assume they did not), they do show that the problem was not wholly ignored. Similarly, the law of 1845 to attract "foreign" settlers through eight-year tithe exemptions and other privileges (V-J21) probably lured few, if any, newcomers to the province, but it is noteworthy as a distant echo of greater Salta's abortive appeal for useful immigrants in the 1820s. As such, it was an ostensibly progressive move, yet its practical effect would have been to lessen the relative importance, demographic and otherwise, of the Indians. That this was even part of its intent is possible, although the records of the legislature provide no clear evidence on the point.

The contribución directa of the Puna Indians was Jujuy's one obvious peculiarity in tax policy. Certainly nothing that can be called fiscal reform ever took place, apart from the ultimate elimination of that disguised form of Indian tribute. Tariff duties were on the whole moderate (V-J9) and were not accompanied by lists of articles prohibited for the benefit of native industries. There were even some expressions of free-trade philosophy in official documents: in 1836 the provincial government introduced a 25 percent levy on Bolivian sugar with a lyric preamble describing "freedom of commerce" as "the prodigious mechanism [*resorte*] which civilization has discovered to spread everywhere comfort and abundance."[56] It is difficult to ascertain how much protection to local producers the duty afforded—or, for that matter, was meant to afford. Overland transportation costs generally gave Jujuy's native industries all the protection needed on their home ground, while the hope of inducing reciprocity for exports or goods in transit to Bolivia was another incentive to avoid protectionist extremes. Moreover, as it had been with Salta before the separation of Jujuy, a heavy reliance on specific duties and on various kinds of transit taxes makes it unusually difficult to assess the real economic impact of the province's tariff measures.[57]

In political organization, Jujuy achieved a more elaborate written constitution (V-J11, 18) than Salta's bare outline of one, but both were generally unremarkable. One of the few unusual features of Jujuy's provincial charter was the article that precluded extraordinary appeals on grounds of nulidad e injusticia notoria (which does not mean that such appeals were never countenanced in practice). After one false start in a democratic direction (V-J7), Jujuy opted in its constitution for the kind of socially restrictive suffrage—with the exclusion of day laborers, domestic servants, and others of the same class—that Salta had adopted in 1834 after abandoning its own experiment with electoral democracy (V-S4).

The treatment of religion in Jujuy's constitution was less restrictive than some, yet the general guarantee of freedom of expression was qualified by denying anyone the right to "publish ideas" that conflicted with either "public tranquility" or the preservation of Roman Catholicism. Free expression was a tricky concept in any case during times of civil strife, when all citizens could be required by official decree to refer "leaflets" and "libels" to the proper authorities for inspection (V-J14). Jujuy finally fell into line with the rest of Argentina (and Uruguay) in the treatment of municipal governments by abolishing the cabildo of its capital city, which had been exempted from the abolition measure adopted by Salta in 1825. According to the decree of extinction, the cabildo was a violation of the desired institutional uniformity within the Argentine Confederation and a relic of "Gothic times" (V-J16). There is little else to say about political structure and related developments in Jujuy until the first part of 1851, when a provincial legislature of crypto-Unitario leanings embarked on a brief frenzy of liberal reform.

The most striking of the reforms of 1851 was the abolition of the fueros, accomplished in terms closely paralleling the measure inspired by Rivadavia at Buenos Aires (V-J25). Abolition of the fueros was accompanied by a broader judicial reform designed to make the constitutional separation of powers effective by eliminating various judicial and quasi-judicial functions still exercised by the provincial executive.[58] This legislation was followed by a law again democratizing the suffrage (V-J27), and harking back to another Rivadavian model. The same legislature moved to repeal the Indian tribute established for the Puna (V-J26), and the list of its accomplishments could easily be extended. But all this had little effect in the short run, because once longtime Federalist caudillo José Mariano Iturbe regained control, he repealed all recent enactments of supposedly Unitario inspiration (V-J28).[59] Iturbe gained additional distinction by giving himself at this point the Suma del Poder Público directly, instead of arranging to have it thrust upon him by the people or their representatives.[60] Yet no sooner was Rosas overthrown than Iturbe was also disposed of, and the reforms went back into effect. The fact that they were adopted at all, like the latter-day abolition of the fueros in Entre Ríos and Corrientes, should be considered one more harbinger of the far greater changes just ahead.

The Center: Córdoba

While Jujuy stagnated in its remote corner of the republic, easily over-looked by sister provinces, Córdoba was too central to ignore. And dur-ing the Rosas era, as before, Córdoba was the interior province with much the greatest quantity and variety of resources and a population ex-ceeded only by Buenos Aires. Through the port of Buenos Aires, Cór-doba participated marginally in the Atlantic economy, but the province was far enough inland for its local industries to derive added protection from the cost of transportation. This geographic position facilitated trade not just with Buenos Aires but with Cuyo and the North, and Córdoba did not easily put aside its pretensions to leadership.

The fall of Rivadavia was generally welcomed in Córdoba, some of whose citizens now visualized the creation of a truly federal system for the Argentine nation with themselves at the head of it. That was not to be, but Córdoba did enjoy a brief predominance, at least in the interior, when the cordobés José María Paz—ablest of the Unitario generals—returned to his native province at the close of the war with Brazil and from 1829 to 1831 made Córdoba the center of a system of alliances and political-military influence that extended to the borders of Bolivia and Chile. This power network rested, however, on a weak foundation: in the last analysis, the interior was not only poor but predominantly Fed-eralist in sentiment, and Buenos Aires, where Rosas was building his strength, was not prepared to tolerate a serious rival. The fortuitous cap-ture of Paz in May 1831 was followed by a collapse of his political system that was not fortuitous at all. The province of Córdoba came first under the control of the brothers Reinafé, close allies of the Federalist governor Estanislao López of Santa Fe. After they were evicted from power for complicity in the death of Juan Facundo Quiroga, Manuel López, a rural militia officer who in turn was the creature of Rosas, became governor. It was a humiliation for proud Córdoba to have its governor imposed from outside, but Manuel López was not without his good points, and he re-mained in power, with one brief interruption, for over fifteen years. Ló-pez never remotely threatened his porteño mentor, but he was milder than Rosas in his treatment of Unitario savages and (ultimately) Jesuits as well.

The institutional profile of Córdoba was not greatly affected by the succession of Paz, the Reinafés, and López in the seat of local power. Of the provinces studied, Córdoba had been the least inclined to imitate the liberal reformism charted by Buenos Aires during the early and middle 1820s. This inherent traditionalism, along with the priority inevitably accorded military matters at times of active civil conflict, served to ward off major innovations even while the followers of Paz were in provincial office. Thus the reaction against the Paz regime (whose acts, with certain exceptions, were formally declared null and void),[61] or, for that matter, the reaction that soon overtook the Reinafés, had more to do with personal and factional rivalries and with extraprovincial alignments than with anything else. The subsequent reign of the rather stolid Manuel López was admirably suited to the further preservation of the status quo.

With few exceptions, from 1827 to the end of the Rosas regime the province of Córdoba was not the focus of any kind of change. In religious matters, the period began with Governor Juan Bautista Bustos's promise to foreigners of freedom of conscience (V-CA1); later, church burials were forbidden inside the city limits (except for the case of nuns being interred within their own convents) (V-CA18); there was repeated interference with tithes; and the provincial government moved to reform mourning practices in the manner of Rosas at Buenos Aires (V-CA27). Yet the first of these developments stopped short of permitting the establishment of Protestant churches and was little more than official confirmation of a de facto situation for foreigners. Cemetery reform, though it may have been intended originally as an attack on unenlightened ecclesiastical tradition and met vigorous opposition when first proposed in Córdoba (III-CA1), had ceased to be a serious matter of controversy by the time it was finally adopted. Its importance, explained Governor López, was that it allowed the city to rid itself at last of "corrupting miasmas."[62] Various suspensions of or exemptions from the tithes were almost continual, favoring frontier settlers (V-CA4, 28), the producers of wool, cheese, and certain other commodities (V-CA13), and, for a number of years, the entire rural livestock industry, to help it recover from Indian depredations and natural disasters (V-CA16, 24). But exemptions sacrificed ecclesiastical interests only to immediate practical considerations and did not represent first steps toward the abolition of compulsory tithing as happened in Buenos Aires. Neither was the "suspension" in 1843 of the understaffed Mercedarian convent a step toward its suppression, since an outwardly normal status was restored three years later (V-CA17). And dispositions adversely affecting church interests and traditions were amply counterbalanced by a continuing and strengthened official commitment to Roman Catholic exclusivism (V-CA22). That commitment found expression (as did the official, though not truly exclusivist, Catholicism of the Rosas regime during its formative period) in at least one order for public incineration of heretical literature.[63] It was reflected, too, in restoration of the governor's religious oath (V-CA6), which had been deleted in 1826 as a gesture of obeisance to the luces del siglo.

While in control of Córdoba, the Unitario chieftain, José María Paz, was no exception in seeking to maintain good relations with the local church; if he was less than fully successful, it was because of the political allegiance of a large part of the clergy to the opposing faction and not because of his religious policies.[64] On the other hand, Paz did make one move against the ingrained racial prejudice of his native province in decreeing that pardos must have access to the public educational system (V-CA3). This reform was accompanied by shocked newspaper comment on the barriers against teaching blacks in the southern United States.[65] However, the reform apparently did not affect the University of Córdoba. The cause of equality at the university level received official support in 1832–33 during the ill-fated Reinafé regime when Acting Governor Benito Otero compelled the University of Córdoba, over its bitter protest, to accept pardo students on equal terms (V-CA9), but any advance made was later undone by Manuel López, who flatly prohibited pardo admissions (V-CA19). Significantly, one of the reasons cited for such retrogression was the existence of discrimination in voting rights in the very text of the provincial constitution.[66] Meanwhile, in Córdoba as elsewhere, the attrition of slavery continued under the impact of military conscription (V-CA5) as well as continued operation of the free-birth principle. But Córdoba provides examples of the occasional unreliability of the military-service road to freedom: cordobés slaves serving in the forces of Facundo Quiroga and captured by Paz were returned to their masters (for a payment of ten pesos each), while at least some slaves drafted by Paz were returned to bondage on the basis of the sweeping annulment of acts of the Paz regime by the succeeding legislature.[67]

Treatment of Córdoba's other racial minority, the Indians, was technically in line with liberal principles but not necessarily beneficial. While the Indians of the frontier were being subjected to military containment, settled pueblos bore the brunt of an effort to liquidate their communal landholdings. In 1837 the legislature authorized sale of the lands in question, adding that the rights of current occupants, whether Indian or not, would be respected; a later directive specified that the Indians should receive both individual shares of the former communal property and continuing access to common pastures (V-CA12). The details of implementation of the measure, which was analogous to efforts to extinguish traditional Indian communities in other provinces, are far from clear. However, it is interesting to note that it was not introduced (as in Buenos Aires in 1812) as a step toward the goal of true civil equality among the races. Rather, it was presented as a means of gaining revenue for the provincial treasury and at the same time bringing under control the assorted undesirables who had established themselves on the lands as the ethnic Indian population inexorably declined.[68]

The cause of civil equality was advanced somewhat, though not very far, by further curtailment of the fueros—at least in those cases arising from the disorders notoriously associated with horse races and cockfighting (V-CA26). Nor was the contribución directa, or tax on capital, that made its appearance in 1845 among the province's tax revenues (V-CA21) introduced for reasons of fiscal rationalization and social justice such as cited (sincerely or not) on behalf of the original Buenos Aires direct tax of 1821 (II-SE4). The tax in Córdoba was one more crass fiscal expedient, and it was quickly found inadequate and abandoned.[69] Indeed, long before adoption of the contribución directa in Córdoba, the province had virtually abandoned the pretense of fiscal reform that marked the formal abolition of alcabala and miscellaneous other taxes in the 1820s (III-CA3). The treasury relied heavily on interprovincial customs duties, which continued to have definite protectionist features—for a time Córdoba prohibited the introduction of shoes and clothing from other Argentine provinces (V-CA8)—but which amounted mainly to a sales tax. Local authorities were prepared to supplement this source of income with almost any form of taxation that came to mind. Though Córdoba was far from poorest of the interior provinces, the 500 or so pesos it obtained annually from the playing-card monopoly (V-CA7) were not scorned, however objectionable the source in principle.[70]

Establishment of the playing-card monopoly, not to mention the brief monopolization of sugar and yerba maté (V-CA11), represented a frank retreat from a reform adopted in the first stage of the Platine revolution. There was also retreat from reforms of the 1820s, even though Córdoba had not adopted many of them. As mentioned, the religious oath taken by the governor of the province was restored in 1832. Prior censorship of the press was reestablished too, and by formal decree (V-CA15, 25), which represented a step backward from the point the province had reached as of the conclusion of a confusing series of press measures in the years 1823–24 (III-CA6). Prior censorship was extended to the theater in 1849 (V-CA25). All these measures were apart from the watering down of individual guarantees in the 1847 revision of the provincial constitution (V-CA22), whose relevance was lessened in any event by the use of the Suma del Poder Público, which Córdoba first instituted under another name in response to the Unitario uprising against Dorrego in

1828 (V-CA2) and then reimplanted in 1835 in timely imitation of Rosas (V-CA10).

Traditionalist Córdoba was prompt in imitating the abolition of carnival, which it did in 1845, but was tardy and reluctant to follow Rosas's example of re-expulsion of the Jesuits, whose initial admission to the province (V-CA14) had represented an instance of explicit reaction against the earlier reform measure of Charles III. Among the interior provinces that extended a welcome to the Jesuits after their return to Buenos Aires, none was more genuinely enthusiastic than Córdoba, a principal center of Jesuit activity before 1767, and this enthusiasm survived the break between the Jesuits and Rosas. Whatever Governor López's personal opinions on the desirability of the Jesuit presence, his conspicuous delay in imitating Rosas's expulsion decree—something he did only in 1848 and under thinly veiled protest (V-CA23)—is a classic illustration of the fact that even the most servile Rosas puppet could not wholly ignore the voice of local opinion when it differed from that of the porteño dictator. The episode further illustrates the fact that if Rosas felt strongly enough about a matter, the leeway his allies possessed was finite.[71] Despite the vicissitudes of the Society of Jesus, in the last analysis Córdoba is chiefly notable in the degree of continuity in policy and institutions over a period of three decades. In other provinces, too, changes were often superficial, but nowhere was net variation less pronounced than in the cordobés heartland.

Comparative Overview

Tables 5.1–5.6, like those in chapter 3, are intended to facilitate comparison among provinces and recognition of overall tendencies, without pretending to offer quantitative precision. The original number of tables has been doubled to permit distinctions between two subperiods: from mid-1827 to the beginning of 1835, comprising the immediate post-Rivadavian reaction and earlier stages of the ascendancy of Rosas; and from 1835 to the beginning of 1852, the era of the mature Rosas dictatorship. As before, the adoption or nonadoption of a specific measure or policy is indicated and combined scores presented. Changes from the preceding table of the same topical series are indicated. If no change is indicated, it may be that an assumption has been made, in the lack of contrary evidence, that some earlier measure or measures remained in effect. Additional items have been incorporated in some tables, representing issues that had not previously been the subject of official action. Even with these additions, the tables by no means offer comprehensive coverage of what was

TABLE 5.1. Political-Judicial Innovations, 1827–35

	Buenos Aires	Cór-doba	Corrien-tes	E. Ríos	Men-doza	Salta	Uru-guay
Written constitution	0	+	+	+	0	+	[+]
Suffrage extension	+	0	+	−	−	[−]	[−]
Guarantee of press freedom	[0]	−	0	+	−	+	+
Abolition of fueros	+	−	0	0	−	−	[−]
Abolition of cabildos	+	+	+	+	+	−	+
Restriction of "extraordi-nary" appeals	−	0	0	0	0	0	−
Combined scores	7	6	6	7	5	7	9

+ = adoption (2 points).
− = partial or temporary adoption (1 point).
0 = no adoption (0 points).
[] = change from preceding table of same topical series.

or was not accomplished in political, socioeconomic, or religious affairs. They show only what was done concerning a sampling of issues that appear to lend themselves to such treatment.

In table 5.1, the restriction of juicios extraordinarios de nulidad e injusticia notoria has been added. These appeals were officially abolished only in Jujuy but elsewhere were sometimes made the business of a designated higher court, rendering the procedure a little less "extraordinary" and thus partially meeting the objections raised against such appeals as fundamentally arbitrary and illiberal. Apart from this addition, few changes occurred through 1834. In Buenos Aires and Salta there was backsliding on the legal status of press freedom and extension of the suffrage. The majority of changes from the earlier to the later period are in Uruguay, where the issuance of a first national constitution entailed a retreat from the relatively generous suffrage regulations adopted previously, but at the same time a start was made toward limiting the fueros. In the period 1835–52, backsliding in official treatment of the press and related matters was widespread, while the increasing use of the Suma del

TABLE 5.2. Political-Judicial Innovations, 1835–52

	Buenos Aires	Cór- doba	Corrien- tes	E. Ríos	Men- doza	Jujuy	Uru- guay
Written constitution	0	[−ª]	+	[−ª]	0	+	+
Suffrage extension	+	0	+	−	−	−	−
Guarantee of press freedom	0	[0]	0	+	−	[−]	[−]
Abolition of fueros	+	−	[+]	[+]	−	−	[+]
Abolition of cabildos	+	+	+	+	+	[+]	+
Restriction of "extraordi- nary" appeals	−	0	0	[−]	0	[+]	−
Combined scores	7	4	8	9	5	9	9

+ = adoption (2 points).
− = partial or temporary adoption (1 point).
0 = no adoption (0 points).
[] = change from preceding table of same topical series.
a. Denoting use of the Suma del Poder Público on a more sustained and regular basis, as distinct from limited or sporadic delegations of legislative and judicial authority to the executive. Under such conditions, the value of a written constitution was particularly questionable.

Poder Público by provincial executives tended to undermine the significance of written constitutions where they existed. Yet Jujuy at last abolished its cabildo, and Corrientes, Entre Ríos, and Uruguay completely abolished the fueros. This apparent progress toward liberalization in Corrientes and Entre Ríos was an accomplishment only of the closing years of the period and should not be overstated. Nevertheless, it allows Entre Ríos to tie with Jujuy and Uruguay for the top ranking that formerly belonged to Buenos Aires.

In socioeconomic reforms, too, Uruguay, making up for its late start, assumed a leading position, while Buenos Aires equivocated on slavery in the early 1830s, ostensibly reversed itself on both immigration and tariff policy, and in the later 1830s began the liquidation of its experiment in emphyteusis (tables 5.3 and 5.4). Jujuy, which adopted a unique system of emphyteusis just as others were abandoning the system, and which

TABLE 5.3. Social-Economic Innovations, 1827–35

	Buenos Aires	Cór-doba	Corrien-tes	E. Ríos	Men-doza	Salta	Uru-guay
Greater freedom of enterprise	+	−	+	0	0	+	[+]
Freedom of interest/ foreclosures	+	0	0	0	0	+	0
Further moves against slavery	[−]	−	[+]	−	0	0	[+]
Reform of tax system	+	[0]	0	0	[0]	0	+
Tariff moderation	[−]	0	0	+	0	−	[+]
Promotion of immigration	[0]	[−ᵃ]	+	[0]	0	+	[+]
Emphyteusis	+	0	[+]	0	0	0	+
Combined scores	10	3	8	3	0	7	12

+ = adoption (2 points).
− = partial or temporary adoption (1 point).
0 = no adoption (0 points).
[] = change from preceding table of same topical series.
a. Representing both Governor Bustos's reassurance to foreigners on the subject of religion and the practice of granting tithe exemption to frontier settlers.

never fully embraced tariff protectionism, is grouped with Buenos Aires; Mendoza, as in the 1820s, has last place. Among the other provinces, differences in receptiveness to innovation are small, although Corrientes stands out for its apparent volatility.

Regarding particular issues, there was a clear tendency to abandon emphyteusis, at least in the later years, and to move toward greater tariff protectionism and away from the promotion of immigration—though there are always one or more exceptions. Tax reform was not a live issue during any part of the period under consideration, while the record on slavery shows numerous and often inconsistent actions of generally minor scope, with the exception of Uruguay's formal abolition of the practice. At the same time, two new jurisdictions joined the movement to liberate interest rates, and several more formalized or reinforced their adherence to a regime of free private enterprise in still other ways—Cór-

TABLE 5.4. Social-Economic Innovations, 1835–52

	Buenos Aires	Cór-doba	Corrien-tes	E. Ríos	Men-doza	Jujuy	Uru-guay
Greater freedom of enterprise	+	[+]	+	[+]	0	+	+
Freedom of interest/ foreclosures	+	0	[−]	0	0	+ᵃ	[+]
Further moves against slavery	[+]	[0]	[−]	−	[−]	0	+
Reform of tax system	+	0	0	0	[−]	0	+
Tariff moderation	[0]	0	0	[0]	0	−	+
Promotion of immigration	0	−	[0]	0	0	+	+
Emphyteusis	[−ᵇ]	0	[−ᵇ]	0	0	[+]	[−ᵇ]
Combined scores	9	3	5	3	2	9	13

+ = adoption (2 points).
− = partial or temporary adoption (1 point).
0 = no adoption (0 points).
[] = change from preceding table of same topical series.
a. On the assumption that pertinent Salta legislation remained in force in Jujuy after its separation.
b. Representing gradual liquidation of the system.

doba, for example, when it joined the attack on communal lands. Sheer survival and the needs of the treasury may have been overriding economic concerns, but there was considerable acceptance, other things being equal, of what *El Progreso de Entre-Ríos* called "that beautiful economic principle—laissez-faire."[72]

In ecclesiastical innovations (tables 5.5 and 5.6), three items have been added to the later period: the reduction in number of religious holidays, the effort to make mourning customs less elaborate, and the return of the Jesuits. The last change was generally opposed by Latin American liberals of the last century, but it was certainly a change and in a strictly logical (if not historical) usage of the term was as liberal as any lessening of restrictions on non–Roman Catholics. It was more liberal, in the same theoretical sense, than many of the reforms favored by Latin American liberals at the expense of the institutional church. Buenos Aires continued to

TABLE 5.5. Ecclesiastical Innovations, 1827–35

	Buenos Aires	Cór- doba	Corrien- tes	E. Ríos	Men- doza	Salta	Uru- guay
Abolition of tithes	+	[−]	0	[0]	−	0	+
Lesser convents suppressed	[−]	0	−	+	+	0	0
Other church assets taken	+	0	[+]	0	0	[+]	0
Religious professions limited	+	0	0	+	[0]	0	0
Redemption of censos facilitated	+	0	[+]	0	0	+	0
Prohibition of church burials	+	0	+	+	[−]	−	0
Religious toleration	+	0	0	0	0	0	[−]
Reduction of holidays	+	0	0	0	+	0	+
Combined scores	15	1	7	6	6	5	5

+ = adoption (2 points).
− = partial or temporary adoption (1 point).
0 = no adoption (0 points).
[] = change from preceding table of same topical series.

show a greater number of innovations in this category than any other Argentine province or Uruguay. It did so despite the eagerness of Rosas to pose as defender of the faith and despite a partial rollback of the measures taken against the religious orders by Rivadavia. To be sure, the extent of its lead over Uruguay is misleading, since the absence in Uruguay of stricter restraints on the orders and more extensive seizure of church assets must be attributed in part to the relative insignificance of both religious orders and church property holdings in the Banda Oriental. (Only by virtue of its hospitality to Jesuits does Uruguay obtain as many points in the table as Corrientes.) However, there is nothing misleading about the last-place ranking of Córdoba in religious changes: the pattern set in the 1820s continued. Córdoba moved closer to the mean in the last phase only through adoption of three reforms which by that time were hardly controversial: the prohibition of church burials, which was eventually

TABLE 5.6. Ecclesiastical Innovations, 1835–52

	Buenos Aires	Córdoba	Corrientes	E. Ríos	Mendoza	Jujuy	Uruguay
Abolition of tithes	+	−	[−]	[−]	−	[−]	+
Lesser convents suppressed	−	0	[+]	[−ᵃ]	+	[+ᵇ]	[+]
Other church assets taken	+	0	+	0	[+ᶜ]	+	0
Religious professions limited	+	0	0	[−ᵈ]	0	0	0
Redemption of censos facilitated	+	0	+	0	0	+	0
Prohibition of church burials	+	[+]	+	+	[+]	[+]	[+]
Religious toleration	+	0	0	0	0	0	[+]
Reduction of holidays	+	[−ᵉ]	[+]	[+]	+	0	+
Simplification of mourning customs	+	+	0	+	0	0	0
Return of Jesuits	−	−	−ᶠ	−ᵍ	−ᵍ	0	+
Combined scores	18	7	12	10	10	9	12

+ = adoption (2 points).
− = partial or temporary adoption (1 point).
0 = no adoption (0 points).
[] = change from preceding table of same topical series.
a. Implicitly revoked, at least in part, by the invitation issued to the Jesuits. (Where suppression had been directed against designated small convents, on the other hand, an invitation to the Jesuits did not necessarily constitute an exception to the original measure.)
b. Referring not just to the formal extinction of a Franciscan convent that had been largely abandoned but to the government's refusal to allow the order to attempt to revive it.
c. Referring to the reduction, by provincial law, of interest on (among other things) ecclesiastical censos.
d. The earlier restriction of religious professions was implicit in the law that prohibited founding of convents; implicitly, it was now relaxed.
e. Carnival only.
f. Referring to the visit of traveling missions.
g. Invitation that was never acted upon.

enacted everywhere, and the reform of holidays and mourning practices, which did not achieve the same universality but made impressive headway once Buenos Aires took the lead.

Córdoba fell in earlier with the tendency (universal in the later years) to limit, if not actually abolish, compulsory tithing. This movement suffered a few reverses, notably in Entre Ríos and Mendoza, but they were never lasting. As pointed out, the various attacks on the tithe system were not inspired primarily by doctrinaire anticlericalism, and the same can be said concerning most other measures that adversely affected church property and income. The fact remains that such measures were fairly numerous and widespread, which does not prove the age irreligious but does indicate the limits of its devotion.

Only Uruguay joined Buenos Aires in implanting a regime of religious toleration. It is nevertheless of interest that the further innovations in religious matters, however limited in scope, outnumber the instances in which an ecclesiastical reform of the Rivadavian era was repealed in whole or in part. And there was a narrowing of the distance between Buenos Aires and the other areas in religious matters, exactly as occurred in political and socioeconomic affairs. With reference specifically to the Argentine provinces, this might even be seen as one of the developments that paved the way for attainment of definitive national union after the fall of Rosas. And between Argentina and Uruguay, it is a reminder that the Río de la Plata unites as well as separates.

Epilogue

Most of the work of liberal reform in nineteenth-century Argentina left unfinished by the end of the Rivadavian presidency or even initiated by scattered measures in the period of rosista reaction came to fruition in the years following the overthrow of the dictatorship. A constitution on the United States model, enacted in 1853 for the country as a whole, included among its specific provisions a comprehensive list of individual guarantees, which did not stop short of freedom of worship for all inhabitants; decreed the final extinction of slavery; abolished all fueros; made the encouragement of immigration an express function of the national government; prohibited the use of "extraordinary faculties" or the Suma del Poder Público at either national or provincial level; and reiterated or extended numerous reform measures adopted from 1810 onward.[1] The constitution did not deal directly with the suffrage but by subsequent interpretation was held to extend the vote by implication to all adult male citizens. (It set only an age requirement for election as national deputy, from which it followed that to require more stringent qualifications for the voters choosing the deputy would be an unconstitutional anomaly.)[2] The constitution offered few explicit provisions on socioeconomic matters but established a tone of laissez-faire economic policy that succeeding governments would generally follow.

The liberal thrust discernible in the national constitution and its various corollaries was at work in the province of Buenos Aires as well, although a secessionist regime refused to ratify the constitution and kept Buenos Aires outside the Argentine Confederation until 1861. The most striking exception was the failure of Buenos Aires to follow the example of the

Confederation in ending the institution of slavery. The separated province of Uruguay, however, liquidated the last vestiges of slavery in the same year the constitution was adopted, 1853, and remained generally faithful to the liberal course it had already charted.

The constituent convention of 1853, convened at Santa Fe, having extended religious toleration from Buenos Aires to the rest of the nation under the terms of the constitution, by separate legislation made all provinces exempt from compulsory tithing.[3] However, no new attack was made on church property or the religious orders, nor was there any attempt to revive the prohibition of baptism with cold water (I-24). This relative moderation in religious policy reflects the predominant influence of the interior provinces in drafting the constitution and in the first national administration. Such moderation also reflects the fact that ecclesiastical power was no longer perceived as threatening, having been weakened by the work of Rivadavia and his imitators and by the general political and economic circumstances of the first half of the nineteenth century. Argentina was to experience a recrudescence of liberal anticlericalism in the last quarter of the century, triggered in part by debate over religious instruction in the public schools, but as of the 1850s that was not yet a critical issue.

A comprehensive examination of the mid-century round of liberal innovation is outside the scope of this study, but clearly the sharpest differences between it and the independence and early post-independence periods are the successful resolution of the problem of constitutional organization and the lessened importance of the religious question. The second difference is most striking if, for the earlier period, one looks only at the high point of ecclesiastical reform in Buenos Aires in the time of Rivadavia; it is less marked if one takes into account the record of the interior provinces during that interval. Yet even in religious policy the contrast between Buenos Aires and the others was never absolute. In this as well as other matters, the reforming impulse was shared to some extent by all the provinces studied and was not wholly abandoned in the era of Rosas. The activism of the Assembly of the Year XIII or of Rivadavia and his followers may have gone against some aspects of the Argentine *ser nacional* (national identity), but the latter could nevertheless assimilate an appreciable dose of Europeanizing modernization. So could the *ser oriental*. If Uruguay in the 1850s failed to experience a true second wave of reform activity, one reason is that former accomplishments left virtually no unfinished business from preceding decades other than the last touch on abolition of slavery.

Although a systematic comparison of the Argentine experience with that of other Spanish American nations is also beyond the scope of this monograph, certain peculiarities of the Argentine or Argentine-Uruguayan "profile" stand out alongside common features. The precocity of the liberal reform measures of the revolutionary governments at Buenos Aires in the midst of the independence struggle has been emphasized in chapter 1, and though the nation for which the measures were intended was soon in a state of dissolution, few of the reforms were explicitly reversed. For the postwar decade of the 1820s, the advanced standing of Buenos Aires province under Rivadavia vis-à-vis the rest of Argentina and Latin America is also apparent. Nowhere else did freedom of worship and of interest rates, as well as suppression of tithes and fueros and alcabala, all go hand in hand. Within the Central American federation, the state of Guatemala, in a brief flurry of liberal anticlericalism, came close to matching the record of Buenos Aires, and Guatemala joined the rest of Central America in the outright abolition of slavery. But early Guatemalan liberalism was fragile, and its effects were ephemeral in comparison to the legacy of Rivadavia.[4] At the same time, Argentina generally, as represented by some arbitrary midpoint between the extremes of Buenos Aires and Córdoba, would perhaps have come close to an equally arbitrary midpoint between Guatemala and, say, Bolivia. The last not only rejected the invitation of Bolívar to abolish slavery but gave a cool reception to the modest educational and fiscal reforms attempted by Sucre in his brief presidency.[5]

During the next two decades, when liberal innovation was not favored in Spanish America as a whole, Argentina came close to the norm whether one considers Buenos Aires only or some arbitrary mean as representative of the Argentine case. There was no general rollback of reforms, although steps backward did occur in specific instances as well as scattered examples of new steps forward—net change was not great. A comparable situation prevailed in a majority of Spanish American nations, with recently independent Uruguay and Venezuela the principal exceptions. Uruguay, as noted in chapter 5, tended to emulate during the decade of the 1830s Buenos Aires of the 1820s. In the same years Venezuela, under the rule of the so-called Conservative Oligarchy, was introducing freedom of worship, liberating interest rates, and suppressing the tobacco monopoly and the military fuero, retrogressing only in the key area of slave emancipation, where the manumission law inherited from Gran Colombia was brazenly watered down.[6] That Venezuela should have backtracked on slavery is logical enough, in view of an agroexport economy resting in part on slave labor. However, that same economy, with attendant openness to external stimuli and models, was a logical foundation for the classical liberalism displayed by Venezuela's Conservatives in other respects. It also gives a further dimension to the parallel with Uruguay or with the province of Buenos Aires, which even under Rosas adhered more closely in nonpolitical questions to the canons of liberalism than did the rest of Argentina.

It is only at mid-century that the Argentine profile diverged noticeably from the larger pattern. As for political and economic liberalism, in the letter of the law and the constitution Argentina left little to be desired. But concern with the church's status, obsessive in Mexico and Colombia and a subject of running controversies in other countries, was distinctly of secondary importance to Argentina. Measures adopted on religious issues aroused opposition, but one easily overcome,[7] and the failure to impose more sweeping reforms—or even to expel the Jesuits—makes a curious contrast with such movements as the Mexican Reforma. The upsurge of clericalism in Ecuador under Gabriel García Moreno or in Guatemala under José Rafael Carrera, at a time when the fortunes of the church were elsewhere at a low ebb, provides a greater contrast, but neither of those two anomalies was to last.

A final question necessary in a comparative perspective is the extent to which Paraguay resembled or diverged from its immediate neighbors. In generalizations about Latin American history, particularly up to the War of the Triple Alliance, Paraguay tends to be dismissed as too deviant a case to consider. But as a part of the larger Platine area, Paraguay cannot be ignored, and currently it is held up by assorted revisionist scholars as a more appropriate model for 'Latin America than the foreignizing liberalism this study has emphasized. That Paraguay was different is obvious enough: even Rosas was more attentive to the appearances of political liberalism than was the famous Dr. Francia, and only defeat by slave-owning Brazil eradicated black slavery in Paraguay. On the other hand, Carlos Antonio López had instituted the principle of free birth some thirty years after the Assembly of the Year XIII issued its free-birth decree which it naïvely and incorrectly assumed would apply to Paraguay. Likewise, a number of measures adopted by Francia in the course of his long reign would have seemed quite familiar to the subjects of Rivadavia: attacks on clerical power and privilege, abolition (or at least renaming) of the tithes, and virtual elimination of the alcabala.[8] This is not to say that the intent or effect of such policies was the same in Paraguay as in Buenos Aires, but the measures serve as a reminder that Paraguay was never unique. It was merely different, neither adhering to a particular rhythm of reform and reaction nor adopting more than a handful of the specific innovations common farther south. In this sense, as well as in

Francia's tactic of political and commercial quasi-isolation, Paraguay cut itself off from the Platine community.

The rest of the Platine community, including Uruguay, adhered to policies that were not identical from one province to another but were never as distinctive as those of Paraguay. Neither did Uruguay and Argentina ever cut ties with the outside world: Britain and France imposed a blockade against Rosas, but he never sought to close the port. Indeed, the years from 1810 to 1852 were a period of preparation for the surge of outward-directed growth of the later nineteenth century quite as much as for the adoption, in Argentina, of definitive forms of national organization. Or, to be more precise, the forms were believed definitive by those who adopted them. The eventual exhaustion, in the twentieth century, of the model of outward growth would cause increasing numbers of Argentines to question the liberal institutional model itself—without, unfortunately, achieving consensus on an acceptable alternative.

Abbreviations Used in References

AHM-EI	Archivo Histórico de Mendoza. Epoca Independiente.
AHPC	Archivo Histórico de la Provincia de Córdoba.
AHPS	Archivo Histórico de la Provincia de Salta.
Ahumada	Ahumada, Manuel de. *Código de las leyes, decretos y acuerdos que sobre administración de justicia se ha dictado la provincia de Mendoza.* Mendoza, 1860.
Angelis	Pedro de Angelis, comp., *Recopilación de las leyes y decretos promulgados en Buenos Aires.* 2 vols. Buenos Aires, 1836–41.
Bagú	Bagú, Sergio, *El plan económico del grupo rivadaviano (1811–1827).* Rosario, 1966.
BANH	*Boletín de la Academia Nacional de Historia* (Buenos Aires).
Bruno	Bruno, Cayetano, *Historia de la iglesia en la Argentina.* Buenos Aires, 1966–.
Constituciones	Arturo Enrique Sampay, comp. *Las constituciones de la Argentina (1810–1972).* Buenos Aires, 1975.
Córdoba, *Compilación*	*Compilación de leyes, decretos, acuerdos de la Excma. Cámara de Justicia y demás disposiciones de carácter público dictadas en la provincia de Córdoba desde 1810 á 1870.* 49 vols. Córdoba, 1870–1911.
Entre Ríos, *Recopilación*	*Recopilación de leyes, decretos, y acuerdos de la Provincia de Entre-Ríos desde 1821 á 1873.* 11 vols. Concepción del Uruguay, 1875–76.

Jujuy,
   Compilación   *Compilación de leyes y decretos de la provincia de Jujuy desde el año 1835.* 3 vols. Jujuy, 1885–88.

RA   *El Redactor de la Asamblea.*

Ramos   Ramos, Juan Pedro. *El derecho público de las provincias argentinas.* 3 vols. Buenos Aires, 1914–16.

RIHD   *Revista del Instituto de Historia del Derecho* (from vol. 13 titled *Revista del Instituto de Historia del Derecho Ricardo Levene*).

RM   Mendoza, *Registro Ministerial.*

RN   *Registro Nacional de la República Argentina que comprende los documentos desde 1810 hasta 1891.* 14 vols. Buenos Aires, 1879–91. (First volume bears title *Registro Oficial.*)

RO   *Registro Oficial* (of Buenos Aires, unless otherwise indicated; if not italicized, a manuscript collection).

Rodríguez   Rodríguez, Adolfo. *Colección de leyes, decretos del gobierno, tratados internacionales y acuerdos del superior tribunal de justicia de la República Oriental del Uruguay.* Montevideo, 1856.

ROPC   *Registro Oficial de la Provincia de Corrientes.* Corrientes, 1929–.

Uruguay,
   Compilación   *Compilación de leyes y decretos 1825–1930.* 58 vols. Montevideo, 1930–32.

Notes

INTRODUCTION

1. See both Charles Hale's *Mexican Liberalism in the Age of Mora, 1821–1853* (New Haven, 1968) and his article "José María Luis Mora and the Structure of Mexican Liberalism," *Hispanic American Historical Review* 45 (1965): 196–208.

2. Perhaps the most glaring exception to this pattern is Venezuela, whose "Conservative Oligarchy" in the 1830s carried out many of the same reforms accomplished by Mexican or Colombian liberals of the 1850s. Uruguay is another. On both of these exceptions, more will follow later.

3. *Constituciones*, 84. Naturally the separation of powers, tentatively enshrined at the level of principle, was repeatedly set aside in practice, whether on grounds of political emergency or merely from habit. The exercise of judicial functions by the executive has been thoroughly discussed by Luis Méndez Calzada, *La función judicial en las primeras épocas de la independencia* (Buenos Aires, 1944).

4. Best known to North American readers is Miron Burgin's classic *The Economic Aspects of Argentine Federalism, 1820–1852* (Cambridge, Mass., 1946). But see also the fine monographic articles of José María Mariluz Urquijo, "Aspectos de la política proteccionista durante la década 1810–1820," *BANH* 37 (1965): 115–54, and "Protección y librecambio durante el período 1820–1835," *BANH* 34, sec. 2 (1964): 697–717.

1. THE FIRST DECADE

1. David Bushnell, "El sufragio en la Argentina y en Colombia hasta 1853," *RIHD* 19 (1968): 12.

2. José A. Craviotto, *Historia de Quilmes desde sus orígenes hasta 1941* (La Plata, 1967), pp. 91–97, 101–104; Bruno, 8: 100–101. The actual distribution of lands (most apparently going to white residents) was not carried out until 1818.

3. *RN*, 1: 121.

4. This was directly copied from a decree of the Cortes of 10 November 1810. See Víctor

Tau Anzoátegui, "La junta protectora de la libertad de imprenta en Buenos Aires," *BANH* 38, sec. 2 (1965): 280.

5. In the case of playing cards, local producers were freed from all taxes "*en el giro y extracción,*" for the sake of encouraging paper manufacturing. A similar rejection of monopolies can be seen in the executive decree of April 1813 annulling as "entirely opposed to the liberal order of principles" a privilege just extended by the *Intendente de Policía* to conduct a lottery; the decree authorized anyone at all to conduct a lottery on payment of a fee (*RN*, 1: 215).

6. For example, in the treaty signed with the autonomous Paraguayan junta on 12 October 1811 (*RN*, 1: 120).

7. *RN*, 1:213–14.

8. *RN*, 1:200–201. The assembly also reaffirmed abolition of the slave trade, ordering on 4 February that all foreign slaves who entered the United Provinces be considered free "*por sólo el hecho de pisar el territorio*" (*RN*, 1:194)—a rule that was subsequently modified to except Brazilian runaways (*RN*, 1:250).

9. *RN*, 1:213. The practice referred to was also taken up by Córdoba and perhaps other interior cities. See Nelly Beatriz López, "Algunos elementos para el estudio del esclavo y del liberto en Córdoba en el lapso 1810–1835," in Academia Nacional de la Historia, *Primer congreso de historia argentina y regional* (Buenos Aires, 1973), p. 555.

10. For further examples and discussion, see *RN*, 1:378–79, 382, 391–94; José Luis Masini, "La esclavitud negra en la República Argentina —época independiente," *Revista de la Junta de Estudios Históricos de Mendoza*, 2a. época, 1 (1961):142–45; José María Mariluz Urquijo, "La mano de obra en la industria porteña (1810–1835)," *BANH* 33, pt. 2 (1963):594–601; López, "Algunos elementos para el estudio del esclavo y del liberto en Córdoba en el lapso 1810–1835," pp. 555–60.

11. José María Mariluz Urquijo, "Aspectos de la política proteccionista durante la década 1810–1820," *BANH* 37 (1965):119–31.

12. *Colección de los decretos y órdenes que han expedido las Córtes generales y extraordinarias*, 10 vols. (Madrid, 1820–23), 3:211–12; Hugh M. Hamill, Jr., *The Hidalgo Revolt* (Gainesville, Fla., 1966), p. 136.

13. *El pensamiento constitucional hispanoamericano hasta 1830*, 5 vols. (Caracas, 1961; Biblioteca de la Academia Nacional de la Historia, vols. 40–44), 5:87, 93, 356.

14. *Gaceta de Buenos Aires*, 10 October 1811. The decree in question gave veteran status to certain pardo and *moreno* militiamen. It cited as one practical consideration the "*prejuicios que disminuyen la masa operante en la gran causa de nuestra libertad.*"

15. See, e.g., Masini, "La esclavitud negra," pp. 141–46.

16. Roberto I. Peña, "La aplicación del derecho castellano indiano por los tribunales judiciales de Córdoba (1810–1820)," *RIHD* 18 (1967):144–56; Robert J. Turkovic, "Race Relations in the Province of Córdoba, Argentina, 1800–1853" (Ph.D. dissertation, University of Florida, 1981), pp. 362–63.

17. José Armando Seco Villalba, *Fuentes de la constitución argentina* (Buenos Aires, 1943), p. 268. This was proposed again at the Congress of Tucumán: see Guillermo Furlong, ed., *El Congreso de Tucumán* (Buenos Aires, 1966), p. 368.

18. On the significance of tribute collections at the treasury of Buenos Aires, see Herbert S. Klein, "Structure and Profitability of Royal Finance in the Viceroyalty of the Río de la Plata in 1790," *Hispanic American Historical Review*, 53 (1973):458–63.

19. *RN*, 1:203.

20. Carlos A. Luque Colombres, *Gaspar de Medina, conquistador y genearca* (Córdoba, 1948), pp. 15n, 16n, 17n. One of the title-holders was the Marqués del Valle de Tojo, estab-

lished at Yavi in the present province of Jujuy, but with holdings that lay partly in what is now Bolivia; the other was a Buenos Aires countess who had inherited a title originally located in Lima.

21. Furlong, *Congreso de Tucumán*, p. 87.

22. *El pensamiento constitucional hispanoamericano*, 5:297.

23. *Constituciones*, pp. 277–78.

24. The pope's recovery of the freedom he lost at the hands of Napoleon had made the legitimacy of the previous measure particularly doubtful; see Bruno, 8:58–60.

25. Mariluz Urquijo, "Aspectos de la política proteccionista," *BANH* 37 (1965):142 and passim; Carlos S. A. Segreti, "La política económica porteña en la primera década revolucionaria," *Investigaciones y Ensayos* 25 (julio–diciembre 1978):46–50, 57–60.

26. *RN*, 1:425; another prohibition, justified on the grounds of a Spanish invasion threat, was issued 16 August 1819 (*RN*, 1:527). See Tulio Halperín Donghi, *Politics, Economics and Society in Argentina in the Revolutionary Period* (Cambridge, England, 1975), pp. 103–5.

2. The Second Decade

1. Tulio Halperín Donghi, *Politics, Economics and Society in Argentina in the Revolutionary Period* (Cambridge, 1975), pp. 345–46, 364–70, and passim; Bagú, pp. 19–24; Sergio Bagú, "Los unitarios; el partido de la unidad nacional," in *Unitarios y federales* (Buenos Aires, 1974), pp. 40–42.

2. Víctor Tau Anzoátegui, "La administración de justicia en las provincias argentinas (1820–1853)," *Revista de Historia del Derecho* 1 (1973):233–34.

3. Ricardo Levene, *Historia del derecho argentino*, 11 vols. (Buenos Aires, 1945–58), 5:325–38; José María Sáenz Valiente, *Baja la campana del cabildo* (Buenos Aires, 1952), pp. 399–437.

4. See also Víctor Tau Anzoátegui, "La junta protectora de la libertad de imprenta en Buenos Aires," *BANH* 38, sec. 2 (1965):290.

5. The *Tribunal de Comercio* continued to be referred to in practice as *Consulado*, yet even before the latter's demise its duties in the promotion of commerce and related matters had been absorbed by other official or quasi-official agencies. On mercantile jurisdiction, see further Julio César Guillamóndegui, "La justicia consular patria (1810–1867)," *BANH* 36, sec. 2 (1964):219–20, 230.

6. As noted in chapter 1, Venezuela formally abolished the fuero as early as 1811, but the innovation did not last and had to be repeated later.

7. Jorge Cabral Texo, "La ley de abolición de los fueros personales de la provincia de Buenos Aires; su subrogación por los fueros de causa," in *Homenaje a Salvador de la Colina* (Eva Perón [La Plata], 1952), p. 105.

8. David Bushnell, "El sufragio en la Argentina y en Colombia hasta 1853," *RIHD* 19 (1968):21.

9. *Constituciones*, p. 310.

10. The same decree reaffirmed restrictions, for purposes of conservation, on the use of *public* wealth by forbidding the hunting of ostriches altogether and limiting that of nutrias to the months of April through July.

11. Bagú, pp. 151, 203–4, 211; on the treatment of drunks, vagrants, and beggars (begging being "*necesariamente un fraude y, frecuentemente, un crimen*" according to the decree against it), see Bagú, pp. 160–61, 185–86. For colonial precedents, see Emiliano Endrek,

El mestizaje en Córdoba, siglo xviii y principios del xix (Córdoba, 1966), pp. 32–34, and Ricardo Rodríguez Molas, "Realidad social del gaucho ríoplatense (1635–1852)," *Universidad* (Santa Fe) 55 (enero–marzo 1963):112–18.

12. *The British Packet, de Rivadavia a Rosas; I, 1826–1832* (Buenos Aires, 1976), p. 207. But they were revived, at least briefly, in the 1830s; see José Luis Busaniche, *Estampas del pasado* (Buenos Aires, 1959), p. 457, and chapter 4, below.

13. Miron Burgin, *The Economic Aspects of Argentine Federalism, 1820–1852* (Cambridge, Mass., 1946), pp. 96–98, emphasizes the purely fiscal objectives of the measure; Bagú, pp. 84–91 and passim, sees more far-reaching social objectives.

14. *RO* (1825), pp. 121–22; Ricardo Rodríguez Molas, "El negro en el Río de la Plata," *Polémica; primera historia argentina integral* 2 (1970):49; George Reid Andrews, "The Afro-Argentine Officers of Buenos Aires Province, 1800–1860," *Journal of Negro History* 64 (1979):86–95. Special treatment also continued to be accorded to pardos in such matters as notary fees, set lower in their case by law—a beneficial application of discriminatory principle.

15. As early as 15 May 1820, or even before the inauguration of the Rodríguez-Rivadavia regime, the provincial Junta de Representantes had abolished the alcabala on sale of slaves, on the grounds that it fell upon the slaves themselves (i.e., slaves who were purchasing their freedom); see *RN*, 1:554.

16. Cf. David Bushnell, *The Santander Regime in Gran Colombia* (Newark, Del., 1954), pp. 81–83.

17. Bagú, pp. 216–24. The lessening of governmental dependence on customs duties and thus on the level of foreign trade was also one of the objectives of the system of emphyteusis.

18. Rivadavia had already held out the prospect of religious toleration as an incentive for immigrants before the measure was passed. See Bagú, p. 245 and passim, for Rivadavia's correspondence on immigration.

19. At the same time, the provincial government revoked a decree of 24 June 1820, which had suspended collection in the countryside of tithes owed for 1819, but it let stand another of 4 April which excused new settlers of Marihuencal, on the southern frontier, from payment of tithes (*RN*, 1:547, 556).

20. Bruno, 9:83–87.

21. The administration had proposed the complete suppression of religious orders (Bruno, 8:470), which was not done. But neither had it included suppression of the ecclesiastical fuero, incorporated in the final version, in its original proposal (Cabral Texo, "La ley de abolición," 103n).

22. Guillermo Gallardo, *La política religiosa de Rivadavia* (Buenos Aires, 1962), pp. 79–104.

23. Gallardo, *Política religiosa*, p. 228, points out the essentially Benthamite approach of Rivadavia to religious matters.

24. Carlos Correa Luna, *Historia de la Sociedad de Beneficencia*, 2 vols. (Buenos Aires, 1923–25), 1:57–74 and passim.

25. *RN*, 2:52.

3. Innovation in Other Provinces

1. Nelson de la Torre, Julio C. Rodríguez, and Lucía Sala de Touron, *La revolución agraria artiguista: 1815–1816* (Montevideo, 1969).

2. See, by the same authors, *Después de Artigas: 1820–1836* (Montevideo, 1972).

3. Though I have not found mention of formal repeal, later references to such a tax apparently refer to a *patente* or license tax that was "direct" but a little different from the original *contribución directa*.

4. For example, a 28 November 1822 tariff measure contained a sliding scale on wheat and flour that was similar to the Uruguayan but did not go quite so high (*RN*, 2:24).

5. Ernesto J. A. Maeder, "La estructura demográfica y ocupacional de Corrientes y Entre Ríos en 1820," *Trabajos y Comunicaciones* (La Plata) 12 (1964):128. On decline of the cattle industry, see Oscar F. Urquiza Almandoz, "Aspectos económicos de la historia entrerriana; ganadería—agricultura—(1550–1830)," *Investigaciones y Ensayos* 18 (enero–junio 1975), pp. 260–67.

6. The Spanish text of the preamble is worth quoting: "Nada hay más justo ni conveniente que imitar la conducta de los pueblos que nos preceden en la carrera de la civilización, adoptando para nosotros aquellas instituciones suyas de una utilidad bien conocida y que por otra parte en nada chocan con nuestras circunstancias. La que sigue no puede ofrecer a lo visto en la actualidad grandes ventajas; pero bastará adelantar un poco la reflexión para conocer que ella, al paso que da uniformidad y decencia al clero, cierra desde ahora la puerta a las pretensiones de una clase que, una vez admitida, se haría con el tiempo numerosa, y que ejerciendo la influencia que arrastra su carácter en favor de los intereses del Cuerpo, fundándose éstos sobre opiniones erróneas y envejecidas, no podrían menos que presentarse en oposición tenaz con la tendencia de las del siglo, y por consiguiente con las instituciones que en lo sucesivo serán resultado. . . ."

7. Juan José Segura, *Historia eclesiástica de Entre Ríos* (Nogoyá, 1964), pp. 89–90, 92; Entre Ríos, *Recopilación* 2:297. Yet some who failed to become secularized did have to leave the province.

8. There is, however, considerable evidence of voluntary payments still being made (Segura, *Historia eclesiástica*, p. 84).

9. Horacio Pereyra, "Notas sobre la economía del litoral argentino," *Humanidades* (La Plata) 35 (1960):147, 149.

10. Entre Ríos, *Recopilación* 1:422, 459–60; Urquiza Almandoz, "Aspectos económicos," pp. 268–69.

11. In addition to the source cited in the Appendix, see Filiberto Reula, *Historia de Entre Ríos*, 3 vols. (Santa Fe, 1963–71), 1:228, and Rubén H. Zorrilla, *Cambio social y población en el pensamiento de Mayo (1810–1830)* (Buenos Aires, 1978), pp. 197–98. This refers to only one of a number of agreements made for settlement of immigrants in Entre Ríos, but the others do not appear to have been carried out even in part (Reula, 1:227–28; Entre Ríos, *Recopilación* 2:53).

12. Beatriz Bosch, *Gobierno del coronel Lucio Mansilla* (Paraná, 1942), p. 61, suggests that the measures of the 1813 assembly, apparently including the free-birth legislation, had not been effectively carried out in Entre Ríos.

13. José María Sáenz Valiente, *Bajo la campana del cabildo* (Buenos Aires, 1952), pp. 453–56.

14. Maeder, "La estructura demográfica y ocupacional," p. 122.

15. Ibid., p. 118; Ernesto J. A. Maeder, *Historia económica de Corrientes en el período virreinal 1776–1810* (Buenos Aires, 1981), pp. 267–90.

16. John P. and William P. Robertson, *Letters on South America: Comprising Travels on the Banks of the Paraná and Río de la Plata*, 3 vols. (London, 1843), 1:69–70.

17. José María Mariluz Urquijo, "Protección y librecambio durante el período 1820–1835," *BANH* 34, sec. 2 (1964):712–713.

18. Law of 22 May 1827, *ROPC*, 2:112–14.

19. *ROPC*, 1:407–9, 2:77–78.

20. On Mendoza, see Arturo Andrés Roig, *La filosofía de las luces en la ciudad agrícola* (Mendoza, 1968), pp. 16–17 and passim.

21. Mariano de Vedia y Mitre, et al., *La Carta de Mayo, 1825–15 de julio–1925* (Buenos Aires, 1925); José Aníbal Verdaguer, *Historia eclesiástica de Cuyo*, 2 vols. (Milan, 1931–32), 1:804–7.

22. *El Eco de los Andes* (Mendoza), 30 September, 11 October 1824; Damián Hudson, *Recuerdos históricos sobre la provincia de Cuyo*, 2 vols. (Buenos Aires, 1898), 1:463–70, 482–85.

23. Of the other provinces, only Uruguay formally adopted a contribución directa, but it was not joined (as in Buenos Aires and Mendoza) to an attempt to abolish the alcabala. Uruguay did ultimately decree abolition of the latter, but implementation of the measure was indefinitely suspended (see below, chap. 5).

24. The contribución directa was still being collected in the early 1830s (*RM*, 4 August 1831), but this must have involved either arrears still owed from earlier years or some fairly minor application of the tax that had remained in effect.

25. I have seen no specific reference to the enforcement of racial restrictions in voting in Mendoza, but there were numerous occasions when provincial authorities reaffirmed the provisions of the 1819 constitution (which contained those restrictions) in all matters in which they had not been expressly superseded. See, e.g., the oath of deputies to the Sala de Representantes, in AHM-EI, carpeta 399 bis, año 1822, f. 12v.

26. Silvestre Peña y Lillo, *Gobernadores de Mendoza*, 2 vols. (Mendoza, 1937–38), 2:126; Enrique Martínez Paz, *Un episodio eclesiástico en Cuyo (1824)* (Córdoba, 1938), pp. 16–19; Verdaguer, *Historia eclesiástica*, 1:975–77. The declining Augustinian convent had not been permitted to dispose of its own income since 1820; see José Luis Masini Calderón, "Aspectos económicos y sociales de la acción de los Agustinos en Cuyo (Siglos xvii, xviii y xix)," *Revista de Historia Americana y Argentina* (Mendoza) 17/18 (1979):88–90.

27. Guillermo Gallardo, *La política religiosa de Rivadavia* (Buenos Aires, 1962), pp. 281–82. The proposed subjection to the ordinaries had earlier evoked strong protest from the Dominican community in Mendoza, which in turn induced the legislature to rule that this would not exclude "spiritual" subordination to the provincials. See AHM-EI, carpeta 399 bis, año 1823, ff. 41v–42r, 51v–52r. De facto it appears that both Dominicans and Franciscans remained until 1830 under the immediate authority of their provincials, while the Mercedarian, Augustinian, and Bethlehemite friars had been placed under diocesan authority since 1823 by the capitular vicar of Córdoba (Verdaguer, *Historia eclesiástica*, 1: 962–64, 966).

28. AHM-EI, carpeta 399 bis, *acta* of 31 September 1824; *El Eco de los Andes*, 11 November 1824.

29. Verdaguer, *Historia eclesiástica*, 1:809. Cf. Edberto Oscar Acevedo, "Proceso a un hereje en Mendoza; aporte para la historia de las ideas en el interior," *Investigaciones y Ensayos* 19 (julio–diciembre 1975):275–304.

30. Avelino Ignacio Gómez Ferreyra, comp., *Viajeros pontificios al Río de la Plata y Chile (1823–1825)* (Córdoba, 1970), 474n.

31. The motive for retaining the cabildos of Jujuy and Orán is suggested in AHPS, Libro 255, Actas de la H. Junta Provincial, 21 Diciembre 1825–26 Marzo 1825, f. 16.

32. AHPS, Libro 335, Correspondencia del Gobierno, 9 December 1825.

33. Ibid., Gobernador interino to Junta de Representantes, 13 October 1825.

34. At least I have not identified the measure that did this, if it existed. Cf. Atilio Cornejo, *El derecho privado en la legislación patria de Salta* (Buenos Aires, 1947), pp. 26–29, 34–35.

35. Efraín U. Bischoff, *Historia de la provincia de Córdoba*, 3 vols. (Buenos Aires 1968–70), 1:191.

36. Domingo F. Sarmiento, *Life in the Argentine Republic in the Days of the Tyrants; or, Civilization and Barbarism* (New York, 1868, facsimile reprint, 1960), pp. 114–29.

37. The provision displayed *"magnífica liberalidad"* in the words of Roland M. Riviere, *El gobernador Juan Bautista Bustos* (Córdoba, 1958), p. 78.

38. David Bushnell, "El sufragio en la Argentina y en Colombia hasta 1853," *RIHD* 19 (1968):15–16. In Córdoba a circular of 7 February 1820 seemingly authorized all men twenty years of age or over to vote for *jueces pedáneos*, but it is doubtful that this was meant to apply to pardos, and in any case it was soon superseded. See Roberto Peña, "Contribución a la historia del derecho patrio de Córdoba," *RIHD* 11 (1961):115.

39. Ernesto H. Celesia, *Federalismo argentino*, 3 vols. (Buenos Aires, 1932), 3:174–75, 302, 304–5.

40. Above, p. 5.

4. The Reaction in Buenos Aires

1. At least until 1825, in the judgment of Tulio Halperín Donghi, *Politics, Economics and Society in Argentina in the Revolutionary Period* (Cambridge, England, 1975), p. 365.

2. This decree followed, by three days, an order for the suspension of three specified newspapers; *RO* (January 1832), p. 13. On the general process of official interference with the press, see also Félix Weinberg, "El periodismo en la época de Rosas," *Revista de Historia* 2 (2 trim. 1957):81–83.

3. Adolfo Enrique Rodríguez, *El régimen electoral en el lapso 1827–1828* (Buenos Aires, 1965), pp. 64–65.

4. Víctor Tau Anzoátegui, "Las facultades extraordinarias y la suma del poder público en el derecho provincial argentino (1820–1853)," *RIHD* 12 (1961):70.

5. *RO* (February 1832), pp. 6–8.

6. Ricardo Levene, *Historia del derecho argentino*, 11 vols. (Buenos Aires, 1945–58), 8:16.

7. Luis Méndez Calzada, *La función judicial en las primeras épocas de la independencia* (Buenos Aires, 1944), p. 107; Ricardo Levene, *Contribución a la historia del tribunal de recursos extraordinarios* (Buenos Aires, 1952), pp. 18–38. The extent of opposition to the practice of *recursos de injusticia notoria* in newly independent Spanish America can be inferred from the fact that they are explicitly forbidden in the constitution drafted by Simón Bolívar for Bolivia (article 116).

8. Price controls were also extended in 1831 from the city proper to San Isidro and San Fernando (Levene, *Historia del derecho argentino*, 8:75–76).

9. Letter from Manuel V. de Maza and Manuel de Yrigoyen to Junta de Representantes, 10 February 1835, in Archivo de la Provincia de Buenos Aires (La Plata), Junta de Representantes 1835, Legajo A, no. 8.

10. Gabriel A. Puentes, *El gobierno de Balcarce; división del Partido Federal (1832–1833)* (Buenos Aires, 1946), p. 118.

11. *RO* (September 1832), pp. 5–6.

12. See, for example, decree of 3 June 1829 from the period of civil war between Lavalle and Rosas, *RN*, 2:238.

13. *RO* (May 1832), p. 8.

14. George Reid Andrews, *The Afro-Argentines of Buenos Aires, 1800–1900* (Madison, Wis., 1980), p. 56.

15. Actually, there was one more minor change made, in a provision of the law not cited in the discussion in chapter 2. Rosas, in a decree of 26 April 1830 issued for the purpose of enhancing the prestige of rural curates, restored to them the immediate responsibility for financial administration of their respective parishes. By the 1822 reform this had been assigned to syndics appointed by secular authority. See *RN*, 2:265.

16. Alberto Levaggi, "Las capellanías bajo la reforma religiosa de Rivadavia," *Investigaciones y Ensayos* 16 (enero–junio 1974):396, suggests that the redemption provisions—which were merely permissive—were not in fact widely used. And naturally the new law applied to more *censos* than those whose redemption was specifically authorized in the law of 1822.

17. Juan José Sebreli, *Apogeo y ocaso de los Anchorena* (Buenos Aires, 1972), p. 170.

18. *British Packet and Argentine News* (Buenos Aires), 2 March 1833.

19. José María Mariluz Urquijo, "Los matrimonios entre personas de diferente religión ante el derecho patrio argentino," *Revista de la Facultad de Derecho y Ciencias Sociales* (Buenos Aires) 3 época, 3 (1948):365–70. The first mixed marriages had been performed by a Protestant minister, with the Catholic parties in effect abjuring their faith. A protest by Bishop Medrano over one such marriage led to its nullification by an ecclesiastical court, which in turn led to the intervention of the legislature in March 1833. See also Américo A. Tonda, *La iglesia argentina incomunicada con Roma* (Santa Fe, 1965), pp. 182–221.

20. Religious holidays were cut back pending approval from Rome which eventually came, though with certain modifications (*RO* [1834], pp. 336–38; Bruno, 9:393). A Rivadavian precedent was the decree of 31 August 1821 stating that public offices would stay open on lesser holidays (*días feriados de sólo precepto de misa*); see *RO* (1821), pp. 35–36.

21. Tulio Halperín Donghi, *Argentina de la revolución de independencia a la confederación rosista* (Buenos Aires, 1972), pp. 319–27 and passim.

22. E.g., *RO* (1850), pp. 91–93, on the occasion of the birth of a prince.

23. John Lynch, *Argentine Dictator: Juan Manuel de Rosas, 1829–1852* (Oxford, 1981), pp. 175–77.

24. E.g., decree of 27 May 1835 requiring all teachers and children in both public and private schools to wear the Federalist red ribbon, *RO* (1835), pp. 128–30. In a somewhat similar vein, Rosas's decree of 27 January 1836 prohibited the awarding of doctoral degrees by the University of Buenos Aires to any candidates whose good behavior and adherence to the Federal cause had not been certified by the government (*RO* [January 1836], p. 14).

25. More specifically, the Junta resolved that it would take up only those matters that Rosas as governor submitted to it (Levene, *Historia del derecho*, 8:412–13).

26. Not only did Rosas himself routinely act as criminal judge (Manuel Ibáñez Frocham, *La organización judicial argentina (ensayo histórico)* [La Plata, 1938], pp. 240–43), but judges appointed by Rosas to the Cámara de Apelaciones might also be high executive officials or members of the legislature (Méndez Calzada, *La función judicial*, pp. 409–11).

27. *RO* (1837), pp. 380–81; Ibáñez Frocham, *La organización judicial*, pp. 227–38; Levene, *Contribución a la historia del tribunal*, pp. 18–38.

28. Miron Burgin, *The Economic Aspects of Argentine Federalism 1820–1852* (Cambridge, Mass., 1946), pp. 218–26, 237–46; José María Mariluz Urquijo, "Protección y librecambio durante el período 1820–1835," *BANH* 34, sec. 2 (1964):706, 709–15; Juan Carlos Nicolau, *Industria argentina y aduana 1835–1854* (Buenos Aires, 1975), pp. 27–49.

29. José Gil Fortoul, *Historia constitucional de Venezuela*, 5th ed., 3 vols. (Caracas, 1967), 2:70–72, 255–56. The Buenos Aires ruling meant also that no creditor could be compelled to grant a delay or reduction (*espera* or *quita*) by majority vote of other creditors as in the past (Levene, *Historia del derecho*, 8:460–61).

30. "Proyecto de Juan Manuel de Rosas sobre la escasez y la carestía de la carne," in Arturo Enrique Sampay, *Las ideas políticas de Juan Manuel de Rosas* (Buenos Aires, 1972), pp. 89–96. On the operation of the system, see Jorge María Ramallo, "Algunos aspectos de la economía en la época de Rosas," *Nuestra Historia* (Buenos Aires) 24 (1979):355–58.

31. Burgin, *Economic Aspects of Argentine Federalism*, pp. 252–55; Andrés M. Carretero, *La propiedad de la tierra en época de Rosas* (Buenos Aires, 1972), p. 16 and passim.

32. Robert C. Means, "Codification in Latin America: The Colombian Commerical Code of 1853," *Texas Law Review* 52/1 (December 1973):30; José María Mariluz Urquijo, "Las sociedades anónimas en Buenos Aires antes del código de comercio," *RIHD* 16 (1965):44–47. The 1837 ruling in effect superseded the provision of Rivadavia's decree of 24 August 1826, which generally appears with a misprint that destroys its meaning, as Mariluz Urquijo observes. Means suggests that in Colombia the equivalent reform was introduced somewhat absentmindedly, without fully realizing the significance of what was done; in Buenos Aires such was hardly the case. But Argentina's post-Rosas commercial code restored the requirement (Means, "Codification," p. 34).

33. *RO* (1838), pp. 32–37. Rosas likewise closed the *Casa de Espósitos* and provided that its wards be distributed among volunteer families (ibid., pp. 29–30).

34. Paul Verdoveye, "*Corridas* et *Carnaval* dans le presse argentine avant 1835," *Caravelle* 10 (1968):9, 12; decree of 29 February 1832, *RO* (February 1832), pp. 13–14.

35. Cf. *RO* (1850), p. 180.

36. Raúl H. Castagnino, *Rosas y los jesuitas* (Buenos Aires, 1970), pp. 75–85 and passim.

37. Antonio Santa Clara Córdoba, *La orden franciscana en las repúblicas del Plata* (Buenos Aires, 1934), 224. The older convent, however, continued its long-time decline (ibid., pp. 309–10). Nor did Rosas move rapidly in reopening the Recoleta convent, which he had been petitioned to do as early as 1836 (Bruno 9:512–13).

38. Córdoba, *La orden franciscana*, p. 217; *Mensajes de los gobernadores de la Provincia de Buenos Aires 1822–1849*, 2 vols. (La Plata, 1976), 1:105; *RN*: 2:393–94.

39. Cf. his message of 1 January 1837 to the legislature, in *Mensajes de los gobernadores de la Provincia de Buenos Aires*, 1:105.

40. *RN*, 2:357–58.

41. Mariluz Urquijo, "Los matrimonios," p. 377.

42. *Gaceta Mercantil* (Buenos Aires), 31 March 1837.

43. Bruno, 9:429.

44. This time the pope refused to give his approval (Bruno, 10:187).

45. Luis Alberto Romero, in *La feliz experiencia 1820–1824* (Buenos Aires, 1976), pp. 275–76, does emphasize the continuity between Rivadavia and Rosas in that both sought "to assure the expansion of livestock and create for the *hacendados* and their associates, the foreign merchants, the adequate political and social framework for their development." He omits to point out explicitly that the "framework" in question necessarily entailed a substantial liberal element.

5. The Reaction Outside Buenos Aires

1. The constituent assembly itself was elected by a broader suffrage, despite at least one attempt—abandoned as a result of strong protests—to impose the restrictive standards of the *Brazilian* constitution. See *Gaceta Mercantil* (Buenos Aires), 22 and 31 October 1828.

2. See also Eduardo Acevedo, *Anales históricos del Uruguay*, 6 vols. (Montevideo, 1933–36), 2:183–84.

3. José Pedro Barrán, *Apogeo y crisis del Uruguay pastoril y caudillesco* (Montevideo, 1974), p. 31.

4. *Actas de la H. Cámara de Representantes*, 6 vols. (Montevideo, 1905–8), 3:83.

5. The Consulado was later ordered reestablished by the government of Manuel Oribe (24 August 1850); see Mateo J. Magariños de Mello, ed., *El gobierno del Cerrito; colección de documentos oficiales emanados de los poderes del gobierno presidido por el brigadier general D. Manuel Oribe 1843–1851*, 2 vols. (Montevideo, 1948–61), 1:225. As in all other citations from this volume of Magariños, the page number refers to the documentary section, which is numbered separately from the preliminary text.

6. *El Nacional* (Montevideo), 10 December 1838.

7. Uruguay, *Compilación*, 3:227–28.

8. Magariños de Mello, *El gobierno del Cerrito*, 1:12–13, 81, 132–46, which also covers some of the precedents on the part of both Uruguayan regimes.

9. Ema Isola, *La esclavitud en Uruguay desde sus comienzos hasta su extinción (1783–1852)* (Montevideo, 1975), pp. 312–19.

10. Uruguay, *Compilación*, 1:57–59, 162.

11. *Actas de la H. Cámara de Representantes*, 3:58–60, 68–69, 73–74; Uruguay, Senado, *Diario de Sesiones* (Montevideo, 1882–), 3:159–61.

12. The law did not apply to Artigas donataries who had received confiscated private lands, although some sought to take advantage of it by claiming that their parcels were actually part of the public domain. See Nelson de la Torre, Lucía Sala de Touron, and Julio Carlos Rodríguez, *Después de Artigas (1820–1836)* (Montevideo, 1972), pp. 182–83.

13. Acevedo, *Anales*, 1:357, 430.

14. Ibid., 1:527; Magariños de Mello, *El gobierno del Cerrito*, 2:194.

15. Rafael Pérez, *La Compañía de Jesús restaurada en la República Argentina y Chile, el Uruguay y el Brasil* (Barcelona, 1911), pp. 224–35, 247–48, 287–89, 341–45, 480–85, 502–3, 528–32, 587–601. The Jesuit *colegio* in Montevideo did suffer harassment from some elements of the Colorado administration, but it survived.

16. *El Nacional*, 1 March 1844.

17. Cf. police decree of 9 Feburary 1839 (*El Nacional*, 9 February 1839).

18. Uruguay, *Registro Nacional* (1834), pp. 163–64.

19. On the latter, see Juan José Antonio Segura, *Historia eclesiástica de Entre Ríos* (Nogoyá, 1964), pp. 128–29, and Entre Ríos, *Recopilación*, 4:161, 5:434–35.

20. Entre Ríos, *Recopilación*, 3:107.

21. E.g., 2 October 1829 tariff in Entre Ríos, *Recopilación*, 2:88–90.

22. Víctor Tau Anzoátegui, "Las facultades extraordinarias y la suma del poder público en el derecho provincial argentino (1820–1853)," *RIHD* 12 (1961):77–78.

23. Law of 2 December 1837, Entre Ríos, *Recopilación*, 4:339.

24. Gualeguaychú, 6 August 1849; *dejad hacer* in the Spanish original.

25. The measure did not last, however, and a maximum price for the entire province was fixed by *acuerdo* of 15 May 1852 (Entre Ríos, *Recopilación*, 6:222).

26. A fairly typical instance is the law of 27 February 1835 permitting mechanized establishments for the extraction of animal grease but specifying that processors must be prepared to halt operations at any time on government demand and that horses must not be killed for either hides or grease from August through November (Entre Ríos, *Recopilación*, 4:149–51.

27. Jonathan C. Brown, *A Socioeconomic History of Argentina, 1776–1860* (Cambridge, England, 1979), p. 215; John Lynch, *Argentine Dictator: Juan Manuel de Rosas 1829–1852* (Oxford, 1981), p. 315.

28. Decree of 1 August 1848, Entre Ríos, *Recopilación*, 5:277–79.
29. Beatriz Bosch, *Urquiza y su tiempo* (Buenos Aires, 1971), pp. 133, 144, 145.
30. *ROPC*, 4:283.
31. *Administración de Justicia de la Provincia de Corrientes* (Concepción del Uruguay, 1850), p. 3, which reproduces the remarks of the president of the provincial congress. The reform had also been reenacted in December 1840, by a law that Ferré vetoed on the ground that its wording left no room for military and church courts to continue handling even service-related offenses (Pedro Ferré, *Memorias del brigadier General Pedro Ferré* [Buenos Aires, 1921], pp. 767–68, 773–74).
32. Hernán F. Gómez, *Instituciones de la Provincia de Corrientes* (Buenos Aires, 1922), pp. 342–43. The process of abandonment began even before the authorization to sell such lands that was adopted in June 1844 (V-CS22).
33. *El Republicano* (Corrientes), 22 October 1843. See also discussion in the issues of 1, 8, 15, and 29 October.
34. There were, naturally, fluctuations in the degree of protectionism (Gómez, *Instituciones*, p. 300), but as late as 1849 Corrientes was putting duties of 50 percent on certain competing agricultural products and charging 80 percent on foreign liquors (Corrientes, *RO* [1849], p. 11).
35. Corrientes, *RO* (1853, Buenos Aires, 1874), p. 6; below, p. 102.
36. Corrientes, *RO* (1883), p. 23; *El Nacional Correntino* (Corrientes), 17 March, 17 April 1842.
37. *RM*, March 1845; AHM-EI, carpeta 403, doc. 37, f. 1; Jorge Comadrán Ruiz, "Notas sobre la creación y evolución de la Legislatura en Mendoza, 1820–1854," *RIHD* 24 (1978):49.
38. *RM*, 1 January 1828; *Suplemento a la Ilustración Argentina* (Mendoza), November 1849; Comadrán Ruiz, "Notas sobre la creación y evolución de la Legislatura," pp. 29–30, 32–33.
39. The clarification as to intended scope of the measure is contained in a marginal note (not by Aldao) to the text of the decree in the provincial archives. For another example of the prohibition of subversive publications, see *bando* of 20 January 1840, *RM*, February 1840.
40. Carlos S. A. Segreti, "Las explotaciones mineras en las provincias argentinas, 1823–1827," *Investigaciones y Ensayos* 18 (enero–junio 1975):136–53.
41. Carlos S. A. Segreti, *La economía del interior en la primera mitad del siglo xix (Correlación de documentos); I, Cuyo* (Buenos Aires, 1981), pp. 177–84, covers both the adoption and repeal of the measure. Segreti may well assume too much in discussing the practical effect of restrictions on interest, but he does make clear that the repeal was defended on strictly economic grounds.
42. The suppression was much debated and passed by a narrow margin. Archivo de la Legislatura, Mendoza, "Resúmenes," 19 November–28 December 1828.
43. AHM-EI, carpeta 399 bis, año 1822, f. 12v; *RM*, March 1835.
44. The Mercedarian convent, however, was almost empty, having only two members as of mid-1827 (José Aníbal Verdaguer, *Historia eclesiática de Cuyo*, 2 vols. [Milan, 1931–32], 1:968).
45. Verdaguer, *Historia eclesiástica*, 2:233–34; also Pérez, *La compañía de Jesús restaurada*, pp. 97–98, who notes that the Jesuits had already accepted Molina's invitation when his successor declined to go through with the plan.
46. Archivo de la Legislatura, "Resúmenes," 21 May, 3 June 1845.

47. Verdaguer, *Historia eclesiástica*, 2:234–36; Raúl H. Castagnino, *Rosas y los jesuitas* (Buenos Aires, 1970), pp. 109–11.

48. Miguel Angel Vergara, *Estudios sobre historia eclesiástica de Jujuy* (Tucumán, 1942), pp. 369–70. Actually, the government had already been putting *fincas capellánicas* up for sale before this law was passed, trying to obtain ecclesiastical concurrence, though it is not clear with what success. See AHPS, Libro 185, Correspondencia oficial 27 de febrero de 1831–9 de mayo de 1831, message of Gobernador delegado to Cabildo eclesiástico, 26 April 1831, and to Gobernador propietario, 28 April 1831.

49. Vergara, *Estudios*, pp. 374–79; Jujuy, *Compilación*, 1:201, 215; Gabriel Tommasini, *El convento de San Francisco de Jujuy en la historia y en la cultura cristiana* (Córdoba, 1934), pp. 132–35, 153–57, 171–74. Refusal to allow the restoration of the Franciscan community was justified expressly on the ground that convent assets had been disposed of under the Salta 1831 disamortization law.

50. Jujuy, *Compilación*, 1:176–77. It was, in fact, created on the initiative of a clergyman. See Miguel Angel Vergara, *Zegada sacerdote y patricio de Jujuy* (Jujuy, 1940), pp. 69–70 and passim.

51. Law of 14 February 1829 in Salta, *RO* (1829), 3:34–35.

52. The arbitrariness of Salta's policy was emphasized by the president of the Jujuy constituent assembly of 1835, who appealed to the tradition of the *leyes de Indias* whereby the state was ultimate owner of the lands, but the Indians had unquestioned usufruct (Archivo Legislativo de Jujuy, Libro primero de Actas, f. 54). Some sales had already been made by the Indians before the situation was frozen by the 7 May 1835 resolution, which appears to have been adopted in response to a proposed new sale; see Archivo Legislativo de Jujuy, Libro I, 1835, Despachos de Comisión, 7 May 1835, and Comunicaciones del Ejecutivo, letter from *Juez territorial* of Humahuaca, 24 April 1835.

53. See "Estado gral. q presenta el Mtro. de Haz.ª," 25 November 1843, in Archivo Legislativo de Jujuy, Libro 3, Comunicaciones del P. Ejecutivo; and "Estado jeneral qe presenta el Ministro de Hacienda . . . 1 de Enero hasta el 31 de Diciembre de 1845," in Archivo Legislativo de Jujuy, Libro 6, Cuadernillo 14, Despachos de Comisión, 1846. Specifically with regard to the Puna, a great part of the land had been technically brought under private ownership in the colonial period, although the Indians apparently retained a traditional belief in their communal ownership of the land. See Ian Rutledge, "The Indian Peasant Rebellion in the Highlands of Northern Argentina, 1872–75," *Journal of Peasant Studies* (London), 4:2 (June 1977):228–36.

54. Jujuy, *Compilación*, 2:43–44. The motive of using the lands as loan security was explicitly acknowledged. Archivo Legislativo de Jujuy, Libro 2, Borradores de actas, 4 March 1839.

55. Discussion of the circumstances surrounding adoption of the tribute is based on debates in the legislature concerning its later abolition, in Archivo Legislativo de Jujuy, Libro 3 de Actas, ff. 260–62. Insofar as payment was the price of exemption from militia duty, those who opted for such service did not have to pay; however, as the contribución directa came to represent 20 to 25 percent of provincial revenues, it would seem that most Indians did pay. See "Estados" cited in note 53, above.

56. Jujuy, *Compilación*, 1:57–58.

57. Ibid., 1:154, for reference to one effort, apparently unsuccessful, to elicit Bolivian reciprocity, and Norberto Aurelio López, "El comercio en la provincia de Jujuy durante el transcurso del siglo xix," in Academia Nacional de la Historia, *Cuarto Congreso Nacional y Regional de Historia Argentina* (Buenos Aires, 1979–), 1:476, for an attempt to put pressure on Bolivia by raising tariffs. Examples of earlier tariff legislation of Salta are the law of 19

July 1832 in Salta, *RO* (1832), pp. 37–38, and decree of 12 March 1833, in Salta, *RO* (1833), p. 69. The last of these measures placed a duty on sugar, and its purpose was frankly stated to be that of fomenting provincial industry without unduly burdening the public; it placed a duty of 12 *reales* on each *arroba* of sugar brought into the province but provided that the duty should be suspended if the price of the local product exceeded $5. The provision linking import duty to the internal price level parallels certain measures giving limited protection to wheat growers in other provinces.

58. Jujuy, *Compilación*, 1:300–317.

59. Jorge A. Bidondo, *Notas para la historia de los gobernadores de Jujuy* (Jujuy, 1971), pp. 27, 32. Yet it should be noted that the law abolishing fueros bore the heading "*Mueran Los Salvajes Unitarios*" (original text in Archivo Provincial de Jujuy, Caja año 1851, enero–junio). Nor can it be assumed that all the laws in question were necessarily implemented, even prior to Iturbe's return to power.

60. Tau Anzoátegui, "Las facultades extraordinarias," pp. 91–92, regards this as a unique case of auto-investiture. It was not unique but certainly unusual.

61. Bando of 7 September 1831, in *Gaceta Mercantil* (Buenos Aires), 10 October 1831.

62. *Mensage del gobierno de Córdoba a la décima tercia legislatura* (Córdoba, 1847), p. 19.

63. Decree of 20 April 1848, in AHPC, RO, tomo 5, f. 299.

64. José María Paz, *Memorias,* ed. José Luis Lanuza, 4 vols. (Buenos Aires, 1968), 2:244–49 and passim.

65. *La Aurora Nacional* (Córdoba), 27 August 1830. Two sons of pardos were to be given scholarships for secondary study; but the whole measure was presumably rescinded by the blanket annulment of Paz's acts after his fall (Ignacio Garzón, *Crónica de Córdoba*, 3 vols. [Córdoba, 1898–1902], 2:366–67). Though it did not specifically refer to the matter, one can assume that some form of segregation of pardo students remained in effect even under the Paz decree. Cf. José Luis Masini Calderón, "Consideraciones sobre la esclavitud en Córdoba; época independiente," in Academia Nacional de la Historia, *Primer Congreso de Historia Argentina y Regional* (Buenos Aires, 1973), p. 549.

66. AHPC, Gobierno 1844, tomo 191, f. 580.

67. Nelly Beatriz López, "Algunos elementos para el estudio del esclavo y del liberto en Córdoba en el lapso 1810–1853," Academia Nacional de la Historia, *Primer Congreso*, pp. 560–62.

68. Letter from Manuel López to Sala de Representantes, 28 February 1837, AHPC, Gobierno, Honorable Asamblea, 1833 a 1852, ff. 61–62. See also Robert J. Turkovic, "Córdoba's Pueblos de Indios: Decline and Extinction," *Latinamericanist* (Gainesville, Florida), 1 December 1979. It appears that the division of communal lands still was not fully implemented (Gastón Gabriel Doucet, personal communication to author, Córdoba, 1 September 1976).

69. *Archivo de la H. Cámara de Diputados de la Provincia de Córdoba*, 7 vols. (Córdoba, 1912–), 6:253.

70. Córdoba, Governor, *Mensaje a la décima séptima legislatura* (Córdoba, 1837), table, and *Mensage del gobierno de Córdoba a la décima tercia legislatura*, table.

71. Castagnino, *Rosas y los jesuitas*, pp. 94–96, 112; *Mensajes de los gobernadores de la provincia de Buenos Aires, 1822–1849*, 2 vols. (La Plata, 1976), 2:73–76.

72. 6 August 1849.

EPILOGUE

1. *Constituciones*, pp. 358–72.
2. David Bushnell, "El sufragio en la Argentina y en Colombia hasta 1853," *RIHD* 19 (1968):28.
3. *RN*, 3:87.
4. Mario Rodríguez, *The Cádiz Experiment in Central America, 1808–1826* (Berkeley and Los Angeles, 1978), esp. pp. 199–211, 222–26. For Guatemala, the high point of liberal innovation came during the first part of the decade of the 1830s—only to be obliterated in the reaction led by José Rafael Carrera at the end of that decade.
5. William Lee Lofstrom, *The Promise and Problem of Reform: Attempted Social and Economic Change in the First Years of Bolivian Independence* (Ithaca, 1972).
6. José Gil Fortoul, *Historia constitucional de Venezuela*, 5th ed., 3 vols. (Caracas, 1967), 2:55, 63–65, 70, 184.
7. David Peña, *La materia religiosa en la política argentina* (Buenos Aires, 1960), pp. 13–53.
8. Richard Alan White, *Paraguay's Autonomous Revolution 1810–1840* (Albuquerque, 1978), pp. 93–94, 108.

Appendix 1. The First Decade

I-1. *8 June 1810.* Integration of Indian militia units into white battalions, on the ground of natural and complete equality of Spaniards and Indians (*RN*, 1:34).

I-2. *3 December 1810.* Circular of Junta stating that all foreigners not at war with the new regime may come and freely live under its protection, with all rights of citizenship (*RN*, 1:91–92).

I-3. *20 April 1811.* Press reglamento abolishes prior censorship except in the case of writings on religious matters, which remain "subject to the prior censorship of the ecclesiastical ordinaries" but with procedural controls to assure fairness. This measure was subsequently confirmed by a more definitive reglamento of 26 October 1811, which ordered the creation of a regular system of juries for trial of press offenses (*RN*, 1:108–9, 124–25).

I-4. *1 September 1811.* Suppression of Indian tribute (*RN*, 1:115).

I-5. *23 November 1811.* Decree of First Triumvirate guaranteeing protection of civil rights and judicial due process; no prisoner to be held incommunicado more than ten days; homes are considered sacred; anyone can remain in or leave the territory of the state as he wishes, etc. (*RN*, 1:128–29).

I-6. *9 April 1812.* Prohibition of slave trade (Bagú, p. 122).

I-7. *12 May 1812.* First Triumvirate orders selection by lot of four slaves who will receive freedom in honor of the coming anniversary of the May Revolution (Rafael Castellano Sáenz Cavia, "La abolición de la esclavitud en las Provincias Unidas del Río de la Plata, 1810–1860," *Revista de Historia del Derecho* 9[1981]:84–85.

I-8. *27 June 1812.* Decree specifies that militia will enjoy the fuero only when in actual service (Abelardo Levaggi, "Los fueros especiales, contribución al estudio de la administración de justicia en el Río de la Plata," *RIHD* 22[1971]:70).

I-9. *14 August 1812.* The Indian community of Quilmes is declared formally open on equal terms to "every class of persons." The separate jurisdiction and "privileges" of the Indians are ended, but Indians will be protected in "possession of the lands they occupy," pending ultimate distribution of communally owned lands as individual private property (*RN*, 1:174).

I-10. *18 August 1812.* Decree of First Triumvirate ends "perpetual" offices in municipal government on the ground that they constitute a tyrannical abuse, but "without prejudice" to current possessors of such posts (*RN*, 1:174).

I-11. *22 August 1812.* Tobacco monopoly abolished. The same measure applies to associated ramos estancados, such as playing cards (*RN*, 1:176–77).

I-12. *4 September 1812.* Decree expressly invites foreign immigration, offering newcomers land and, if they enter mining, duty-free importation of equipment (*RN*, 1:177–78; Bagú, pp. 123–24).

I-13. *11 September 1812.* The First Triumvirate ends the requirement (in practice widely evaded) that foreigners use native merchants as consignees rather than selling directly in wholesale commerce (the Assembly of 1813 returns to the consignment system, then abandons it again) (*RN*, 1:178; Bagú, p. 125; *RA*, 23 October 1813).

I-14. *31 January 1813.* Effective date of the free-birth principle, adopted for gradual abolition of slavery (*RN*, 1:194).

I-15. *12 March 1813.* While reaffirming the previous abolition of tribute and complete equality of Indians with other inhabitants in all matters, the assembly further extinguishes the mita and all forms of "personal service of the Indians," including that performed on behalf of the church (*RN*, 1:203).

I-16. *27 March 1813.* Inquisition abolished. The ecclesiastical ordinaries inherit its function to watch over "purity of belief," but by "canonical means" and in accord with "the spirit of Jesus Christ" (*RN*, 1:206–7).

I-17. *7 May 1813.* Project for encouragement of the mining industry adopted which specifically recognizes the right of foreign entrepreneurs and their employees "to worship God inside their houses privately, according to their customs" (*RN*, 1:211–12).

I-18. *19 May 1813.* Titles of nobility abolished. As a corollary, a subsequent law of 26 October forbids the use of coats of arms and other distinctions of nobility on houses (*RA*, 29 May, 20 November 1813).

I-19. *19 May 1813.* Use of torture prohibited. Instruments of torture to be "*inutilizados*" by official executioner (*RA*, 29 May 1813).

I-20. *19 May 1813.* Minimum age of thirty set for professions in religious orders (*RA*, 29 May 1813).

I-21. *31 May and 23 June 1813.* Decree of the assembly, complemented by an order of the ministry of finance, creates the first *batallón de libertos*, composed of former slaves who will eventually obtain full freedom in return for military service (*RN*, 1:218, 221).

I-22. *28 June 1813.* Having severed ties between the religious orders and their superiors in Spain on 4 June, the assembly establishes a Comisaría General de Regulares to exercise authority formerly vested in the latter (*RA*, 12 June, 17 July 1813).

I-23. *5 July 1813.* All assets belonging to hospital orders (the Bethlehemite friars) placed under secular administration (*RA*, 17 July 1813).

I-24. *4 August 1813.* Baptism of infants with cold water prohibited, ostensibly as a health measure in order to "save from death so many innocents who are scarcely going to touch the threshold of life." The measure is reiterated by Supreme Director Juan Martín de Pueyrredón in a decree of October 1816, in which he takes note of poor enforcement (*RA*, 14 August 1813; *RN*, 1:385).

I-25. *13 August 1813.* Founding of entailed estates (mayorazgos) prohibited (*RA*, 21 August 1813).

I-26. *9 October 1813.* Decree of Second Triumvirate prohibits "the barbarous practice" of punishing school children by whipping (*RN*, 1:234–35).

I-27. *22 September 1814.* Supreme Director Gervasio Posadas reduces tithes in the provinces of Entre Ríos and Corrientes, as well as in Uruguay, by half, for a twenty-year period (*RN*, 1:285).

I-28. *5 May 1815.* Estatuto Provisional issued as a temporary national constitution pending the adoption of a permanent replacement. It is generally unremarkable, with conventional provisions for separation of powers and individual guarantees. There are two features of particular interest: (a) full citizenship rights, including the suffrage, are extended to "every free man" but are to be automatically suspended in the case of domestic servants and others who lack property or some "lucrative and useful profession" ("*oficio lucrativo y útil al país*"), and they are withheld in the case of individuals descended in any degree from African slaves ("*originarios por cualquiera línea de Africa, cuyos mayores hayan sido esclavos en este continente*"), unless their fathers had been born free; (b) an appendix to the Estatuto Provisional repeals "the laws and decrees which the last assembly made on religious professions" as well as the Second Triumvirate's prohibition of the use of the lash on school children (*Constituciones*, pp. 211–32).

I-29. *12 October 1816*. Congress of Tucumán abolishes the Comisaría General de Regulares in view of the doubtful legitimacy of its authority and therefore probable "nullity" of its acts (*RN*, 1:383).

I-30. *20 December 1816*. Decree of Supreme Director Pueyrredón returns the administration of hospitals and their assets to Bethlehemite friars (*RN*, 1:400; Bruno, 8:44–45).

I-31. *January 1817*. Pueyrredón introduces a new tariff schedule with sharply increased duties, especially on articles that compete with domestic industries (José María Mariluz Urquijo, "Aspectos de la política proteccionista durante la década 1810–1820," *BANH* 37 [1965]:142).

I-32. *15 May 1817*. Privateering regulation stipulates that slaves seized by Argentine corsairs will, if suitable for bearing arms, serve four years and then receive their freedom; their captors will receive a reward of $50 for each one (*RN*, 1:418).

I-33. *3 December 1817*. Reglamento Provisorio adopted by the national congress confirms most provisions of the 1815 Estatuto but reinstates the decree against whipping of school children that the latter had annulled (*RN*, 1:441–54, 511).

I-34. *January 1819*. Directorial decree prohibits bullfighting at Buenos Aires, where the last *corrida* (at least for a time) takes place on 6 January (*Diccionario histórico argentino*, 6 vols. [Buenos Aires, 1953–54], 6:635).

Appendix 2. The Second Decade

Political Innovations

II-P1.   *14 August 1821*. Provincial law grants the right to vote to all free adult males (*RO* [1821], p. 18).

II-P2.   *3 September 1821*. Rivadavia decree repeals all restrictions on the introduction of books, paintings, engravings (*RO* [1821], p. 37).

II-P3.   *24 October 1821*. Rivadavia eliminates the standing requirement to obtain government permission for printing any "paper" by an author not in the province (*RO* [1821], p. 109).

II-P4.   *24 December 1821*. Law suppresses the cabildos of Buenos Aires and Luján, the only ones in the province (*RO* [1821], pp. 201–2).

II-P5.   *25 April 1822*. Rivadavia decree provides that the Tribunal de Comercio (which has replaced the former Consulado of Buenos Aires in its judicial role) will hear all cases dealing with actos de comercio regardless of individuals involved and further defines an acto de comercio. The mercantile fuero is thereby abolished (*RO* [1822], pp. 171–73).

II-P6.   *10 October 1822*. Law on press abuses reaffirms essential features of the system established in 1811, including a form of jury, though attempting to provide more summary handling of cases (*RO* [1822], pp. 295–96).

II-P7.   *5 July 1823*. Law abolishes personal fueros in civil and criminal matters. Exceptions concern criminal offenses committed by treasury and postal employees in discharging their functions, which will continue to be handled by "the respective ministry." A subsequent decree of Rivadavia (8 July) specifies that there is to be no change in "civil exemptions or social consideration" of any individuals formerly enjoying fuero (*RO* [1823], pp. 119–21).

Socioeconomic Innovations

II-SE1.   *22 August 1821.* Law expressly authorizes the provincial executive to make arrangements for introduction of immigrants (Bagú, p. 143).

II-SE2.   *10 November 1821.* Rivadavia decree forbids taking pregnant slaves to "foreign territory" to give birth as a means of evading the free-birth principle. The decree similarly forbids removal abroad of free-born offspring of slave mothers while still under the owners' tutelage, i.e., pending age of full emancipation (Bagú, p. 150).

II-SE3.   *22 November 1821.* Decree of Rivadavia, noting that "free use of property is as important for its increase as is security in its possession," repeals existing restrictions on slaughter of cows. The most recent restriction had been decreed by Rivadavia himself on 2 August (Bagú, pp. 140, 152).

II-SE4.   *17 December 1821.* Provincial law establishes the contribución directa, a direct tax on capital, at a variable rate initially set at one to eight mills depending on nature of the capital (*RO* [1821], pp. 196–97).

II-SE5.   *18 December 1821.* Companion measure provides for general abolition of the alcabala or sales tax, although that on auction sales survives (*RO* [1821], p. 195; *RO* [1822], p. 295).

II-SE6.   *1 January 1822.* Effective date of new tariff which taxes imported merchandise at basic rate of 15 percent ad valorem; though it does establish a moderate protectionism on behalf of some national products, this is not a general tendency. With modifications, this tariff lasts out the decade (Miron Burgin, *The Economic Aspects of Argentine Federalism, 1820–1852* [Cambridge, Mass., 1946], pp. 70–72; José María Mariluz Urquijo, "Protección y librecambio durante el período 1820–1835," *BANH* 34, sec. 2 [1964]:701–7).

II-SE7.   *4 January 1822.* Decree of Manuel José García prohibits bullfights "without special permission of the chief of police" and requires that bulls first be dehorned (*RO* [1822], p. 3).

II-SE8.   *February 1822.* In answer to a query from the Tribunal de Comercio, Rivadavia authorizes suspension of traditional legal restrictions which held rates of interest (in theory, though not in practice) to a maximum of 6 percent. Pending adoption of new legislation on the subject, which in fact was not forthcoming, lenders are allowed to charge the amount the government had been known to pay (up to 3 percent per month) (Alberto Palcos, *Rivadavia, ejecutor del pensamiento de Mayo*, 2 vols. [La Plata, 1960], 1:618).

II-SE9.   *21 June 1822.* Provincial law is adopted which contains just one article: "The inviolability accorded to properties by law of the province is extensive to all those found in its territory, of whatever ownership." Though not explicitly stated, the primary purpose is to guarantee the property of Spanish subjects (Bagú, pp. 166, 208).

II-SE10.   *1 July 1822.* Decree of Manuel José García prohibits the sale of public lands, which are to be distributed instead by long-term leases under the system of emphyteusis (Bagú, p. 167).

II-SE11.   *2 December 1822.* Provincial law abolishes the sisa, a former municipal levy on foodstuffs, and the media anata, a tax on first-year salaries of appointees to civil and ecclesiastical office (*RO* [1822], pp. 323–24).

II-SE12.   *29 August 1825.* Law providing for the military recruitment of slaves in the war with Brazil offers them full freedom but requires them to serve six years beyond the time the state reimburses itself from their pay for whatever sums given former owners (*RO* [1825], pp. 68–69).

II-SE13.   *10 March 1826.* Decree of Rivadavia, as president of Argentina, awards outfitters of the corsair *Lavalleja* $50 for each black taken in the war with Brazil. The blacks receive conditional freedom as libertos, but to provide for their "education" as well as repay the public treasury for the expenditures on their behalf, they are hired out for six years or assigned to military duty for eight years (Bagú, pp. 328–29).

II-SE14.   *18 May 1826.* Law of the constituent congress extends the system of emphyteusis adopted for Buenos Aires in 1822 to public lands of the entire republic (Bagú, p. 378).

II-SE15.   *15 December 1826.* Rivadavia rules that the government cannot compel urban artisans to do harvest labor, as had been customary, but it will make sure that the high wages offered for harvest work are announced in the press (José María Mariluz Urquijo, "La mano de obra en la industria porteña, 1810–1835," *BANH* 33, sec. 2 [1962]:619–20).

II-SE16.   *28 March 1827.* Elaborating on his March 1826 decree, Rivadavia extends its provisions to all blacks on ships taken by corsairs, specifically including crew members and personal servants. The military service term is reduced to four years (*RN* [1827], pp. 51–57).

II-SE17.   *4 May 1827.* Two decrees of Rivadavia lift price controls from bread and meat as of 1 January 1828, on the ground that free competition has been effective in other lines of commerce and is supported by the "experience of the most civilized peoples" (Bagú, pp. 450–53).

Religious Innovations

II-R1.   *14 November 1820.* Provincial legislature grants a ten-year, 20 percent reduction in tithes, to aid recovery from economic dislocations caused by the independence struggle (*RN*, 1:555–56).

II-R2.   *January 1821.* First cemetery for non–Roman Catholics is established on land donated by the government (José Antonio Wilde, *Buenos Aires desde setenta años atrás, 1810–1880* [Buenos Aires, 1960], pp. 85–86).

II-R3.   *28 November 1821.* Rivadavia decree forbids clergy to enter the province without prior governmental permission (*RN*, 1:596).

II-R4.   *13 December 1821.* Rivadavia decree withdraws Mercedarian friars from obedience to their provincial, placing them under immediate protection of the government and subject, in spiritual affairs, only to the "ordinary ecclesiastical authority." The same is ordered with respect to Franciscans by a decree of 8 February 1822 and for all regulars in the province of Buenos Aires on 1 July 1822 (Bruno, 8:437; *RN*, 2:4, 19).

II-R5.   *13 December 1821.* Rivadavia orders that all burials be made in two public cemeteries to be constructed west of the city of Buenos Aires. Though the stated purpose is to end the unhygienic practice of burials within churches, actual prohibition of the latter is delayed pending inauguration of the new facilities (*RO* [1821], p. 181; *RO* [1822], pp. 3–4).

II-R6.   *22 March 1822.* Decree of Rivadavia establishes special controls over the assets of Santa Catalina convent (Dominican
nuns) while authorizing the redemption of its censos (ecclesiastical mortgages) in 6 percent government notes (*RN*,
2:11).

II-R7.   *1 July 1822.* Rivadavia decree suppresses the Franciscan convent of Recoleta and reassigns its property for a new cemetery
(*RN*, 2:18–19; Bruno, 8:439–41).

II-R8.   *1 July 1822.* Noting with distress that the sanctuary of Luján
has as its sole purpose the cult of an image, Rivadavia directs
the ministry of finance to take possession of all its properties
except those directly used in the cult (*RN*, 2:18).

II-R9.   *1 July 1822.* Two more decrees of Rivadavia—it was a busy
day—remove the men's hospitals and their assets from control
of the Bethlehemite friars and the women's hospital from that
of the Hermandad de la Caridad, which is abolished. The
women's hospital is subsequently transferred to the control of
a new Sociedad de Beneficencia. Of the men's hospitals, one is
suppressed and the other placed under state administration; affected friars may continue working there at $1 per day or retire
on a state pension (*RO* [1822], pp. 235–39, 253–60; Angelis,
1:443).

II-R10.   *17 July 1822.* Regulation for Recoleta cemetery states that cadavers must be taken directly to the cemetery from the mortuary, bypassing the church (Angelis, 1:392).

II-R11.   *28 November 1822.* Rivadavia decree authorizes redemption of
the capital of capellanías (chantries) in public treasury notes,
though still requiring agreement of the "patron" (*RO* [1822],
p. 303).

II-R12.   *21 December 1822.* Comprehensive "law of reform of the
clergy" adopted by Junta de Representantes. In addition to detailed provisions concerning organization and management of
the secular clergy—in particular the cathedral chapter now
converted into *Senado del Clero*—it provides that
a. the ecclesiastical fuero be abolished;
b. tithes be abolished, the public treasury to assume responsibility for expenditures previously made with their proceeds;
c. the diocesan seminary be converted into the Colegio Nacional de Estudios Eclesiásticos, to be maintained by the state;
d. houses of Bethlehemite friars and other male orders with

less than sixteen religious be suppressed and no order be allowed more than thirty members;

e. provincials of the religious orders not be allowed to exercise
authority within Buenos Aires, the diocesan ordinary to act
in their place for maintenance of discipline;

f. ordinary be encouraged to act upon requests of friars or nuns
for secularization, with the government offering maintenance
allotments, as needed, to those who become secularized;

g. no professions in religious orders be allowed before age
twenty-five;

h. the convent of Santa Catalina not have more than thirty
nuns and that of Capuchin nuns retain the maximum number set by its present constitution (thirty-three);

i. property of suppressed houses pass to the state, and the
value of real estate owned by those not suppressed be converted to treasury notes;

j. principal owed to capellanías and *memorias pías* (pious foundations) of the regular orders be repaid (if so desired) in 6
percent treasury notes, at par (Guillermo Gallardo, *La política religiosa de Rivadavia* [Buenos Aires, 1962], pp. 277–280;
Bruno, 8:477).

II-R13.   *14 and 17 January 1823.* Government takes possession of all
properties of the cathedral and Senado del Clero except those
essential for religious services and the temple itself (Bruno,
8:489; *RO* [1823], pp. 16–18).

II-R14.   *15 February 1823.* Provisor Mariano Zavaleta, acting "in agreement with the superior government," declares the Mercedarian
convent extinguished for lack of sufficient members (Bruno,
8:482).

II-R15.   *24 February 1823.* Government orders suppression of the small
Franciscan convent at the town of San Pedro (Bruno, 8:485).

II-R16.   *4 March 1823.* Members of the one remaining Franciscan convent, in the city of Buenos Aires, and of the only Dominican
male convent, are ordered by Zavaleta to become secularized
or to leave the province. Protests cause him to withdraw his
order on 10 March, but by then too many Dominicans have
already committed themselves to one or the other of the op-
tions, and on 4 April the convent is suppressed for lack of sufficient members (Bruno, 8:483–84, 487).

II-R17.   *2 February 1825.* Treaty signed between the United Provinces
of the Río de la Plata and Great Britain expressly grants free-

dom of conscience and worship to British subjects in Argentina (Bruno, 9:74).

II–R18.   *8 October 1825.* Decree of Governor Juan Gregorio Las Heras repeals the prohibition of clergy entering the province without prior government permission (*RN*, 2:88).

II–R19.   *12 October 1825.* Freedom of worship granted by law to all residents of Buenos Aires province (*RN*, 2:89).

II–R20.   *14 June 1826.* Rivadavia decree on primary education requires that schoolmasters demonstrate their knowledge of the Lancasterian "system of mutual instruction" and their personal moral character but conspicuously omits any reference to religious orthodoxy (*RN*, 2:137).

Appendix 3. Innovation in Other Provinces

Uruguay

III-U1.   *17 June 1825.* Instructions for the election of a first provincial assembly grant the suffrage to all free males over twenty years of age, though under a system of indirect voting (Uruguay, *Compilación*, 1:6).

III-U2.   *7 September 1825.* Assembly expressly endorses the prohibition of the slave trade and the principle of free birth (Uruguay, *Compilación*, 1:15–16).

III-U3.   *30 December 1825.* Provincial assembly abolishes tithes on livestock and grain (Uruguay, *Compilación*, 1:20).

III-U4.   *3 February 1826.* For protection of Uruguayan agriculture, law places heavier duties—exact rate to vary with local price levels—on foreign grains and flour. This measure is soon superseded, however, by the Argentine law of 13 March 1826 that brings all customs legislation and administration under national control (*Actas de la h. Junta de Representantes de la Provincia Oriental, Años 1825–26–27* [Montevideo, 1920], pp. 68–69, 114; Bagú, p. 335).

III-U5.   *8 July 1826.* Provincial law of "guarantees" affirms that "industry will be entirely free of all the obstacles that may oppose its increase." With respect to press freedom, the law excludes the use of prior censorship (Uruguay, *Compilación*, 1:30).

III-U6.   *17 October 1826.* Suppression of cabildos (Uruguay, *Compilación*, 1:30–32, 122).

III-U7.   *31 March 1827.* Uruguayan assembly accepts the Argentine constitution of 1826, which was conventionally republican but highly centralist and restrictive in its treatment of the suffrage (*Registro Oficial del Gobierno de la Provincia Oriental* [Canelones, 1827], pp. 78–79); *Constituciones,* 309–22).

III-U8.   *9 April 1827.* Press law issued which is substantially similar to the October 1811 regulation (I-3); a special jury is to hear cases of alleged abuses (Uruguay, *Compilación,* 1:40–43).

III-U9.   *10 April 1827.* Uruguay adopts a law of contribución directa broadly patterned on that of Buenos Aires, with the minimum rate of $3 per $1,000 of capital, rising to $10 per $1,000 for merchants (*Registro Oficial del Gobierno de la Provincia Oriental,* pp. 102–4).

Entre Ríos

III-ER1.   *1820.* Instructions of Francisco Ramírez, Jefe Supremo of the "Republic" of Entre Ríos, convoke all "inhabitants . . . without distinction of class or person" to take part in forthcoming elections (Aníbal Vásquez, *La República de Entre Ríos* [Paraná, 1930], pp. 64–72).

III-ER2.   *3 October 1821.* Entre Ríos adopts a tariff law that establishes generally moderate import duties (Entre Ríos, *Recopilación,* 1:13–16).

III-ER3.   *4 March 1822.* First provincial constitution (Estatuto Provisorio) creates a government that is formally representative, with nominal separation of powers. Citizenship rights are restricted when compared to the instructions of Ramírez: to enjoy full citizenship, including the right to vote, one must have a useful occupation and (beginning in 1840) know how to read and write. The constitution also reaffirms press freedom under the terms of the October 1811 reglamento and the measures on slavery adopted by the Assembly of the Year XIII (Ramos, 1:199–216).

III-ER4.   *8 March 1822.* Separate law repeats the constitutional guarantee of press freedom but with specification that it does not authorize anyone to attack "the dogmas of our religion, promote maxims contrary to morality," or espouse sedition (Entre Ríos, *Recopilación,* 1:166–68).

III-ER5.   *11 March 1822.* Another separate enactment reiterates the adherence of Entre Ríos to abolition of the slave trade and to the principle of free birth (Entre Ríos, *Recopilación*, 1:160–62).

III-ER6.   *20 January 1823.* Decree of Governor Lucio Mansilla makes payment of tithes purely voluntary. Recognizing that such a measure should have been adopted by law rather than by executive decree, he explains that he wished to act in time to prevent still another year of injustice and irregularities in tithe collection. On 13 March, the legislature adds its approval (Entre Ríos, *Recopilación*, 1:249–51, 256–57).

III-ER7.   *13 November 1824.* Law calls for the establishment of cemeteries at a proper distance from all towns, while forbidding burials in churches (Entre Ríos, *Recopilación*, 1:447–48).

III-ER8.   *14 December 1824.* Decree of Governor León Sola repeats the prohibition, by the 1813 assembly, of lashing as a punishment in schools—noting that it had been commonly ignored in Entre Ríos—and extends it to cover use of the rod (Entre Ríos, *Recopilación*, 1:457–58).

III-ER9.   *17 January 1825.* Law for reform of religious orders prohibits "forever . . . the establishment of convents or monastic houses of any sort." Regulars serving curacies or chaplaincies must request secularization or leave; any coming to Entre Ríos in the future must obtain official permission to stay (Entre Ríos, *Recopilación*, 2:7–9).

III-ER10.   *1825–1826.* A group of English colonists is brought to Entre Ríos by the Río de la Plata Agricultural Association, under a contract with the provincial government that offered tax exemptions and other privileges. They do not stay long (J.A.B. Beaumont, *Viajes por Buenos Aires, Entre Ríos y la Banda Oriental, 1826–1827* [Buenos Aires, 1957], pp. 144–45, 191, 194–96, 202–4).

Corrientes

III-CS1.   *11 December 1821.* First provincial constitution creates a conventional three-power structure of government. It includes a strong and unqualified statement of the position of Roman Catholicism as the "religion of the State," which all must respect. No restrictions are placed on citizenship, including voting rights, of native-born, free male adults (*ROPC*, 1:24–34).

III-CS2.   *22 September 1824.* Revised constitution retains the above features and further includes among specific faculties of the provincial congress that of providing two years' subsistence (on a reimbursable basis) for new settlers. It orders the suppression of cabildos, effective 1 January 1825 (*ROPC*, 1:245–60).

III-CS3. *26 January 1825.* Corrientes adopts a tariff law that levies generally protectionist duties on tobacco products, liquors, and imported manufactures. It allows books to be imported free of duty, provided they are not opposed to the Roman Catholic religion—in which case they are prohibited (*ROPC*, 1:347–50).

III-CS4. *14 February 1825.* Law extinguishes the Indian community of Itatí. Families native to the town, even if not presently living there, are to receive a house lot in town plus a farm lot (*chacra*), which will be alienable only after four years. (A subsequent decree of Governor Pedro Ferré, 18 May 1826, offers fewer privileges to nonnative residents.) Excess lands are to be sold (*ROPC*, 1:367–68; 2:15–16, 20, 45–47).

III-CS5. *6 January 1826.* Ferré decree prohibits burials within churches, but not until 15 September 1827 does a law make special provision for construction of a cemetery (*ROPC*, 2:131; Corrientes, *RO* [1826], p. 2).

III-CS6. *28 February 1826.* Law authorizes sale of property belonging to the only surviving Indian community, Santa Lucía (*ROPC*, 2:12).

III-CS7. *1 July 1826.* Noting the state of "nullity" to which the Dominican convent has been reduced, with one resident friar, a provincial law authorizes the governor to name chaplains to Dominican capellanías that are not being served and to make "pious" disposition of the convent's assets. Assured (incorrectly) that new friars will be sent, Ferré suspends implementation, but the law remains technically in force and is in fact carried out in 1842 (V-CS-19) (*ROPC*, 2:19, 25–26; Bruno, 10:176).

III-CS8. *29 November 1826.* Law creates a Cuerpo de Enseñanza Pública to take charge of education throughout the province, under close official supervision. The measure is in response to a proposal of Governor Ferré in which he stated the need for government control of education and observed that educational functions "have no necessary connection" with those of religious worship (*"no tienen connección alguna necesaria con las funciones del culto"*) (Corrientes, *RO* [1826], pp. 49–64).

III-CS9.   *28 September 1827.* Law orders formal extinction of the Indian community of Santa Lucía. Land will be assigned both to natives of the town and to others who request it (*ROPC*, 2:134).

Mendoza

III-M1.   *28 November 1820.* Law of provincial Sala de Representantes strips common soldiers of the military fuero, except during active duty (AHM-EI, Carpeta 199, doc. 4, f. 18).

III-M2.   *12 July 1822.* Sala forbids printing of "defamatory papers" (*papeles infamatorios*), which are not otherwise defined (Ahumada, p. 11).

III-M3.   *25 October 1822.* Sala repeals the preceding measure as ineffective, restores press freedom on the basis of the October 1811 reglamento (Ahumada, p. 16; *RM*, 16 November 1822).

III-M4.   *25 February 1823.* General tax decree explicitly recognizes protection of local industries as a goal in setting import duties and at the same time orders restoration of the playing-card monopoly, which had been abolished in 1812 (I-11) (AHM-EI, Carpeta 399 bis, año 1823, f. 21v; *RM*, 16 March 1823).

III-M5.   *11 April 1823.* Sala repeals the playing-card monopoly in favor of a 6 percent import tax on cards (*RM*, 23 April 1823).

III-M6.   *15 July 1823.* *Reforma de regulares*, enacted by provincial Sala, orders all religious to "observe their primitive institutions . . . and common life"; also forbids religious profession by anyone not yet twenty-two years old. The diocesan ordinary is instructed to enforce these provisions (*RM*, 7 August 1823).

III-M7.   *16 December 1823.* In arranging for withdrawal of counterfeit money from circulation, legislators resolve that the operation be financed in part with money "borrowed" from the proceeds of the tithes. Despite promise of repayment, the cathedral chapter of Córdoba, to which diocese Mendoza belongs, vigorously protests (AHM-EI, Carpeta 52, doc. 105, Carpeta 399 bis, 16 December 1823 and 31 September 1824; *El Eco de los Andes* [Mendoza], 11 November 1824).

III-M8.   *7 July 1824.* Judicial functions of municipal *alcaldes* are transferred to specialized judicial officers, as first step in abolition of the cabildo (Ahumada, p. 28).

III-M9.   *23 December 1824.* (I have not seen a copy of the complete law but infer the date from, e.g., Ahumada, p. 43.) New tax law creates a Mendozan version of Buenos Aires's contribución directa. In place of various taxes on importation and sales, such as the alcabala, merchants will pay a flat 4 percent of their operating capital; other groups are to pay rates geared to their economic activities (*El Eco de los Andes*, 20 March 1825; Silvestre Peña y Lillo, *Gobernadores de Mendoza*, 2 vols. [Mendoza, 1927–28], 2:27, 93–96, 276).

III-M10. *12 April 1825* Governor Juan de Dios Correas decrees suppression of the Augustinian convent (one of only two of that order in Argentina) for lack of members: the prior had sought and obtained permission to secularize, and only a lay brother remained. The convent's temporalities go to the public treasury (Ahumada, p. 38).

III-M11. *11 May 1825.* Sala de Representantes pronounces final suppression of the cabildo (Ahumada, pp. 39–40).

III-M12. *17 November 1825.* Another decree of Governor Correas (later confirmed by the Sala) puts the final touches on Mendoza's reforma de regulares. Convents are placed under immediate authority of the ordinary, not the provincials of their respective orders, and no religious may enter Mendoza without government license (*RM*, 20 December 1825, 12 April 1826).

III-M13. *4 November 1826.* Law reestablishes alcabala, at a rate as high as 40 percent on items such as foreign footwear, clothing, and furniture. Contribución directa is largely abandoned (*RM*, 11 November 1826).

III-M14. *17 May 1827.* New election law supersedes suffrage provisions of the 1815 Estatuto Provisional (I-28), which had remained technically in force in Mendoza and which imposed socioeconomic and racial restrictions on political participation. A voter must still own real property, or practice an "industrious occupation in sciences, arts, or commerce," or hold a "civil or military office," or in the absence of any of these "have obtained . . . some reward for services to the cause of Liberty"; but racial discrimination is eliminated (AHM-EI, Carpeta 199, doc. 4, f. 29).

III-M15. *22 May 1827.* Two local newspapers are simultaneously suppressed by executive decree. Issued in the name of "enlightenment" and inaccurately citing the absence of any law in the province to regulate press freedom, the decree emphasizes that no one may print anything that "offends public decency" (Félix Weinberg, *Juan Gualberto Godoy: literatura y política* [Buenos Aires, 1970], 115n, 116n).

Salta

III-S1.   *May 1820.* Salta provincial assembly restores the playing-card monopoly to help meet emergency military expenditures. This is done on a short-term basis, but the monopoly reappears in another set of emergency tax levies of 8 November 1821 (AHPS, Carpeta 34, ff. 8–13; Marta de la Cuesta Figueroa, "El origen del poder legislativo en Salta," *Revista de Historia del Derecho* 3 [1975]:367–68).

III-S2.   *December (?) 1820.* Dr. José Ignacio de Gorriti, acting governor, prohibits bullfights (*Diccionario histórico argentino*, 6 vols. [Buenos Aires, 1953–55], 6:636).

III-S3.   *9 August 1821.* Salta adopts a provisional frame of government which serves as a written constitution, though it is less comprehensive than most. It outlines both form and major functions of the branches of government (granting executive and legislature a significant share of judicial power) and guarantees freedom of press under the terms of the October 1811 regulation. It contains no detailed treatment of citizenship requirements. (Atilio Cornejo, "Las constituciones de la provincia de Salta," *RIHD* 13 [1962]:25–27).

III-S4.   *5 September 1823.* Junta Provincial adopts an electoral reglamento extending the suffrage to all free men (AHPS, Libro 3° de las sesiones de la Hon.ᵉ Junta Provincial de Salta, f. 156).

III-S5.   *21 October 1823.* Junta prohibits religious orders from alienating property without approval of the diocesan ordinary (Gabriel Tommasini, *El convento de San Francisco de Jujuy en la historia y en la cultura cristiana* [Córdoba, 1934], p. 133; AHPS, Libro 506, ff. 199–200).

III-S6.   *22 September 1824.* Legislature authorizes provincial executive to negotiate with private interested parties for the redemption of censos pertaining to ecclesiastical capellanías; government may receive the principal and assume obligation for future payments (AHPS, Libro 4° de las sesiones. . . , Acta of 22 September 1824).

III-S7.   *2 November 1824.* Salta suppresses the military fuero in civil cases, also that of fiscal employees except in "what pertains to the conduct of their offices" (Atilio Cornejo, *El derecho privado en la legislación patria de Salta* [Buenos Aires, 1947], pp. 26–29).

III-S8.   *12 February 1825.* Law suppresses the cabildo of Salta but not those of Jujuy and Orán (Cornejo, *Derecho privado*, p. 31).

III-S9.   *10 March 1825. Reglamento de policía* for the cities of Salta and
             Jujuy adopted by Governor Juan Antonio Alvarez de Arenales
             (and approved by the Junta on 21 March) stipulates that no
             fuero can be invoked in police matters (AHPS, Libro 255, ff.
             97–98).

III-S10.   *23 September 1825.* Junta authorizes the governor to plan a
             cemetery outside the city of Salta (AHPS, Libro 334, f. 42).

III-S11.   *5 December 1825.* Junta prohibits the granting of moratoria to
             debtors without the consent of creditors, to protect the prop-
             erty rights of the latter (AHPS, Libro 66, pp. 240, 244, 246–
             47, 255).

III-S12.   *19 December 1825.* Legislature grants authority to the provin-
             cial executive to divide communal lands of Indian villages
             among the Indians as private property. Governor Arenales re-
             ports the following April that preparations for distribution are
             under way and that the measure "at the same time as it will
             provide some indemnity for the heroic sacrifices of those
             brave defenders of liberty, will give a new impulse to agricul-
             ture and increase the population" (Cornejo, *Derecho privado*,
             pp. 35–36; AHPS, Libro 66, p. 274).

III-S13.   *29 December 1825.* Law signed by Governor Arenales and pub-
             lished in English and French as well as Spanish declares: "Every
             inhabitant of the globe who shall employ his capital and indus-
             try in the province shall enjoy the full protection of the gov-
             ernment and laws for the safety of his person, the inviolability
             of his property and liberty of opinion, upon the same footing
             as the natives of the province." For encouragement of mining
             enterprises in particular, mines "are declared to be the private
             property of whoever shall discover them and work them," and
             various tax exemptions are provided, although the granting of
             exclusive privileges in the mining industry is expressly pro-
             hibited (Ricardo Rojas, ed., *Archivo capitular de Jujuy*, 4 vols.
             [Buenos Aires, 1913], 1:lxxiii–lxxiv).

III-S14.   *1826.* Provincial government refuses to recognize the superi-
             ors of the Franciscan convents in Salta and Jujuy, named (from
             Córdoba) by the provincial chapter, on the ground that regu-
             lars should be subject to the diocesan ordinary (Antonio Santa
             Clara Córdoba, *La orden franciscana en las repúblicas del Plata*
             [Buenos Aires, 1934], pp. 79–80).

Córdoba

III-CA1. *6 December 1820.* Provincial legislature instructs the executive
to protect the right of citizens to bury cadavers in churches—a
right the diocesan provisor is seeking to limit (*Archivo de la
H. Cámara de Diputados de la Provincia de Córdoba*, 7 vols. [Cór-
doba, 1912–], 1:61–63).

III-CA2. *30 January 1821.* Córdoba adopts a written constitution, and
most of its essential provisions would last until after the fall of
Rosas. Among other provisions, it:

a. expressly forbids any public worship other than Roman
Catholic, or the teaching of any doctrines "contrary to that
of Jesus Christ";

b. declares the promotion of "common happiness" to be
one purpose of government, so that functions of the provincial authorities include that of aiding "the indigent and
unfortunate";

c. makes certain that the indigent will not vote, by limiting
suffrage to those who own 4,000 pesos in property, or practice a liberal art or science, or have some "lucrative and useful profession," with the further stipulation that pardos may
vote only if they pass the special test contained in the national regulations of 1815 and 1817;

d. includes a long statement of individual rights in which it is
pledged that no sort of "work, culture, industry or commerce will be prohibited";

e. grants the fuero to members of the disciplined militia (*milicia nacional*) only when on active service and denies it to a
milicia cívica composed essentially of individuals who meet
the provincial suffrage requirements (Ramos, 1:153–87).

III-CA3. *21 January 1822.* Tax law abolishes the alcabala (except on real
estate), as well as various other taxes on commerce, to be replaced by a single list of import duties, which are clearly protectionist in intent (Córdoba, *Compilación*, 1:14–15).

III-CA4. *15 November 1823.* Governor Juan Bautista Bustos issues a
provisional decree on press freedom that offers nominal guarantees but expressly prohibits any attack on the "constituted
authorities" or "Religion of the State" (Ernesto H. Celesia,
Federalismo argentino, 3 vols. [Buenos Aires, 1932], 3:299–
300).

III-CA5. *3 June 1824.* Bustos suspends his press decree. The provincial legislature seeks to reinstate it, but he holds out for a new law (Córdoba, *Compilación*, 1:15–16; Celesia, *Federalismo*, 3:174–75, 302, 304–6).

III-CA6. *24 November 1824.* New press law orders observance of the October 1811 regulation (Córdoba, *Compilación*, 1:16).

III-CA7. *31 December 1824.* Suppression of cabildos within the province (Córdoba, *Compilación*, 1:18).

III-CA8. *3 May 1825.* Provincial legislature explicitly rejects article 12 (mutual religious toleration) of the treaty signed with Great Britain (II-R17) (*Archivo de la H. Cámara*, 1:327).

III-CA9. *May 1825.* Legislature authorizes the executive to purchase freedom for a number of slaves in celebration of the May Revolution. The practice continues at least through 1828, the number freed yearly being two—both female (*Archivo de la H. Cámara*, 1:342–43; Robert J. Turkovic, "Race Relations in the Province of Córdoba, Argentina, 1800–1853" [Ph.D. dissertation, University of Florida, 1981], pp. 202–6).

III-CA10. *12 August 1826.* A revision of the provincial constitution deletes the requirement that the governor take a religious oath to fulfill his responsibilities of office, including protection of the Roman Catholic religion; henceforth he must only promise on his honor to do his duty and uphold the law (Celesia, *Federalismo*, 3:246–51).

Appendix 4. Reaction in Buenos Aires

Political Innovations

IV-P1.   *15 September 1827.* Law of Buenos Aires legislature deprives veteran troops of the right to vote for representatives (*RO* [1827], p. 61).

IV-P2.   *8 May 1828.* New press law sponsored by Dorrego reaffirms existing procedure for handling of press offenses but expands the definition of what is illegal, specifically including publications that "attack the religion of the State," "excite to sedition" or encourage disobedience to authorities, or "appear obscene" (*RO* [1828], pp. 45–48).

IV-P3.   *20 October 1829.* Decree of Interim Governor Juan José Viamonte calls for "extraordinary" appeals (against court decisions handed down in what would normally be the final instance) to be handled by the Cámara de Apelaciones, without participation of the executive (Angelis, 2:1012–13).

IV-P4.   *30 October 1829.* Viamonte decree forbids press criticism of the Rosas-Lavalle agreements that brought a temporary end to civil conflict (*RO* [1 November 1829], p. 34).

IV-P5.   *24 December 1829.* Legislature calls for a "public demonstration" against newspaper articles defaming Dorrego and Rosas, which appeared in the wake of Lavalle's December 1828 coup. In fulfillment of this measure, a commission is named to review publications of the period; it orders the burning of offen-

144

sive writings, which is publicly done on 16 April 1830 (*RO* [1 January 1830], p. 4; Adolfo Saldías, *Historia de la Confederación Argentina*, 3 vols. [Buenos Aires, 1968], 1:208n).

IV-P6.   *3 February 1830*. Decree of Governor Rosas orders strict enforcement of "the general resolutions" that forbid leaving the province or traveling through its interior "without the corresponding passport or licence" (*RO* [1 March 1830], pp. 1–2).

IV-P7.   *1 February 1832*. Lamenting press abuses, Rosas decrees that no one may establish a press or publish any periodical without government approval, which a foreigner may obtain only if he renounces diplomatic protection. An editor will be held responsible for all contents of his periodical, without exception (*RO* [February 1832], pp. 1–6).

IV-P8.   *22 June 1833*. The legislature repeals the press decree of Rosas after his resignation as governor and restores the May 1828 press law (*RO* [June 1833], p. 1).

IV-P9.   *15 October 1833*. As conflict intensifies between the administration of Governor Juan Ramón Balcarce and unconditional rosistas, the legislature temporarily suspends all publication of "political writings"; a new press law of 2 November makes the suspension indefinite (*RO* [October 1833], pp. 2–4; *RO* [November 1833], p. 1).

IV-P10.   *26 November 1833*. Juan José Viamonte, again governor, lifts the longstanding requirement of a police passport for travel through the countryside, but rural laborers still need a pass from their employer (*RO* [November 1833], pp. 25–26).

IV-P11.   *19 December 1833*. Legislature ends the suspension of political publications (*RO* [December 1833], p. 2).

IV-P12.   *3 September 1834*. Law puts Rosas's press decree of 1 February 1832 back in effect (*RO* [1834], pp. 229–30).

IV-P13.   *16 October 1834*. Law approves the conduct of the government in expelling Rivadavia on his return to Buenos Aires the previous April and requires others who have gone into exile because of political dissensions since 1 December 1828 to obtain special permission to return (*RO* [1834], pp. 255–56).

IV-P14.   *7 March 1835*. Legislature grants Rosas, as governor, the Suma del Poder Público. The action is confirmed by a popular plebiscite of city voters three weeks later (*RO* [1835], pp. 43–45; José Sartorio, *El plebiscito de Rosas* [Buenos Aires, 1934]).

IV-P15.   *28 November 1835*. Revoking Viamonte's 26 November 1833 decree that abolished the pass requirement for internal travel, Rosas reestablishes his own decree of February 1830 for strict enforcement of that requirement (*RO* [1835], p. 316).

IV-P16. *1 January 1837.* Rosas informs the legislature that his government has circulated a list of recommended candidates for election as representatives, commending this procedure as an honest and straightforward means of establishing "a permanent legal guarantee for Authority" (*RO* [1837], p. 31).

IV-P17. *5 December 1838.* Law establishes Tribunal de Recursos Extraordinarios to hear and decide appeals from court decisions already handed down in what would have been the final instance (Angelis, 2:1556–59).

IV-P18. *26 May 1844.* A Rosas decree requires government permission and proof of loyalty to both Federalism and Roman Catholicism for anyone who would open or teach in a private or a public school. Moreover, permission must be renewed annually (*RO* [1844], pp. 28–30).

Socioeconomic Innovations

IV-SE1. *12 September 1827.* Decree of Governor Dorrego, purporting both military and humanitarian objectives, grants outfitters of corsairs capturing blacks in the war with Brazil a right of patronage over captives taken, except for one-tenth of the total who must be ceded to the government for military service. Though no longer technically slaves, captives must work for their patrons (who may transfer the right to others) for a variable term depending on age. By a subsequent *acuerdo* of 28 June 1828, Dorrego settles certain difficulties of "interpretation," making clear that the measure would apply to any slaves belonging to members of the crew or to private citizens (*RO* [1827], pp. 27–31; Archivo General de la Nación, Acuerdos 1826–30, X-44-6-17).

IV-SE2. *29 December 1827.* Dorrego suspends (until one month after the end of the war) the abolition of price controls on bread and meat decreed by Rivadavia on 4 May 1827 (II-SE17); in practice, suspension is indefinite (*RO* [1827], pp. 107–8).

IV-SE3. *2 January 1829.* Governor Juan Lavalle decrees the termination of all outstanding contracts with immigration agents. As governor the following year Rosas abolishes the Comisión de Inmigración created in 1824 (Miron Burgin, *The Economic Aspects of Argentine Federalism 1820–1852* [Cambridge, Mass., 1946], pp. 33, 258–59).

IV-SE4.   *29 December 1829.* Rosas decrees that henceforth the Defensor de Pobres y Menores will have the further title of Protector de Naturales (*RO* [1 January 1830], p. 15).

IV-SE5.   *14 October 1830.* Decree of Juan Ramón Balcarce, acting governor in the absence of Rosas, explicitly continues racial segregation in the Buenos Aires militia: any "free man of color" is assigned to the *Batallón Defensores de Buenos Aires* (*RO* [October 1830], p. 14).

IV-SE6.   *27 November 1830.* Law authorizes the provincial executive to free fifteen slaves serving in the men's hospital (*RO* [1 November 1830], pp. 7–8).

IV-SE7.   *14 December 1830.* Another Balcarce decree directs that anyone who falsely claims to own a man who is free must purchase two slaves for military service; it also condemns to service in the regular army anyone who, to elude militia duty, falsely claims to be a slave (*RO* [December 1830], p. 17).

IV-SE8.   *19 and 26 February 1831.* Noting that freedmen must feel a special obligation to perform military service, Rosas orders all to enlist for the militia in both city and countryside. By a decree of 7 March, he organizes the urban contingent as *Milicia Activa de Infantería, Libertos de Buenos Aires* (*RO* [February 1831], pp. 30–34; *RO* [March 1831], pp. 22–23).

IV-SE9.   *15 October 1831.* Decree jointly signed by the ministers of provincial government, but not by Rosas, permits the sale of slaves legally brought in by foreign owners as personal servants. The decree notes that with the slave trade in fact extinguished there is no longer a need to guard against evasion of the prohibition of the slave trade by forbidding the sale of slaves thus lawfully introduced (*RO* [October 1831], pp. 13–14).

IV-SE10. *16 November 1833.* Decree of Governor Viamonte ends the requirement for outgoing overseas correspondence to pass through the post office and pay fees; considerations of commercial efficiency are cited in justification, although the same freedom is not extended to incoming correspondence (*RO* [November 1833], pp. 48–49).

II-SE11. *26 November 1833.* Viamonte revokes the 15 October 1831 decree on the sale of personal servants, observing that it has been abused to permit illegal importation of slaves; strict controls are reestablished (*RO* [November 1833], pp. 22–24).

IV-SE12. *11 December 1834.* That they may now do something for the land that gave them freedom, corsair-seized slaves whose legal period of tutelage as libertos is over are ordered to present themselves for enlistment in provincial militia (*RO* [1834], pp. 352–53).

IV-SE13. *3 January 1835.* Legislature declares free "the sale of water, meat, and bread." Only the size or weight of units in which they are sold—not price—will remain subject to control. The provincial executive, however, fails to carry out the measure (*RO* [1835], pp. 1–3; letter from Manuel V. de Maza and Manuel de Yrigoyen, 10 February 1835, Archivo de la Provincia de Buenos Aires, Junta de Representantes 1835, legajo A, no. 8).

IV-SE14. *April 1835.* Bullfights are held in celebration of Rosas's return to power (John Lynch, *Argentine Dictator: Juan Manuel De Rosas, 1829–1852* [Oxford, 1981], p. 165).

IV-SE15. *18 December 1835.* New customs tariff attempts to meet partway the protectionist demands of the interior provinces and of specific interest groups within the province of Buenos Aires (*RO* [1835], pp. 361–69).

IV-SE16. *29 March 1836.* Rosas decree abolishes the judicial procedures of delay and acquittance (*espera* and *quita*) among debtors and creditors and provides that under no circumstances may the appeal court grant a moratorium to a debtor (*RO* [March 1836], pp. 61–64).

IV-SE17. *9 June 1836.* Stating that the need has ceased, Rosas rescinds decrees of February 1831 on compulsory enlistment of libertos (*RO* [June 1836], pp. 41–42).

IV-SE18. *1 October 1836.* Rosas moves to implement, at least partially, the law of 3 January 1835 freeing the price of bread, water, and meat. The price of meat is permitted to fluctuate, provided it does not exceed the maximum figure set by a special citizens' committee that Rosas appoints (*RO* [September 1836], pp. 100–113).

IV-SE19. *5 September 1837.* Government attorney rules that official permission to establish limited liability corporations will no longer be required, since the action is a purely private one (José María Mariluz Urquijo, "Las sociedades anónimas en Buenos Aires antes del código de comercio," *RIHD* 16 [1965]: 47).

IV-SE20. *1 April 1840.* Rosas decrees that only legitimate parents of libertos who are themselves free and of good conduct may buy libertos' release from service still owed former masters under the tutelage system established in 1813 (*RO* [1840], p. 58).

IV-SE21. *15 May 1840.* Rosas ratifies treaty of 24 May 1839 with Great Britain for suppression of the slave trade (*RN*, 2:406–13).

IV-SE22. *22 February 1844.* Rosas decrees abolition of carnival "forever"—for reasons of morality, health, industry (*RO* [1844], pp. 9–10).

Religious Innovations

IV-R1. *5 November 1827.* Provincial legislature sets at forty the number of nuns permissible in the convent of Santa Catalina, repealing the limit of thirty set by the ecclesiastical reform of 1822 (II-R12) (*RO* [1827], p. 81).

IV-R2. *30 April 1828.* Law orders that repayment of the capital of censos of obras pías be made exclusively in metallic currency or its equivalent (Angelis, 2:921).

IV-R3. *8 May 1828.* Press law (IV-P2 above) tightens restrictions on religiously unorthodox publications (*RO* [1828], pp. 45–48).

IV-R4. *5 April 1830.* Cornerstone is laid for Anglican chapel, on land donated by the provincial government of Rosas (*The British Packet, de Rivadavia a Rosas: I, 1826–1832* [Buenos Aires, 1976], p. 307).

IV-R5. *26 April 1830.* Rosas decree, issued at San Nicolás, forbids burials in the local church or churchyard and provides for establishment of a public cemetery outside the town (*RO* [1 May 1830], pp. 5–6).

IV-R6. *20 December 1830.* Decree of Interim Governor Juan Ramón Balcarce repeals the regulation of 17 July 1822, of Rivadavian origin, against taking cadavers into church for services prior to burial (II-R10) (Angelis, 1:392, 2:1079).

IV-R7. *8 February 1831.* Balcarce decree, deploring the neglect of religious education in some primary schools, provides that such schools not be allowed to operate unless they employ teachers of good morals and known Catholicism and devote every Saturday to teaching catechism (*RO* [February 1831], pp. 13–15).

IV-R8. *12 April 1831.* Minister of Government Tomás Manuel de Anchorena permits a secularized Bethlehemite friar to resume wearing the habit; subsequently the friar is authorized to serve again in hospital (Bruno, 9:377).

IV-R9. *3 October 1831.* Another Anchorena decree specifies that it is illegal to sell or circulate "books that manifestly tend to attack the wholesome morality of the Gospel, the truth and holiness of the religion of the State, and the divinity of JESUS CHRIST its author." It is illegal even to place obscene art works on view (*RO* [October 1831], pp. 5–6).

IV-R10. *12 December 1831.* Law authorizes sale of up to one million pesos of publicly owned property including assets seized from religious corporations, with proceeds to be used for amortization of public debts (*RO* [December 1831], pp. 1–2).

IV-R11. *13 November 1832.* Edict of Bishop Mariano Medrano, who acknowledged prodding by the provincial government, reduces to eleven the number of full religious holidays other than Sundays (*RN*, 2:302–4; Américo A. Tonda, *La iglesia argentina incomunicada con Roma* [Santa Fe, 1965], pp. 230–33).

IV-R12. *26 March 1833.* Legislature authorizes the granting of dispensations for mixed marriages between Protestants and Roman Catholics (*RO* [March 1833], p. 2).

IV-R13. *2 December 1833.* Decree of Governor Viamonte gives the former Mercedarian convent to the Sociedad de Beneficencia, for a school for orphaned girls (*RO* [December 1833], pp. 11–13).

IV-R14. *22 October 1835.* Rosas allows the suppressed Dominican convent to be reestablished and to follow the same rules that applied before the 1822 clergy reform. He further provides it with capital endowment and an estancia (*RN*, 2:355–56; Bruno, 9:355–62).

IV-R15. *8 March 1836.* Police announcement that, by order of Rosas, all those guilty of obscene language are condemned to military service—except slaves, who instead receive a hundred lashes for a first offense (*RO* [March 1836], pp. 64–65).

IV-R16. *26 August 1836.* Rosas reassigns to recently arrived Jesuits the building which had housed the Jesuit college at Buenos Aires prior to the expulsion decree of Charles III (*RN*, 2:364–65).

IV-R17. *2 November 1836.* In a note to Bishop Medrano, Rosas prohibits until further notice funeral masses de cuerpo presente, for health reasons (*RN*, 2:365).

IV-R18. *7 December 1836.* Two related decrees provide a monthly subsidy to the Jesuits and authorize them to resume educational activities; the rector of the University of Buenos Aires is instructed to place any excess equipment and furnishings at their disposal (*RN*, 2:366).

IV-R19. *19 January 1837*. Rosas forbids the practice of wakes (*RO* [1837], pp. 92–93).

IV-R20. *23 August 1837*. With an expression of alarm over theater performances which offend religion, morality, and "principles of social order," Rosas decrees establishment of a committee for prior censorship of plays, the diocesan provisor to be among its members (*RO* [1837], pp. 284–85).

IV-R21. *29 January 1838*. Decree returns the church of San Ignacio to the Jesuits (*RN*, 2:393).

IV-R22. *22 March 1843*. Rosas decrees the expulsion of Jesuits from Buenos Aires (Ricardo Levene, *Historia del derecho argentino*, 11 vols. [Buenos Aires, 1945–58], 9:240n).

IV-R23. *18 May 1844*. Rosas orders simplification of mourning customs and apparel, to curtail excessive expense for families (*RO* [1844], pp. 24–25).

IV-R24. *26 May 1844*. Decree on control of education (IV-P18) establishes a strict standard of religious orthodoxy (*RO* [1844], pp. 28–30).

IV-R25. *20 August 1844*. Rosas returns Recoleta convent to the Franciscans (Bruno, 10:170).

IV-R26. *27 July 1846*. Rosas creates a special commission to review school texts for theological (and political) correctness (*RO* [1846], pp. 52–54).

IV-R27. *2 January 1849*. After continual official prodding, Medrano orders a further reduction in the number of full holidays (other than Sundays) to four (*RN*, 2:451–52).

Appendix 5. Reaction Outside Buenos Aires

Uruguay

V-U1.   *9 March 1829.* First comprehensive tariff law establishes gener-
         ally moderate duties, rising to a maximum of 25 percent on
         articles such as wine and tobacco (Horacio José Pereyra, "Con-
         sideraciones sobre legislación aduanera en el Río de la Plata
         (época de Rosas)," *RIHD* 11 [1960]: 127–29).

V-U2.   *13 April 1829.* Law abolishes the alcabala, to be superseded by
         license taxes (*patentes*); in practice the alcabala continues until
         1852 (Rodríguez, pp. 48–49).

V-U3.   *4 June 1829.* Press law generally reiterates the previous guaran-
         tee of freedom and handling of abuses (III-U8), though speci-
         fying that any attack on "the dogmas of our Holy Religion" is
         an abuse to be punished (Uruguay, *Compilación*, 1:106–10).

V-U4.   *12 August 1829.* Regulation on administration of justice estab-
         lishes a formal procedure for cases of nulidad e injusticia noto-
         ria, which will be heard by three judges from the regular Tri-
         bunal de Apelaciones plus "eight good men" chosen by lot, i.e.,
         a quasi-jury (a subsequent law of 6 July 1839 replaces the good
         men with further professional judges) (Uruguay, *Compilación*,
         1:120–21; Enrique Sayagués Laso, *Recurso extraordinario de
         nulidad notoria* [Montevideo, 1934], pp. 18–21).

V-U5.   *24 September 1829.* Decree of provisional government expressly
         states that public lands will remain subject to the system of
         emphyteusis implanted in Uruguay by the Argentine law of

1826 (Uruguay, *Compilación*, 1:166; Nelson de la Torre, Lucía Sala de Touron, and Julio Carlos Rodríguez, *Después de Artigas (1820–1836)* [Montevideo, 1972], pp. 103–4).

V-U6.   *22 January 1830.* Special law extends to all parts of the state where they "have not yet been observed," i.e., those which had been under Brazilian occupation, the principle of free birth and prohibition of the slave trade (Uruguay, *Compilación*, 1:177).

V-U7.   *15 March 1830.* Slaves who fled from Brazil or were seized by military forces in Brazil during the recent war are declared free, as are slaves confiscated from emigrés (Uruguay, *Compilación*, 1:192–93).

V-U8.   *16 March 1830.* Law abolishes fuero of militiamen in cases not related to military discipline (Uruguay, *Compilación*, 1:195–96).

V-U9.   *18 July 1830.* The Uruguayan constitution (a) establishes a conventional republican regime on a basis of restricted suffrage with citizenship suspended for hired servants, day laborers, and common soldiers, as well as for illiterates after 1840; (b) declares the Roman Catholic apostolic religion to be that of the state but puts no express limitation on other religious activities; (c) instructs congress to provide for general introduction of the jury system; and (d) prohibits the founding of entails (Uruguay, *Compilación*, 1:243–44, 259, 261–62).

V-U10.   *7 February 1831.* Decree of José Ellauri, minister of government, prohibits the observance of carnival (Uruguay, *Registro Nacional* [1831], p. 43).

V-U11.   *17 March 1831.* Government is authorized by congress to sell commercial property comprising the ejido of Montevideo (Uruguay, *Compilación*, 1:302–3).

V-U12.   *14 May 1833.* Law of emphyteusis, applicable to public grazing lands not privately possessed for over twenty years. The lands are to be leased for five years, after which time the possibility of sale is foreseen (Uruguay, *Compilación*, 1:356–57; De la Torre, et al., *Después de Artigas*, pp. 182–83).

V-U13.   *21 June 1833.* Decree of Apostolic Vicar Dámaso Larrañaga, issued in agreement with civil authorities, exempts rural inhabitants for one year from going to mass on lesser holidays and limits the number of full or major holidays. The number is set lower for nonwhites. The next year (1 July 1834) Larrañaga broadens the decree to cover all inhabitants, who will enjoy the same dispensations from holiday observances approved by the papacy for Buenos Aires (Uruguay, *Registro Nacional* [1833], pp. 73–74; *Registro Nacional* [1834], pp. 163–64).

V-U14. *August 1834*. Government provides subsidies to assist prospective immigrants with passage money. Similar, mostly ad hoc measures to promote immigration continue in subsequent years (Eduardo Acevedo, *Anales históricos del Uruguay*, 6 vols. [Montevideo, 1933–36], 1:413–14, 495).

V-U15. *April 1835*. Bullfighting prohibited, but the prohibition is lifted before the end of the year (Acevedo, *Anales históricos*, 1:530–1).

V-U16. *10 October 1835*. Cemetery regulation prohibits burials in churches or churchyards of Montevideo and environs (Rodríguez, p. 138).

V-U17. *24 December 1835*. Government of President Manuel Oribe decrees that freedom of the press does not extend to criticism of a friendly foreign country (meaning, in effect, attacks on Rosas) (Juan E. Pivel Devoto, *Historia de los partidos y de las ideas políticos en el Uruguay*, vol. 2 [Montevideo, 1956], pp. 139–40).

V-U18. *16 June 1837*. Law states that all blacks are free on entering the republic except fugitive slaves, who will be extradited, and slaves who come with their owners, for up to one year; slaves introduced illegally will be placed under the tutelage of private employers for three years, or until they reach majority if it is longer (Uruguay, *Compilación*, 2:150–51).

V-U19. *15 July 1837*. Decree of Acting President Carlos Anaya removes controls from the weight and price of bread (Rodríguez, pp. 155–56).

V-U20. *6 March 1838*. Law abolishes all personal fueros in civil and criminal cases; ecclesiastical and military courts will henceforth try offenses "that only can be committed" by members of their respective institutions, plus in the case of the military those committed "within the barracks, on march, on campaign or in acts of the service" (Uruguay, *Compilación*, 2:163–64).

V-U21. *4 April 1838*. Law grants private contracting parties full freedom to determine the rate of interest (Uruguay, *Compilación*, 2:167).

V-U22. *25 November 1838*. Police instructions require all free blacks and pardos to have a legal contract with their employers similar to those in force for rural peons in Uruguay, as in Buenos Aires and other Argentine provinces, and to carry a document proving their free status (*El Nacional*, 29 November 1838).

V-U23. *7 December 1838.* Decree of newly installed President Fructuoso Rivera suppresses the Montevideo Consulado; five days later, he creates a *Juzgado de Hacienda y Comercio* as an integral part of the national judiciary to handle cases formerly referred to the Consulado (Uruguay, *Compilación*, 2:244–46, 264–66).

V-U24. *31 December 1838.* Rivera decree suppresses the only convent in Uruguay, of the Franciscan order, for lack of sufficient friars; its assets pass to the state. The Franciscans themselves are told to leave Uruguay for wherever they can properly observe "the institutes of their order." The same applies to non-Franciscans who had for any reason taken shelter in the convent (Rodríguez, p. 181; Pacífico Otero, *La orden franciscana en el Uruguay* [Buenos Aires, 1908], pp. 111–12; *El Nacional*, 21 January 1839).

V-U25. *13 July 1839.* Treaty with Great Britain for suppression of the slave trade, not formally ratified until January 1842 (Ema Isola, *La esclavitud en Uruguay desde sus comienzos hasta su extinción 1743–1852* [Montevideo, 1975], pp. 317–19).

V-U26. *1841.* Jesuits begin returning to Uruguay (Rafael Pérez, *La Compañía de Jesús restaurada en la República Argentina y Chile, el Uruguay y el Brasil* [Barcelona, 1911], pp. 224–35).

V-U27. *12 December 1842.* Law of Colorado government declares slavery abolished, but able-bodied male slaves are ordered into military service, while all others remain "for now" under tutelage and in the service of their former owners (Uruguay, *Compilación*, 2:351).

V-U28. *1 January 1844.* Cornerstone laid for first Protestant (Anglican) church in Montevideo (*El Nacional*, 11 January 1844).

V-U29. *1844.* Government establishes monopoly of bread in Montevideo as a fiscal expedient. It is discontinued in August 1845, revived in mid-1848 (Acevedo, *Anales históricos*, 2:224).

V-U30. *28 October 1846.* Law of rival Blanco regime also abolishes slavery, with compensation to be paid to owners when civil war is ended. Minors, however, remain under the patronage of previous owners until they come of age (Mateo J. Magariños de Mello, *El gobierno del Cerrito; colección de documentos oficiales emanados de los poderes del gobierno presidido por el brigadier general D. Manuel Oribe 1843–1851*, 2 vols. [Montevideo, 1948–61], 1:134–43).

Entre Ríos

V-ER1.   *4 December 1829.* Decree of Governor León Sola provides for
ecclesiastical inspection of incoming book shipments to keep
out heretical literature (Entre Ríos, *Recopilación*, 3:102–3).

V-ER2.   *4 May 1833.* Provincial law orders restoration of the tithes on
the traditional footing (subsequent law of 26 February 1834
appropriates a part of the proceeds for use in secondary education) (Entre Ríos, *Recopilación*, 4:29–31, 81–82).

V-ER3.   *26 January 1835.* Provincial legislature adopts a law declaring
hacendados free to dispose of their cattle, horses, and mules as
they wish, slaughtering or selling them both in and outside
the province. The representatives accept Governor Pascual
Echagüe's objection to allowing free export of mares but urge
him to be liberal in granting special permission for that purpose in the name of "free use" of private property. Less than
two weeks later the legislature asks the governor to suspend
publication of this law altogether (Entre Ríos, *Recopilación*,
4:121–22, 126–27).

V-ER4.   *5 February 1836.* Customs law issued in the same protectionist
mold as the Buenos Aires tariff of December 1835. It contains
a long list of items that are prohibited if imported from a foreign country (e.g., articles of clothing and, unless the market
price reaches a certain level, wheat). The law also reaffirms the
absolute prohibition of anti-Catholic books and obscene pic-
tures, although there is no explicit reference to ecclesiastical
review of shipments (Entre Ríos, *Recopilación*, 4:203–5).

V-ER5.   *14 March 1836.* General law on administration of justice provides for establishment of (among other things) a separate Tribunal de Recursos Extraordinarios for cases of nulidad e injusticia notoria. The law is suspended the following year for
lack of funds to implement it (Entre Ríos, *Recopilación*, 4:233,
343).

V-ER6.   *12 August 1836.* Sala de Representantes invests Governor Echagüe "fully with all ordinary and extraordinary faculties" (Entre Ríos, *Recopilación*, 4:260–61).

V-ER7.   *2 December 1837.* Law passed at Echagüe's request authorizes
bringing Jesuits into the province for educational work (none
arrive, however) (Entre Ríos, *Recopilación*, 4:335–37; Juan
José Antonio Segura, *Historia eclesiástica de Entre Ríos* [No-
goyá, 1964], p. 124).

V-ER8.   *7 March 1842.* Noting that tithe payments have been suspended because of the combined effects of drought and civil war, the legislature instructs the governor to find other funds to support the cult in Paraná's main parish church (Entre Ríos, *Recopilación*, 5:51–52).

V-ER9.   *25 June 1847.* Bishop Mariano Medrano of Buenos Aires, at the urging of Governor Justo José de Urquiza, suppresses numerous holidays in Entre Ríos (Segura, *Historia eclesiástica*, p. 130).

V-ER10.   *21 October 1848.* Urquiza decree prohibits carnival celebrations (Entre Ríos, *Recopilación*, 5:287–88).

V-ER11.   *16 November 1848.* For the protection and encouragement of local agriculture, Urquiza decrees a 50 percent duty on cereals, flour, and other vegetable products imported from provinces of the Argentine Confederation; the same articles are prohibited if coming from abroad (Entre Ríos, *Recopilación*, 4:291–92).

V-ER12.   *13 April 1849.* New law on administration of justice abolishes the fuero; in future, military and ecclesiastical courts will be restricted to cases involving offenses that only a military man or member of the clergy can commit. The same law abolishes imprisonment for debt in civil cases for professional men, artisans, and farmers though not for servants and day laborers. The establishment of a Tribunal de Recursos Extraordinarios is ordered once again (Entre Ríos, *Recopilación*, 5:356–57, 369).

V-ER13.   *22 August 1850.* Government communiqué recognizes that drought has led to a shortage of meat but emphasizes that suppliers must be allowed to set any price they wish, since only in that way can they be induced to offer meat for sale; the one qualification is that they must not refuse to sell at retail to the poor (Entre Ríos, *Recopilación*, 6:73).

V-ER14.   *5 February 1851.* Urquiza decree graciously permits mourners to simplify their display of grief, in view of the burdens imposed by the "ancient custom" of full mourning; but compliance remains optional (Entre Ríos, *Recopilación*, 6:109–11).

Corrientes

V-CS1.   *23 May 1828.* Provincial law orders the assets of capellanías, with certain exceptions, turned over to the public treasury, which will use their proceeds as circumstances demand and pay 3 percent yearly on the principal amount of funds received. Implementing decree specifies that real property is to be auctioned off and calls for repayment of loans made from capellanía funds (*ROPC*, 2:239–40, 273–75).

V-CS2. *3 July 1830.* Law establishes that public lands, instead of being sold, will be given in emphyteutic lease. A subsequent decree of Governor Pedro Ferré (16 April 1831) states that emphyteusis is to last fifty years (*ROPC*, 2:374–75, 3:10, 62–65).

V-CS3. *17 May 1831.* Law provides that children of slaves, at fourteen years of age, will come under direct jurisdiction of the government, to be assigned suitable occupations (*ROPC*, 3:26–27).

V-CS4. *20 August 1831.* For better observance of free-birth legislation, Governor Ferré orders priests to report all libertos baptized since 31 January 1813 (*ROPC*, 3:83).

V-CS5. *5 September 1832.* Ferré decrees that new settlers who bring livestock with them be given public lands in emphyteusis, with a three-year exemption from taxes (*ROPC*, 3:137–38).

V-CS6. *29 October 1832.* New tariff, marking a high point of Corrientes protectionism, prohibits importation from abroad of any "effects" produced in the Argentine Confederation except liquor (which is hard to identify by origin) and those things that domestic producers cannot supply in sufficient quantity (*ROPC*, 3:107).

V-CS7. *18 December 1832.* Provincial law equalizes burial charges for all inhabitants regardless of race, repealing the ecclesiastical tariff of fees on this point (*ROPC*, 3:107).

V-CS8. *11 February 1836.* Decree of Governor Rafael Atienza abolishes carnival (*ROPC*, 3:342–43).

V-CS9. *11 February 1837.* Law authorizes executive to exempt farmers whose indigence is "notorious" from payment of tithes (Corrientes, *RO* [1838], p. 9).

V-CS10. *4 July 1838.* Provincial law recognizes the right of Brazilian masters to fugitive slaves; they may either sell them in Corrientes or take them back to Brazil (*ROPC*, 4:64).

V-CS11. *1 January 1839.* Effective date of new provincial constitution that specifically guarantees freedom of religious opinions, though still excluding non–Roman Catholic worship, and abolishes the military (but not the ecclesiastical) fuero; this constitution lasts only three months (Hernán F. Gómez, *Bases del derecho público correntino*, 3 vols. [Corrientes, 1926–27], 1:151, 155, 165, 171).

V-CS12. *24 July 1839*. Law abolishes separate military cuerpo de libertos, but the measure is repealed on 4 December (*ROPC*, 4: 136, 163).

V-CS13. *19 October 1839*. Law introduces freedom of interest rates to stimulate the economy, claiming that such freedom exists "in all the other provinces" (*ROPC*, 4:151–152).

V-CS14. *25 November 1839*. Legislature votes Suma del Poder Público for one year to Governor Pedro Ferré (Corrientes, *RO* [1839], pp. 60–61).

V-CS15. *11 March 1840*. New law, requested by provincial government, repeals freedom of interest. However, a major loophole is left in a distinction between "interest pure and simple," which is illegal, and both the "rent that capital pays" and "insurance paid to the lender, equivalent to the risk of losing his capital in whole or in part" (*ROPC*, 4:233–34).

V-CS16. *23 September 1840*. Governor Ferré by decree cancels tithes for the year 1841 to diminish burdens on ranchers and farmers in the present civil strife (*ROPC*, 4:276).

V-CS17. *16 December 1840*. Provincial congress adopts a law stating that Corrientes can never be governed with extraordinary faculties or with the Suma del Poder. But Ferré refuses to sign the measure, which is repealed 6 February 1841 (*ROPC*, 4:245; Víctor Tau Anzoátegui, "Las facultades extraordinarias y la suma del poder público en el derecho provincial argentino (1820–1853)," *RIHD* 12 [1961]:80).

V-CS18. *16 February 1841*. Law assigns the building and assets of the Mercedarian convent for use of proposed college; for lack of funds, however, the measure is not fully implemented (*ROPC*, 4:341, 5:67–68).

V-CS19. *12 April 1842*. Property of the former Dominican convent, now virtually abandoned, is assigned for use as hospital and school (*ROPC*, 5:47).

V-CS20. *23 April 1842*. Decree of Governor Ferré against the admission of fugitive slaves from neighboring states. An exception is subsequently made on behalf of those serving in the provincial army: they will remain free, their owners to be compensated when conditions permit (*ROPC*, 5:48–49, 180–82).

V-CS21. *22 June 1844*. Law suspends tithe collections until one year after the return of peace (*El Pacificador* [Corrientes], 28 November 1846; *ROPC*, 5:185).

V-CS22. *26 June 1844*. Law authorizes military enlistment of all able male slaves, who will receive freedom in return for service; owners are to be compensated ultimately. (Following the overthrow of the Unitario provincial government by the forces of Urquiza, however, the soldier-slaves are ordered back to enslavement.) The same measure authorizes sale of lands which had been given in emphyteusis (*ROPC*, 5:185–86, 210–11; Miguel Florencio Mantilla, *Crónica histórica de la provincia de Corrientes*, 2 vols. [Buenos Aires, 1928–29], 2:213).

V-CS23. *29 October 1846*. Legislature confirms the circular of Unitario Governor Joaquín Madariaga that abolished the alcabala on sales of slaves and on transfers of patronage over libertos, ostensibly for humanitarian reasons to facilitate the freedom of slaves (*El Pacificador*, 21 November 1846; *ROPC*, 5:356–57).

V-CS24. *21 June 1847*. The law of 23 May 1828 (V-CS1) for assets and obligations of capellanías to be assumed by the provincial treasury is repealed, as in conflict with the free use of property. Anyone henceforth can establish a capellanía in the form he may desire (*ROPC*, 6:14–15).

V-CS25. *6 July 1847*. Law passed under Madariaga's auspices concerning the administration of justice abolishes all fueros. This and other basic provisions of the law are confirmed in a new regulation adopted by the Federalist regime of Governor Benjamín Virasoro (Urquiza's ally) in June 1849 (*ROPC*, 6:18, 144).

V-CS26. *2 January 1849*. Bishop Medrano, at the request of Virasoro, reduces the number of religious holidays to conform with the practice of Buenos Aires (*ROPC*, 6:228–31; *Mensage del Gobierno de Corrientes a la undécima legislatura* [Corrientes, 1850], p. 13).

V-CS27. *22 August 1849*. New tariff of ecclesiastical fees decreed by Virasoro provides lower rates for Indians, pardos, and blacks (*ROPC*, 6:235–38).

Mendoza

V-M1. *7 September 1827*. Legislative decree reestablishes "in all its vigor" the discipline of the church as it affects the Franciscan, Dominican, and Mercedarian orders; the convents of all three are declared again subject to their "legitimate provincials" (*RM*, 1 January 1828).

V-M2. *18 March 1828*. *Reglamento de Policía* declares all inhabitants subject to its provisions, without protection of any fuero (Ahumada, p. 59).

V-M3. *5 July 1828.* Provincial law orders the establishment of cemeteries outside towns; burials in churches or elsewhere inside town limits are forbidden, as is the practice of bringing cadavers into church for prior services. However, no proper cemetery is built in Mendoza for nearly twenty years (Ahumada, pp. 61, 185).

V-M4. *10 September 1828.* New press law prohibits the publication of anonymous writings—only to be repealed in August 1829 (Ahumada, pp. 64–65).

V-M5. *30 December 1828.* Law places the entire proceeds of the tithes for 1829 at the disposal of the provincial executive; compulsory tithe payments are suppressed outright as of 1 January 1830 (*RM*, 20 January 1829).

V-M6. *16 November 1831.* Sala de Representantes prohibits all importation of "foreign liquors." This provision is later "clarified" (7 February 1835) by deleting the word "foreign," but it is not clear how long it remained in effect (AHM-EI, Carpeta 403, doc. 1, f. 1).

V-M7. *4 February 1832.* Law directs the establishment of a fiscal monopoly of yerba, tobacco, and playing cards. The same measure is adopted again in 1838 and on that occasion, at least, the law is implemented (AHM-EI, Carpeta 200, doc. 24, f. 14; *RM*, July, September, October 1838).

V-M8. *30 May 1832.* Sala revokes the law of December 1828 that suppressed the tithes but delays for eight years their reimposition on livestock (*RM*, May 1835; AHM-EI, Carpeta 403, doc. 14, f. 13).

V-M9. *3 June 1833.* The bishop of Cuyo, urged by regional governors, reduces the number of major religious holidays to fourteen (Américo A. Tonda, *La iglesia argentina incomunicada con Roma* [Santa Fe, 1965], p. 238).

V-M10. *September 1834. Reglamento de Administración de Justicia* abolishes all fueros except the ecclesiastical and military and all other forms of personal privilege (Ahumada, p. 102).

V-M11. *28 March 1835.* Sala decrees that slaves who go to Chile with or by order of their masters and obtain freedom under Chilean law cannot lose it on their return. This provision expressly does not apply to runaways (AHM-EI, Carpeta 403, doc. 3, f. 12).

V-M12.   *6 May 1835.* Legislature votes full restoration of tithes effective next year. For the first two years, however, the proceeds are wholly earmarked for frontier defense and settlement. After that the clergy will receive their share but must give baptism and extreme unction without charge (*RM*, May 1835).

V-M13.   *11 October 1835.* Decree of Acting Governor Pedro José Pelliza extends to age twenty-five (or until marriage) the service owed by daughters of slaves to their mothers' masters under the free-birth system. Through administrative confusion, if nothing else, the same extension of servitude appears to have been applied to male libertos (Ahumada, pp. 110–11; José Luis Masini, *La esclavitud negra en Mendoza, época independiente* [Mendoza, 1962], pp. 53, 65–66).

V-M14.   *23 December 1835.* Law exempts miners for six years from *quinto* and other taxes (Ahumada, pp. 112–13).

V-M15.   *14 December 1836.* Rate of tithes cut to ⅟₁₅, "in agreement with the Ecclesiastical Authority" and until "the circumstances of the province improve" (*RM*, December 1836).

V-M16.   *15 December 1836.* Law reduces legal interest rate from 5 to 3 percent per year in view of depressed economic conditions. Though broadly phrased, the measure affects primarily ecclesiastical censos (Ahumada, p. 121).

V-M17.   *18 May 1837.* Sala de Representantes authorizes restoration of the Jesuits, proposing that they be given—among other things—the church and various assets of the former Augustinian convent (Ahumada, p. 128; José Aníbal Verdaguer, *Historia eclesiástica de Cuyo*, 2 vols. [Milan, 1931–32], 2:231).

V-M18.   *8 October 1838.* No Jesuits having arrived, the Sala empowers provincial executive to arrange for the coming to Mendoza of religious of any order (Ahumada, pp. 141–42).

V-M19.   *17 January 1840.* Sala restores interest rate to 5 percent (*RM*, January 1840).

V-M20.   *2 July 1840.* Sala confers the Suma del Poder on Governor Justo Correas. It is returned by the executive on 6 December 1840 (Archivo de la Legislatura, Mendoza, "Resúmenes," 6 December 1840).

V-M21.   *17 January 1843.* Decree of Governor José Félix Aldao prohibits the introduction of "public papers" from Chile, which are to be burned by the public executioner (AHM-EI, Carpeta 201, doc. 16).

V-M22.   *16 March 1843.* Aldao reiterates provisions of the 5 July 1828 law on burials, which still awaits proper implementation (a public cemetery for the city of Mendoza finally opens on a regular basis in 1847) (AHM-EI, Carpeta 201, doc. 13; *RM*, February, April 1847).

V-M23. *4 October 1843.* By decree, Aldao restores tithes to the traditional ⅒. This in turn is suspended by decree of 10 January 1849, which returns the rate to ⅕ and is repealed in turn by decree of 29 March 1852 (AHM-EI, Carpeta 201, doc. 16; *RM*, March 1852).

V-M24. *7 May 1845.* Law declares that no fueros shall apply in cases of robbery and murder (Ahumada, p. 155).

V-M25. *3 June 1845.* Sala de Representantes invites the Jesuits to enter Mendoza, provided they support the "Federal system," and again assigns properties for their support. The next day Governor Pablo Segura notes in a decree that Jesuits do not constitute a "permitted association" and that for them to take advantage of the invitation they must not "live in community" (*RM*, 2 June 1845).

V-M26. *16 March 1846.* Law establishes contribución directa for a period of one year, which begins in 1847 (*RM*, January 1847).

Salta/Jujuy

V-S1. *4 April 1829.* Decree of Unitario Governor Juan Ignacio Gorriti repeats the prohibition of alienating convent property without approval of the diocesan ordinary, noting that the October 1823 measure to this effect (III-S5) had been widely ignored (Salta, *RO*, 4 [1829]:58).

V-S2. *9 June 1831.* Law (passed under Unitario auspices) provides for disamortization of assets of chantries and pious foundations. Though it cites as an antecedent the Spanish disamortization of 1805 (i.e., 1804), supposedly still in effect, the reforms of Rivadavia in Buenos Aires suggest a more immediate model. The provincial executive is authorized to sell real property involved and to accept repayments of loaned capital; the treasury will then be responsible for payment of yearly interest equivalent to 5 percent of the amount received, with half of the province's share of tithe income earmarked for the purpose. Two months later (5 August) the legislature orders a halt to the sale of properties under this law, but a major reduction in ecclesiastical holdings did in fact take place (Miguel Angel Vergara, *Estudios sobre historia eclesiástica de Jujuy* [Tucumán, 1942], pp. 368–72; Atilio Cornejo, *El derecho privado en la legislación patria de Salta* [Buenos Aires, 1947], pp. 38–39; AHPS, Carpeta 369, HH.RR. Leyes y Decretos, Sala de Representantes, 1830–31).

V-S3.   *11 September 1832.* Governor Pablo Antonio Alemán "absolutely prohibits" burial of cadavers in the cemetery of the Iglesia de la Misericordia, located on the city plaza; use of other urban churchyards is still permitted pending construction of a "pantheon" outside the city (Salta, *RO*, 11 [1832]:45).

V-S4.   *4 January 1834.* Decree of Governor Antonio Fernández Castro modifies the democratic suffrage regulation of 1823 (III-S4), establishing more restrictive criteria: domestic servants, those "who live at another's expense," and any who lack a "lucrative or useful occupation" (*oficio lucrativo o útil al país*) are denied the vote. (Atilio Cornejo, *Apuntes históricos sobre Salta*, 2d ed. [Buenos Aires, 1937], p. 221).

V-S5.   *3 May 1834.* Law reiterates the December 1825 authorization to sell "lands which belonged to the Communities of Indigenes" (III-S12) (AHPS, Libro 439, Actas, f. 296; Carpeta 505, H.J. de Gobierno de la Provincia, Libro copiador de oficios, Novena Legislatura, doc. 42).

V-S6.   *16 July 1834.* Law authorizes redemption of censos pertaining to "all the extinguished [abandoned] convents" and sale of their temporalities. This applies to Franciscan and Mercedarian convents in Jujuy and assets of Third Order Franciscans in both Jujuy and Salta (AHPS, Carpeta 505, doc. 53, and Libro 439, Legislatura provincial, Actas, 26 de septiembre 1830–7 diciembre 1834, ff. 279, 326–27).

V-J7.   *28 February 1835.* Law of the newly separate province of Jujuy specifies that municipal elections will follow the Salta regulation of 1823 (Jujuy, *Compilación*, 1:11).

V-J8.   *7 May 1835.* Jujuy legislative resolution prohibits all sale or alienation of Indian community lands, pending further legislation (Jujuy, *Compilación*, 1:17–18).

V-J9.   *13 June 1835.* Jujuy's first comprehensive tariff law levies only 4 percent duty on "effects from overseas" but establishes specific duties for such items as wine and coca from other provinces and from Bolivia; it also incorporates a wide range of transit taxes (Jujuy, *Compilación*, 1:18–21).

V-J10.   *22 September 1835.* "For now and until the settlement [*arreglo*] of the bishopric," the legislature decrees that all proceeds of the tithes will go to the provincial government except the portion corresponding to the clergy of the main parish church (Jujuy, *Compilación*, 1:23).

V-J11.   *23 November 1835.* Provisional constitution (Estatuto Provisorio) provides for representative government with separation of powers, etc., and grants suffrage to all free men "who profess some industry, science or art, without subjection to another in the class of domestic servant"; day laborers and common soldiers are also explicitly excluded. Among other civil guarantees, it grants everyone the right "to publish his ideas freely," provided they do not conflict with "public tranquillity" or the "conservation" of the Roman Catholic religion. Although "private acts" are reserved to divine judgment, all inhabitants must respect the Catholic religion, and freedom of worship is neither granted nor explicitly denied. In the judicial system, extraordinary appeals on grounds of nulidad e injusticia notoria will not be admitted ("Estatuto provisorio para la dirección, y administración de la Provincia de Jujuy—Año de 1835," Universidad Nacional de Tucumán, *Revista Jurídica* 3 [1958]:291–324, 327, 331–32).

V-J12.   *12 July 1836.* Regulation on Indian community lands in the Quebrada de Humahuaca authorizes enrolled militiamen to use such lands without payment of rent but also specifies that communal Indians will continue "in peaceful possession . . . of the part of the land which they have occupied in their service" (Jujuy, *Compilación*, 1:33–35).

V-J13.   *13 July 1836.* Decree prohibits exaction of compulsory labor from tenants by landlords over and above a stipulated cash rent (Jujuy, *Compilación*, 1:33, 198).

V-J14.   *20 July 1836.* Decree requires each citizen to "present" to the authorities any "leaflet or libel which in some manner reaches his hands" (Jujuy, *Compilación*, 1:43).

V-J15.   *22 September 1837.* Having repaired the Franciscan convent and noting the "absolute extinction" of its membership, the provincial government orders the building used for a secondary school. Remaining Franciscan assets continue to be treated as state property (Gabriel Tommasini, *El Convento de San Francisco de Jujuy en la historia y en la cultura cristiana* [Córdoba, 1934], 135n; Jujuy, *Compilación*, 1:180–81).

V-J16.   *1 January 1838.* Date of suppression of Jujuy cabildo, as ordered by a decree of the previous 18 December (Jujuy, *Compilación*, 1:87–88; José María Sáenz Valiente, *Bajo la campana del cabildo* [Buenos Aires, 1952], pp. 467–68).

V-J17.   *1 July 1838.* Law exempts militiamen of Humahuaca and Tumbaya from payment of tithes but is repealed the following year, 9 March 1839 (Jujuy, *Compilación*, 1:116).

V-J18.   *6 February 1839.* Adoption of definitive constitution, which retains features of the 1835 provisional statute noted above (Jujuy *Compilación*, 1:100, 107–9).

V-J19.   *4 March 1839.* Law authorizes sale "under contract of emphyteusis" of lands belonging to the state in Humahuaca, Tilcara, and Purmamarca. The law does not expressly say so, but it applies to Indian community lands (*"terrenos que fueron de comunidad"*). Subsequent regulations for the distribution of lands in emphyteusis give preference to Indian inhabitants (Jujuy, *Compilación*, 1:116, 120–21, 126–27; Archivo Legislativo de Jujuy, Libro 3, Actas 1839–40, 13 and 20 December 1839, 2, 12, and 18 January 1840).

V-J20.   *19 February 1840.* Contribución directa is created by law for inhabitants of the Puna, which amounts in practice to a restored personal tribute of $3 per year (Jujuy, *Compilación*, 1:130).

V-J21.   *18 January 1845.* With a view to increasing the province's population, a law is passed to welcome emigrés from any "foreign republic," granting them among other privileges an eight-year exemption from payment of tithes (Jujuy, *Compilación*, 1: 185–86; Archivo Legislativo de Jujuy, Libro 3, Carpeta varios, *proyecto de ley* of 23 December 1844).

V-J22.   *20 April 1845.* Decree of Governor José Mariano de Iturbe prohibits burials in churches of the capital; burials must be in the cemetery that will be (and soon is) constructed. In rural parishes lacking a cemetery, burials may be in churchyards but not in the churches themselves (Jujuy, *Compilación*, 1:190–91).

V-J23.   *9 August 1845.* Decree prohibits the use of Indian forced labor by priests and civil magistrates in the Puna as "repugnant to reason and good sense" and contrary to the "spirit and intention of the laws" (Jujuy, *Compilación*, 1:197–98).

V-J24.   *14 October (?) 1850.* Decree exempts wool and cheese production of the Puna from payment of tithes (Jujuy, *Compilación*, 1:259–60).

V-J25. *21 January 1851*. Law of Unitario-influenced 11th Legislature abolishes all fueros; military and ecclesiastical courts retain jurisdiction only over acts peculiar to those professions or committed by the military in barracks, march, or line of duty (Jujuy, *Compilación*, 1:267).

V-J26. *6 February 1851*. Law abolishes the personal tribute (i.e., contribución directa) collected in Puna departments (Jujuy, *Compilación*, 1:282).

V-J27. *13 February 1851*. New election law extends suffrage to all free men (Jujuy, *Compilación*, 1:298).

V-J28. *1 and 2 October 1851*. Following restoration of a properly Federalist regime, Governor Iturbe invests himself with the Suma del Poder Público. The next day he revokes the reforms of the 11th Legislature, charging that "some factious savage Unitarios" had too much weight in its proceedings. Included are items V-J25–27 above. But the measures are quickly reenacted (decree of 5 March 1852) once Iturbe is permanently overthrown as a by-product of the fall of Rosas (Jujuy, *Compilación*, 1:331–32, 351).

Córdoba

V-CA1. *September 1827*. Governor Juan Bautista Bustos, in a letter to the English promoter Edmund Temple, pledges freedom of conscience to foreign settlers (Rodolfo Ortega Peña and Eduardo Luis Duhalde, *Facundo y la montonera* [Buenos Aires, 1968], p. 503).

V-CA2. *11 December 1828*. On receiving news of the uprising in Buenos Aires against Governor Manuel Dorrego, the *Comisión General* of the Córdoba legislature invests Bustos with *los tres altos poderes* and dissolves both itself and the provincial court of appeals (*Archivo de la H. Cámara de Diputados de la Provincia de Córdoba*, 7 vols. [Córdoba, 1912–], 3:137–41).

V-CA3. *4 May 1829*. Decree of José María Paz declares public instruction open to pardos (Ignacio Garzón, *Crónica de Córdoba*, 3 vols. [Córdoba, 1898–1902], 2:349–50).

V-CA4. *1 September 1830*. Provincial law exempts frontier settlers from payment of tithes for ten years (Córdoba, *Compilación*, 1:56–57).

V-CA5. *21 October 1830*. Executive decree notes that twenty-eight slaves have obtained freedom through military service in civil war and promises compensation to former owners (AHPC, RO, tomo 1, f. 46).

V-CA6.   *1832.* Governor's religious oath, eliminated in 1826 (III-CA10), is restored (Ernesto A. Celesia, *Federalismo argentino,* 3 vols. [Buenos Aires, 1932], p. 377n).

V-CA7.   *11 August 1832.* Law creates provincial playing-card monopoly as a fiscal expedient (Córdoba, *Compilación,* 1:72).

V-CA8.   *22 September 1832.* Legislature prohibits the introduction of shoes and ready-made clothing even from other Argentine provinces. A subsequent decree of 1836 eliminates this prohibition for Argentine, not foreign, merchandise (Beatriz Rosario Solveira, comp., *La aduana de la Provincia de Córdoba* [Córdoba, 1973], pp. 17, 30–31).

V-CA9.   *7 August 1833.* Acting Governor Benito Otero rules that pardos can receive university degrees. This decision follows a lengthy controversy which began when the provincial government first declared that pardos could be enrolled, then seemingly backed down under violent protests from the university, whose cloister was willing at most to allow a pardo to attend but not to obtain a degree (Garzón, *Crónica de Córdoba,* 2:415–17; Emiliano Endrek, *El mestizaje en Córdoba* [Córdoba, 1966], pp. 62–65).

V-CA10. *8 November 1835.* Governor Sixto Casanova takes the Suma del Poder Público, though not with the intention of exercising it personally; it passes first to his own delegate, then to Colonel Manuel López (AHPC, RO, tomo 3, f. 169; Antonio Zinny, *Historia de los gobernadores de las provincias argentinas,* 5 vols. [Buenos Aires, 1920–21], 3:134–35).

V-CA11. *15 December 1836.* Decree of Governor Manuel López adds sugar and yerba maté to the articles monopolized by the state. Early the following year, the sugar and yerba monopoly is auctioned to a private firm, but in the face of strong outcry over alleged favoritism in the award of the contract, López revokes it and restores free commerce in both articles, subject only to ordinary taxation (Solveira, *La aduana,* pp. 31–35, 39–41; Efraín U. Bischoff, *Historia de la provincia de Córdoba,* 3 vols. [Buenos Aires, 1968–70], 1:261; Garzón, *Crónica de Córdoba,* 3:30).

V-CA12. *15 March 1837.* Legislative decree authorizes the executive to sell lands of the former Indian communities of Quilino, San

Antonio, Cosquín, etc.; the rights of present occupants, few of them actually Indians, are to be protected. The measure provides specifically that "legitimate" occupants may keep what they have and that squatters will be preferred in any sale. Subsequent instructions to the government surveyor state that each town is to have a common pasture, reserved to use by the Indians, who will also receive their own separate plots (Córdoba, *Compilación*, 1:99; Garzón, *Crónica de Córdoba*, 3:31–32).

V-CA13. *4 December 1837.* Executive decree ends tithes on wool, cheese, and certain other articles (AHPC, RO, tomo 4, ff. 90–91).

V-CA14. *14 May 1839.* Sala de Representantes votes to admit the Jesuits, a first contingent having already arrived (AHPC, RO, tomo 4, f. 192; Pérez, *La Compañía de Jesús restaurada*, pp. 140–44, 156–64).

V-CA15. *7 July 1841.* Prior censorship of periodicals established by decree (AHPC, RO, tomo 4, f. 423).

V-CA16. *13 May and 7 June 1843.* Because they have been hard hit by Indian attacks and other disasters, rural departments are granted a twelve-year exemption from payment of tithes on livestock (Córdoba, *Compilación*, 1:117; AHPC, RO, tomo 5, f. 29).

V-CA17. *4 August 1843.* López "suspends" the Mercedarian convent in Córdoba, placing it under direct jurisdiction of the diocesan provisor—apparently on grounds of insufficient members. Three years later it is reorganized, ostensibly on a proper footing, though its existence remains precarious (Bruno, 10:69–71; Bischoff, *Historia de la provincia de Córdoba*, 1:295; *Mensage del gobierno de Córdoba a la décima tercia legislatura* [Córdoba, 1847], pp. 15–16).

V-CA18. *14 September 1843.* Decree forbids burials in churches or churchyards of the city of Córdoba, making exception only for nuns, who may still be buried in their respective convents. Henceforth burials must be in a new cemetery outside the city, which is inaugurated in 1844 (Córdoba, *Compilación*, 1:115–16; *Mensage . . . a la décima tercia legislatura*, p. 18).

V-CA19. *17 December 1844.* Governor López revokes the 1833 decision that permitted pardos to obtain university degrees and provides that in the future no pardos may be admitted (Endrek, *Mestizaje*, p. 67; Garzón, *Crónica de Córdoba*, 3:169–72; Juan N. Garro, *Bosquejo histórico de la Universidad de Córdoba* [Buenos Aires, 1882], pp. 342–43).

V-CA20. *28 January 1845.* López suppresses carnival (*Mensage . . . a la décima tercia legislatura*, pp. 20–21).

V-CA21. *14 April 1845.* Legislative decree authorizes imposition of a contribución directa on capital amounts of $500 or more. However, it is replaced by a patente or license tax in August 1846 (Córdoba, *Compilación*, 1:124; Garzón, *Crónica de Córdoba*, 3:172–73, 175).

V-CA22. *1 February 1847.* Revised provincial constitution retains basic provisions of the 1821 text (III-CA2) except for deletion of certain individual liberties. It also strengthens the original wording with respect to the religious monopoly enjoyed by Roman Catholicism. The principal change is to permit indefinite reelection of the governor while enlarging his legal powers (Celesia, *Federalismo*, 3:69, 237, 324–26, 348–49; Córdoba, *Compilación*, 1:341–49).

V-CA23. *10 May 1848.* López decree withdraws the authorization given to the Jesuits to function in Córdoba, citing the need for uniformity of policy with Buenos Aires (Córdoba, *Compilación*, 1:136).

V-CA24. *10 June 1849.* Tithe exemption granted to rural departments in 1843 is withdrawn ahead of time, with a view to using the proceeds for support of military forces on the southern and eastern frontiers (Córdoba, *Compilación*, 1:140–41).

V-CA25. *12 May 1849.* A special committee is created for prior censorship of all printed or manuscript works that may "directly or indirectly attack the Holy Religion of the State and public morality or the Sacred National Cause of Federation." It will also censor theatrical productions (AHPC, RO, tomo 5, f. 355; Efraín U. Bischoff, "El periodismo cordobés durante la época de Rosas," *Revista de la Junta Provincial de Historia de Córdoba*, 8 [1978]:50, 58).

V-CA26. *5 July and 13 August 1849.* In view of the disorderly conduct often associated with cockfights and horse races, regulations stipulate that those who attend will not be protected by any kind of fuero (Córdoba, *Compilación*, 1:141–42, 144).

V-CA27. *27 September 1849.* Executive decree sets limits on the use of special mourning apparel to spare families excessive costs (Córdoba, *Compilación*, 1:146).

V-CA28. *14 April 1851.* López grants a two-year tithe exemption to Saladillo and Cruz Alta, to encourage settlement of the southern frontier (AHPC, RO, tomo 5, f. 403).

References

As a glance at the reference notes reveals, this monograph is based principally on published and unpublished official documents of the various Platine provinces. Published documents predominate but are supplemented with material contained in a number of archives. The secondary historical literature made an essential contribution, in large part suggesting the questions to be asked and providing the implicit and explicit interpretative frameworks. However, that contribution cannot be fully reflected in the citations, which for the most part make reference only to secondary works from which quotations and certain specialized data are taken. And, if all the published works used at one time or another were to be included in this bibliography, the result would be a list of standard sources plus scattered unstandard ones that would replicate the Argentine history drawer of any major library's card catalog. The list would augment the drawer's contents only to the extent that it further listed scholarly articles, most of which have been routinely annotated in the *Handbook of Latin American Studies*. For these reasons, the bibliography that follows is limited to archival sources, printed documents, and newspapers of the period—several of which are themselves official compilations of printed documents.

Archival Sources

Archivo de la Legislatura, Mendoza.
Archivo de la Provincia de Buenos Aires.
Archivo General de la Nación.

172   References

Archivo Histórico de Mendoza.
Archivo Histórico de la Provincia de Córdoba.
Archivo Histórico de la Provincia de Salta.
Archivo Legislativo de Jujuy.
Archivo Provincial de Jujuy.

PRINTED DOCUMENTS

Administración de justicia de la provincia de Corrientes. Concepción del Uruguay, 1850.

Ahumada, Manuel de. *Código de las leyes, decretos y acuerdos que sobre administración de justicia se ha dictado la provincia de Mendoza.* Mendoza, 1860.

Angelis, Pedro de, comp. *Recopilación de las leyes y decretos promulgados en Buenos Aires.* 2 vols. Buenos Aires, 1836–41.

Argentina. *Registro Nacional de la República Argentina que comprende los documentos desde 1810 hasta 1891.* 14 vols. Buenos Aires, 1879–91.

Bagú, Sergio. *El plan económico del grupo rivadaviano (1811–1827).* Rosario, 1966.

Buenos Aires. Gobierno. *Mensajes de los gobernadores de la provincia de Buenos Aires 1822–1849.* 2 vols. La Plata, 1976.

Córdoba. *Compilación de leyes, decretos, acuerdos de la Excma. Cámara de Justicia y demás disposiciones de carácter público dictadas en la provincia de Córdoba desde 1810 á 1870.* 49 vols. Córdoba, 1870–1911.

———. Cámara de Diputados. *Archivo de la H. Cámara de Diputados de la Provincia de Córdoba.* 7 vols. Córdoba, 1912–.

———. Gobierno. *Mensage a la décima séptima legislatura.* Córdoba, 1837.

———. Gobierno. *Mensaje del gobierno de Córdoba a la décima tercia legislatura.* Córdoba, 1847.

Corrientes. *Registro Oficial de la Provincia de Corrientes.* Corrientes, 1929–.

———. Gobierno. *Mensage del Gobierno de Corrientes a la undécima legislatura.* Corrientes, 1850.

Entre Ríos. *Recopilación de leyes, decretos y acuerdos de la provincia de Entre-Ríos desde 1821 á 1873.* 11 vols. Concepción del Uruguay, 1875–76.

"Estatuto provisorio para la dirección, y administración de la Provincia de Jujuy—Año de 1835." Universidad Nacional de Tucumán, Facultad de Derecho y Ciencias Sociales, *Revista Jurídica* 3 (1958):291–324.

Jujuy. *Compilación de leyes y decretos de la provincia de Jujuy desde el año 1835.* 3 vols. Jujuy, 1885–88.

Magariños de Mello, Mateo J., ed. *El gobierno del Cerrito; colección de documentos oficiales emanados de los poderes del gobierno presidido por el brigadier general D. Manuel Oribe 1843–1851.* 2 vols. Montevideo, 1948–61.

El pensamiento constitucional hispanoamericano hasta 1830. 5 vols. Caracas, 1961.

Ramos, Juan Pedro, *El derecho público de las provincias argentinas.* 3 vols. Buenos Aires, 1914–16.

Rodríguez, Adolfo. *Colección de leyes, decretos del gobierno, tratados internacionales y acuerdos del superior tribunal de justicia de la República Oriental del Uruguay.* Montevideo, 1856.

Rojas, Ricardo, ed. *Archivo capitular de Jujuy.* 4 vols. Buenos Aires, 1913.

Sampay, Arturo Enrique, comp. *Las constituciones de la Argentina (1810/1972).* Buenos Aires, 1975.

———. *Las ideas políticas de Juan Manuel de Rosas.* Buenos Aires, 1972.

Solveira, Beatriz Rosario, comp. *La aduana de la Provincia de Córdoba.* Córdoba, 1973.

Uruguay. *Actas de la H. Junta de Representantes de la Provincia Oriental (Años 1825–26–27).* Montevideo, 1920.

———. *Compilación de leyes y decretos 1825–1930.* 58 vols. Montevideo, 1930–32.

———. Asamblea General. Cámara de Representantes. *Actas de la H. Cámara de Representantes.* 6 vols. Montevideo, 1905–8.

———. Asamblea General. Senado. *Diario de Sesiones.* Montevideo, 1882–.

NEWSPAPERS

El Argos de Buenos Aires. Buènos Aires.
La Aurora Nacional. Córdoba.
The British Packet. Buenos Aires.
El Eco de los Andes. Mendoza.
Gaceta de Buenos Aires. Buenos Aires.
La Gaceta Mercantil. Buenos Aires.
La Ilustración Argentina. Mendoza.
El Nacional. Montevideo.
El Nacional Correntino. Corrientes.
El Pacificador. Corrientes.
El Progreso de Entre-Ríos. Gualeguaychú.
El Redactor de la Asamblea. Buenos Aires.
Registro Ministerial. Mendoza.
Registro Nacional. Buenos Aires.
Registro Nacional. Montevideo.
Registro Oficial. Buenos Aires.
Registro Oficial. Salta.
Registro Oficial del Gobierno de la Provincia Oriental. Canelones.
El Republicano. Corrientes.
El Teo-Filantrópico o el Amigo de Dios y de los Hombres. Córdoba.

Index

Academy of Mathematics, 9
Africa, 17, 126
Agriculture: in Buenos Aires, 61, 129–30; in Cuyo, 38; in Littoral, 37, 38, 74, 77, 119, 157; in Northwest, 41, 121; in Uruguay, 34, 134
Alcabala, 47, 103; in Buenos Aires, 25, 112, 128; in Córdoba, 44, 92, 142; in Corrientes, 78, 160; in Mendoza, 39, 114, 139; in Paraguay, 104; in Uruguay, 70, 114, 152
Aldao, José Félix, 79, 80, 82, 162, 163
Alemán, Pablo, 164
Alvarez de Arenales, Juan Antonio, 43, 141
Anaya, Carlos, 154
Anchorena, Nicolás, 60
Anchorena, Tomás Manuel, 57, 149–50
Andrews, George, 56
Anglicans, 57, 65, 149, 155
Apprentices, 23
Argentine Confederation, 65, 67, 74, 80, 83, 88, 101–2, 157, 158
Artigas, José Gervasio, 33, 68, 71, 118
Assembly of Year XIII, 10–13, 15, 16, 18, 19, 29, 71, 102, 104, 110, 124–26, 135
Atienza, Rafael, 79, 158

Audiencia, 5
Augustinians, 40, 114, 139, 162

Balcarce, Juan Ramón, 55, 57, 58, 145, 147, 149
Baptism, cold-water, 11, 12, 102, 125
Benthamism, 22, 112
Bethlehemites, 18, 27–29, 57, 64, 114, 125, 126, 131, 150
Blacks: Rosas friend of, 55. *See also* Pardos; Slavery
Blancos, 68, 70, 155
Bolívar, Simón, 103, 115
Bolivia, 86, 103, 111, 115; in independence movement, 9–11, 15, 16; and Northwest, 41, 83, 84, 87, 120, 164
Bonaparte, Joseph, 14
Bonaparte, Napoleon, 111
Bourbon reforms, 2
Brazil: constitution of, 117; occupies Uruguay, 6, 32, 153; slavery in, 70, 78, 104, 110, 153, 158; war with, 24–25, 33, 34, 54, 68, 89, 129, 146, 153
British: influence, 10, 13; subjects, 57–58, 65, 136, 167
Buenos Aires: city, 126–27, 130; diocese of, 28, 79, 131–32, 151 (*see*

176   Index

Buenos Aires (*continued*)
  also Medrano); revolutionary government at, 8–10, 14, 16, 17, 103;
  university, 29, 116, 151
Buenos Aires, province, 4, 6, 12, 15;
  and interior, 31, 35–41, 43, 67, 73–
  77, 80–81, 83, 89–90, 93, 100, 102,
  139, 156, 160, 163, 167, 170; and
  Rivadavian reforms, 19–30, 44–49,
  84–86, 88, 92, 103, 112, 114, 127–
  33; under Rosas, 50–66, 94–99,
  104, 116, 117, 144–51; after Rosas,
  101; and Uruguay, 33–34, 68–73,
  135, 154
Bullfighting, 18–19, 24, 43, 48, 63,
  70, 126, 128–29, 140, 148, 154
Bustos, Juan Bautista, 45, 90, 96,
  142–43, 167

Cabildos, 21, 46, 94–95, 127; in inte-
  rior provinces, 36, 37, 40, 41, 44,
  85, 88, 137–40, 143, 166; in Uruguay, 34, 134
Caillet-Bois, Ricardo R., 7
Cámara de Apelaciones, 54, 60, 116,
  144
Capellanías, 28, 42, 78, 84, 120, 131,
  132, 137, 140, 157, 158, 160, 163
Capuchin nuns, 132
Carnival, 63, 65, 149; in interior, 74,
  79, 93, 99n, 157, 158, 170; in Uruguay, 72, 153
Carrera, José Rafael, 104, 122
Casa de Espósitos, 117
Casanova, Sixto, 168
Castañeda, Francisco, 35
Cemeteries, 26–29, 45, 59, 98–99,
  130, 131, 149; in Córdoba, 44, 90,
  142, 169; in Corrientes, 37, 137,
  158; in Entre Ríos, 35, 136; in Men-
  doza, 82, 161, 163; in Salta/Jujuy,
  42, 85, 141, 164, 166; in Uruguay,
  72, 154
Censos, 28, 42, 49, 57, 82, 84, 98–99,
  116, 131, 132, 140, 149, 162–64
Central America, 103
Charles III, 64, 93, 150
Chile, 16, 38; and Mendoza, 41, 79–
  81, 83, 161, 162

Church: assets taken, 27–29, 37, 42,
  49, 57, 65, 66, 78, 84, 85, 98–100,
  102, 120, 125, 126, 131, 132, 137,
  139, 150, 155, 157–60, 163–65;
  controversy over, 30, 47, 56,
  102–4; defense of, 44, 59, 82, 90,
  92, 136, 143, 146, 168; fees, 9, 15,
  38, 55, 78, 158, 160, 162; and Indian labor, 11, 87, 124, 166; regulation of clergy by, 26–27, 40, 53, 65,
  116, 130, 133, 139; religious censorship by, 10, 36, 45, 52, 57, 71, 88,
  90, 123, 135, 137, 142, 144,
  149–52, 156, 165, 170; supports
  Rosas, 66; on usury, 23, 72; weak
  inUruguay, 33. *See also* Cemeteries;
  Censos; Fueros; Papacy; Religious
  orders; Toleration
Civil rights, 10, 13, 92, 101, 123, 125,
  165, 170
Colombia, 29, 62, 103, 104, 109, 117
Colorados, 68, 69, 72, 118, 155
Comisaría General de Regulares, 11,
  18, 125, 126
Commerce: with Bolivia and Chile,
  38, 41, 79–80, 83, 87; in Buenos
  Aires monopoly, 35, 76; code, 117;
  contraband, 73; and foreign merchants, 10, 13, 68, 76, 117, 124. *See
  also* Consulado; Tariffs
Communal lands, 9, 15, 47, 71, 109,
  124; in Córdoba, 91–92, 97, 168–
  69; in Corrientes, 37, 38, 45, 137,
  138; in Salta/Jujuy, 42–43, 85, 86,
  120, 141, 164–66
Congress: constituent (1826), 129;
  constituent (1853), 79, 102; national
  (1816–20), 16–18, 110, 126. *See
  also* Assembly of Year XIII
Conservatism, 1, 2, 12; in interior, 43,
  67; in Venezuela, 61, 103–4, 109
Constitution: of Bolivia (1826), 115;
  of Brazil, 117; of Cádiz, 17; of Uruguay (1830), 68–69, 71, 94–95, 153
Constitutions, Argentine, 5, 15; of
  1819, 8, 17, 41, 114; of 1826, 22–
  23, 34, 46, 68, 135; of 1853, 5, 101,
  102, 104. *See also* Estatuto provisional; Reglamento Provisorio

France, 2, 63, 73, 74, 105
Francia, José Gaspar Rodríguez de,
104–5
Franciscans, 27, 37, 42, 64, 72, 84–85,
99n, 114, 120, 130–32, 141, 151,
155, 160, 164, 165
Free-birth legislation, 10–11, 13, 14,
24, 104, 113, 124, 128, 149; in interior provinces, 78, 81, 91, 135–36,
158, 162; in Paraguay, 104; in Uruguay, 34, 70, 134, 153
Frontier defense and settlement, 112;
in Córdoba, 90, 91, 96, 167, 170; in
Mendoza, 162
Fueros, 14, 46–47, 94–95, 101, 103,
127–28; ecclesiastical, 22, 28, 66,
72, 112, 131; fiscal employees, 43,
128, 140; in interior provinces, 39–
40, 43, 44, 75, 77, 80, 88, 92, 119,
121, 138, 140–42, 158, 160, 161,
163, 167, 170; military, 2, 10, 13,
22, 124; in Uruguay, 69, 72, 153,
154; in Venezuela, 14, 111. *See also*
Consulado
Funeral practices, 28, 58, 65, 82, 131,
149, 150, 161. *See also* Cemeteries

García, Manuel José, 20, 24, 128, 129
García de Zúñiga, Mateo, 35
García Moreno, Gabriel, 104
González, Julio César, 7
Gorriti, José Ignacio de, 140
Gorriti, Juan Ignacio, 163
Great Britain: and antislave trade
treaties, 63, 70, 149, 155; and block-
ade, 73, 105; and 1825 treaty, 26,
44, 132–33, 143; Rosas and, 59
Guatemala, 103, 104, 122
Guanache, past, 41

Hacendados, 75, 117, 156
Hale, Charles, 3
Halperín Donghi, Tulio, 58
Hermandad de la Caridad, 27, 131
Hidalgo, Miguel, 14, 16
Holidays, reduction of, 58, 65, 97–
100, 116, 150, 151; in interior prov-
inces, 74, 79, 82, 157, 160, 161; in
Uruguay, 72, 153

Hospitals, 11, 18, 27, 29, 55, 125,
126, 131, 147, 150, 159
Humahuaca, 166. *See also* Quebrada

Immigration, 9, 11, 13, 26, 28, 36, 47,
48, 56, 95–97, 101, 112, 124, 128,
146–47; in interior provinces, 38,
42, 70, 78, 87, 113, 136, 137, 141,
158, 166, 167; in Uruguay, 70, 154
Imprisonment for debt, 75, 76, 157
Indians: in Buenos Aires, 9, 55, 56,
124; in Córdoba, 90–92, 168–69; in
Corrientes, 37, 38, 45, 137, 138,
160; independence movement and,
9–11, 13–15, 123–24; in Salta/
Jujuy, 41–43, 84–88, 120, 141,
164–67; in Uruguay, 72
Inquisition, 11, 12, 14, 124
Intendant system, 2
Interest rates, 23, 43, 47, 48, 61–62,
96–97, 103, 129; in Corrientes, 77,
159; in Mendoza, 81–82, 99n, 119,
162; in Uruguay, 70, 72, 154
Itatí, 38, 137
Iturbe, José Mariano, 88, 121, 166,
167

Jesuits, 2, 97, 99; interior provinces
and, 74, 83, 89, 93, 119, 156, 162,
163, 169, 170; return to Buenos
Aires, 63–64, 66, 150–51; in Uruguay, 72, 98, 118, 155
Judicial procedure, 10, 11, 21, 59, 60,
88, 109, 116, 123, 138, 140, 148.
See also Cámara; Fueros; Tribunals
Jujuy, city, 41, 140, 141
Jujuy, province, 6, 31, 32, 48, 89, 111;
measures adopted by (1835–52),
84–88, 94, 95, 97, 99, 120, 121,
164–67; as part of Salta, 41, 42, 84
Junta, revolutionary (1810), 5, 8–9,
123
Junta de Representantes, Buenos
Aires, 21, 26, 52, 55, 59, 60, 112,
116, 131
Juries, 34, 69, 123, 127, 135, 152, 153

Lancaster, Joseph, 39, 133
La Rioja, province, 31, 39

UNIVERSITY OF FLORIDA
MONOGRAPHS

Social Sciences